WITHDRAWN
UTSA LIBRARIES

NEW GEOGRAPHY 1970-71

NEW GEOGRAPHY
1970-71

John Laffin

Illustrated with maps and diagrams

ABELARD-SCHUMAN
LONDON   NEW YORK   TORONTO

by the same author

The Hunger to come
(The Food and Population Crises)
New Geography 1966-7
New Geography 1968-9
Anatomy of Captivity
Middle East Journey
Return to Glory
One Man's War
Digger
(Story of the Australian Soldier)
Scotland the Brave
(Story of the Scottish Soldier)
Jackboot
(Story of the German Soldier)
Swifter Than Eagles
(Biography of Marshal of the R.A.F.
Sir John Salmon)
Codes and Ciphers
Anzacs at War
Links of Leadership
Tommy Atkins
(Story of the English Soldier)
Women in Battle
Jack Tar
(Story of the English Seaman)
Surgeons in the Field

© 1971 John Laffin
I.S.B.N. 200.71733.2
L.C.C.C. Number 78 – 158667

LONDON	NEW YORK	TORONTO
Abelard-Schuman	Abelard-Schuman	Abelard-Schuman
Limited	Limited	Limited
8 King Street	257 Park Avenue South	228 Yorkland Boulevard
WC2	NY 10010	425

CONTENTS

	page
About this Book	15
Abu Dhabi	17
Afghanistan	17
Agriculture	18
Alaska	19
Algeria	20
Arctic	22
Argentina	22
Aid	23
Australia	27
Austria	31
Aviation	31
Belgium	35
Bolivia	36
Botswana	37
Brazil	39
British Commonwealth	40
Bulgaria	43
Canada	45
Canary Islands	49
Cayman Islands	49
Central America	50
Ceylon	50
Chile	51
Cities	52
Climate	54
Cocoa	55
Colombia	55
Colombo Plan	56
Common Markets	56

New Geography 1970-71

Continental Drift	page 59
Cook Islands	59
Copper	59
Costa Rica	60
Cuba	60
Cyprus	61
Czechoslovakia	61
Denmark	63
Dubai	64
Earthquakes	66
East Germany	69
Ecology	69
Ecuador	73
Education	73
Eire	74
El Salvador	75
Ethiopia	76
European Economic Community	77
European Free Trade Association	78
Euro-Trade Centres	80
Exploration	80
Finland	81
Fishing	83
Floods	86
Food	87
Food and Agriculture Organization	91
France	93
Fuels	96
Geomorphology	99
Ghana	103
Glaciers	104
Gravel	105
Great Lakes	105

Contents

Greece	*page* 106
Guatemala	107
Honduras	108
Hong Kong	109
Hungary	110
Hurricanes	110
Hydro-electric Power	111
Hydrology	112
Iceland	114
India	115
Indonesia	115
Iran	116
Iraq	117
Irrigation	118
Israel	119
Italy	121
Japan	125
Kenya	129
Kuwait	130
Labour	132
Lebanon	136
Liberia	136
Libya	138
Malawi	140
Malaysia	140
Malta	141
Maps	142
Mauritius	142
Methane	143

New Geography 1970-71

Mexico	page 144
Minerals	144
Mining	147
Mongolia	150
Monsoon	151
Morocco	152
Netherlands	153
New Zealand	153
Nicaragua	155
Nigeria	155
Nile	156
Norway	156
Oceanography	158
Oil	159
Pakistan	163
Panama	164
Papua and New Guinea	165
Paraguay	166
Pearling	167
Peru	168
Philippines	168
Poland	169
Population	170
Portugal	171
Qatar	173
Resources	174
Rhodesia	174
Routes	175
Rumania	177
Saudia Arabia	178

Contents

	page	
Selenology		179
Shipbuilding		179
Sierra Leone		182
Singapore		182
Somalia		183
South Africa		184
South Korea		185
Spain		186
Steel		188
Sudan		188
Sweden		188
Switzerland		189
Tea		191
Thailand		191
Tides		192
Timber		193
Tourism		196
Trade		198
Trinidad and Tobago		199
Tunisia		200
Tunnels		200
Turkey		202
Uganda		204
United Arab Republic		205
United Kingdom		205
United Soviet Socialist Republic		217
United States of America		219
Uruguay		223
Venezuela		225
Vietnam, North		226
Vietnam, South		227
West Germany		229
Whaling		231
Wheat		231

New Geography 1970-71

Windward Islands	page 233
Wool	233
Yugoslavia	234
Zambia	236
Appendix	238
Index	239

LIST OF ILLUSTRATIONS

	page
1. Mining and Agriculture in Canada	46
2. Diagram of the Peruvian Earthquake	68
3. Comparative Diagrams of Pollution in the Rhur Area	72
4. Fishmeal Production in 1966 and 1968	84
5. Power Stations of the Dordogne	94-5
6. Shares in World Consumption of Fuels	97
7. The Great African Rift Valley	100
8. Priority Development Areas in Israel	120
9. Drainage System in the Mezzano Valley	123
10. Distribution of Japanese Trade in 1969	126
11. Table of Migrant Labour	134
12. Libyan Oil Fields	137
12. Mining Seafloor Uranium	148
14. Principal Oil and Natural Deposits in West Germany	160
15. Proposed Routes for Nuclear Canals in Panama	164
16. Thoroughfares between Honshu and Hokkaido	200
17. New Towns and Development Areas in the United Kingdom	210

18. Diagram of British Farm Products   214
19. British Exports   215
20. Main U.S. Exports and Imports   222
21. Rice Production in South Vietnam   227

ABBREVIATIONS

Many organizations are now commonly known only by their initials. This is a list of the principal ones referred to in this book and of other abbreviations used.

ADB	Asian Development Bank
ADC	Andean Development Corporation
ALCAN	Aluminium Company of Canada
bbl	barrels
CACM	Central American Common Market
CARIFTA	Caribbean Free Trade Area
COMECON	Council for Mutual Economic Assistance (Eastern Europe)
EAC	East African Community
EEC	European Economic Community
FAO	Food and Agriculture Organization
EFTA	European Free Trade Association
GNP	Gross National Product
HEP	Hydro-electric Power
IAB	Inter-American Bank
IADB	Inter-American Development Bank
IATA	International Air Transport Association
IBRD	International Bank for Reconstruction and Development
IDA	International Development Association
IFYGL	International Field Year for Great Lakes
IGOSS	Integrated Global Ocean Station System
IISEE	International Institute of Seismology and Earthquake Engineering
ILO	International Labour Organization
IMF	International Monetary Fund
IWP	Indicative World Plan (for Agricultural Development)
LAFTA	Latin American Free Trade Association
m	million
SCOR	Scientific Commission on Oceanic Research
sq.km.	square kilometres
sq.m.	square miles
UNDP	United Nations Development Programme
UNESCO	United Nations Educational, Scientific, and Cultural Association
USAID	United States Agency for International Development
WFP	World Food Programme
WHO	World Health Organization

ACKNOWLEDGMENTS

Several organizations have been helpful in supplying information and illustrations in this book. My thanks are due to: Barclays Bank Economic Intelligence Department for permission to reproduce maps and diagrams; the European Free Trade Association; the *Geographical Magazine* for diagrams; the Department of Economic Affairs; the FAO; *Time Magazine* for diagrams; the U.S. Department of Agriculture; the National Bank of Australasia; UNESCO's *Courier Magazine*; the Petroleum Information Bureau; the British Broadcasting Corporation, Publications Division. Departments of many governments have been co-operative in verifying information.

Individually my chief thanks go to my wife for much research and all the typing and indexing.

ABOUT THIS BOOK

The purpose of *New Geography* is to enable anybody interested in his world to keep abreast of developments in human, physical, economic and scientific geography. All entries in this third edition are completely new, not merely revised, and, naturally, there are some fresh entries.

The book should, ideally, be used in conjunction with *New Geography 1966-67* and *New Geography 1968-69*. Collectively these three books and those which will follow them keep orthodox text books up to date.

The classification is similar to that of the earlier books — alphabetical on the basis of countries, commodities and related geographical matters such as ecology, geology, population, oceanology. Where useful, entries suggest cross-references to a subject. AGRICULTURE, for instance, gives a cross-reference to FOOD AND AGRICULTURE ORGANIZATION and to FOOD.

The index at the rear gives *all* references to a particular subject; wheat, for instance, might be mentioned in reference to a dozen countries. Tourism was referred to no fewer than 32 times in *New Geography 1968-69* and all are shown in the index.

Unless otherwise stated trade figures are correct to December 31, 1969.

ABU DHABI

16,000 sq.m. Pop. 100,000. Japanese interests are heavily involved in developing the oil reserves of the Trucial State of Abu Dhabi and state revenue from oil was expected to pass the 100m-dinar level in 1970. In April-May 1970 Japanese companies made two major strikes offshore. The deep water port must be finished in 1971 if congestion is not to choke sea traffic. The state is reaching the stage of needing to search for channels of diversification, as in the cases of Kuwait and Bahrain, and it has a leading role to play as provisional capital in the Gulf Federation.

Trade with the U.K., 1969: exports to, £20m; imports from, £20m. Trade with the U.S.A., 1969: Exports to, $30m; imports from, $18m.

AFGHANISTAN

250,000 sq.m. Pop. 16.120m. Under the third five-year plan, ending 1971, Afghanistan has made economic progress but foreign aid will remain the decisive factor. The country is determined to earn more foreign exchange through its tourist industry. A growing network of modern roads – built with U.S. and Soviet help – enables the Afghans to plan their future based on a major overland trade route. There are now 2,000 miles of paved road; there were none a decade ago.

Trade with the U.K., 1969: exports to, £3.5m; imports from £6m. Trade with the U.S.A., 1969: exports to, $20m; imports from $45m.

New Geography 1970-71
AGRICULTURE

NEW SEEDS. Development of high-yielding crop varieties in many African countries offers promising opportunities for a dynamic agricultural advance. In some countries the new varieties, used in combination with fertilizers and insecticides on well-irrigated farms, have given three-fold yields per acre. One large-scale planting of the new seeds in any one country can produce a sudden dramatic harvest increase. Advance planning is therefore necessary so that early adjustments can be made in social and economic institutions. The patterns of foreign trade and the internal and regional supply and demand picture may alter considerably.

If higher-yielding cereals are to be produced from smaller proportions of the cultivated area, new crops may have to be introduced. New cropping patterns will be needed and new forms of land use may be essential.

Maize production in Kenya provides an example of higher yield. Production of maize from hybrid seeds began in 1963 on 287 acres. Nearly 3,000 200lb-bags were produced, a yield of 10 bags an acre. In 1966 3,065 acres were devoted to high-yielding seeds and produced 44,350 200lb-bags — an average yield of 16.62 bags per acre. In 1969 there was an approximate maize surplus of 320,000 metric lb of maize, after a deficit in 1965 of 45,000 metric lb.

In Malawi the maize-breeding programme has been running for 15 years and the country will be exporting in 1971. In Ethiopia maize is playing an increasingly important part in the large-scale irrigation schemes now being developed in the lowlands. Maize is gradually ousting sorghum throughout Africa. The higher returns produced by the quick-returning varieties have made it a prestige crop. Sorghum is maintained mainly for beer-making.

Research and development in high yielding seed programmes are not confined to maize. The Rockefeller Foundation is giving assistance to millet, sorghum and maize projects in Ghana, Nigeria, Sierra Leone and Tanzania. In Nigeria the Kano Agricultural Research Station is increasing yields of high protein cowpeas by up to 800 lb on a single crop. New varieties of groundnut seeds have led to 11% production increases in the north, 20% in the central area and 25% in the riverine area.

Egypt has a well-established seed research programme. Liberia has almost completed trials on sorghum and new rice strains are already in production. In Libya both wheat and maize are producing greatly increased yields. Lesotho's maize and wheat seed improvement programmes are giving good results.

Successful sorghum research in Senegal, Upper Volta and Mali has led to the beginning of field production. Early reports from Mali show increased yields of 15–25%. Hybrid millet in Senegal produced a 68% yield increase in 1969. Dahomey had a 35% increase.

Particularly noteworthy results have been obtained by development teams from the Republic of China in African countries where they have introduced their Taiwan Native 1 rice species. Extensive experiments in the Cameroons, Gabon, Gambia, Malawi, Niger, Senegal, Chad and Togo by these teams have more than doubled production obtained with traditional rice strains.

The FAO has begun research into high-yielding varieties of legumes and oil seed crops. Successful high yield research in soya beans and sunflower seeds is already well advanced in Kenya. The importance of this work may be gauged from the fact that most dry legumes contain 20-25% protein — three times the protein value of most cereal grain.

The development and expansion of the high-yielding seeds are among the FAO's main priorities for the Second Development Decade.

(See *Food and Agriculture Organization,* also *Food.*)

ALASKA

586,000 sq. m. Pop. 265,000. The oil strike at Prudhoe Bay in April 1968 is transforming the Alaskan economy; it is potentially one of the world's largest fields. Fairbanks, at the northern end of the Alaska Highway, has become a centre for tourism and trade and a seat of learning. The University of Alaska has 2,400 students, more than 500 of them from other states and foreign countries; 174 are Eskimos, Indians and Aleuts. The Arctic Environmental Engineering Laboratory at Barrow is finding new ways for men to live, work and build in what was once considered the uninhabitable north.

Stimulated by the Prudhoe Bay discovery, a dozen oil companies are exploring the Arctic Slope, stretching more than 500 miles westward from the Canadian border between the Brooks Range and the Arctic Ocean, an area of 69,000 sq. m. Until recently drilling on the Arctic Slope was strictly a winter operation. Not only was the ground too soft but the ice on the lake landing field began to melt in April. The permafrost 1,000 ft. thick, also makes drilling difficult. Now, to prevent thawing of the surface in summer, 5 ft. of gravel is spread to insulate the tundra and lake airfield. The 500,000 yards of gravel needed at Prudhoe comes from the bed of the Sagavanirtok River.

Recent surveys show that Alaska has not only oil but exploitable timber, fish, copper, tin, silver and gold. Fish are particularly important for Alaska has a longer coastline than the rest of the U.S.A. and 64% of the nation's continental shelf. The state's sea trade with Japan and Asia is growing, particularly with sales of natural gas and wood pulp to Japan.

ALGERIA

855,000 sq. m. Pop. 13m. Encouraging progress continues and under the new plan of January 1970, an outlay of £2.230m is forecast. The plan's objectives are twofold: the growth of income per capita and of employment. Algeria's population is growing at a rate of 3.2% – about 400,000 each

Algeria

year recently. In August 1970, 900,000 of a total male work force of 2.5m were entirely unemployed. The creation of 70,000 new jobs a year is planned together with a continuing emigration to France and EEC countries of 30,000 a year. A broad range of new industries is to be developed, notably heavy engineering, petro-chemicals, construction materials, textiles and footwear.

The output of Algerian agriculture is to increase substantially over the four years. The largest rise is likely to be in cereals, with output planned to grow by 600,000 tons, the aim being to reduce wheat imports to around 200,000 tons by 1973. The Algerian fishing fleet is to be increased by 80 trawlers, and 8m dinars are to be invested in canning and cold storage. Output of industrial and export crops, notably of sunflower seed, raw cotton, sugar beet, honey and tomatoes, is to increase greatly.

Between 1966 and mid-1970 500m tons of crude oil were found in Algeria. This industry, which now accounts for nearly 70% of exports, is making great progress. Algeria, through the state oil and gas monopoly, has signed a 25-year contract with a U.S. company to supply 10,000 cubic metres of methane per year from 1973.

Links with France and the Soviet Union are still strong. A French firm is building an important textile factory south of Algiers. During 1970 West German, British, Italian, Belgian and Canadian firms won large contracts in the motor vehicle, methane, wood products and cement industries. Algeria is highly successful in attracting investment, as seen in the Annaba steel complex, opened in mid-1969, which combined investments from France, the Soviet Union, Italy and West Germany.

Trade with the U.K., 1969: exports to, £22m; imports from, £9.5m. Trade with the U.S.A., 1969: exports to, $50m; imports from, $ 30.7m.

New Geography 1970-71
ARCTIC

The Arctic Research Laboratory at Barrow, Alaska, is now producing significant information about the Arctic. To plot the movement of the Arctic ice pack and record currents, weather and ocean depths four stations have been set up on floating ice islands. One, occupied for four years, drifted 4,300 miles. Investigators are studying the animal, fish and plant life of the Arctic.

ARGENTINA

1.1m sq. m. Pop. 23.7m. Political and industrial instability, largely the result of inflation, prevent Argentina from developing some of its industries. No less than 180m dollars were withdrawn from the country between April and September 1969 and this flow has continued. Argentina is one of the U.K.'s largest trading partners in South America and is currently second only to Brazil as a British export market in the continent, but the U.K.'s share of Argentine imports fell from 30% in 1938 to only 9% in 1969. Export sales to the U.S.A. account for 12% of the total. Investment projects are supposed to increase by 36% during 1970-74, notably with the nuclear power plant at Atucha, several HEP schemes and a methane pipeline from Neuquen province to Bahia Blanca. Iron ore and aluminium export terminals are to be built. Much future industrial activity is geared to the £120m aluminium project on the Patagonian coast which is to begin production in 1974. The meat trade has, by concentrating on exports of boneless cuts of beef, recovered from the British ban on imports of carcasses.

Trade with the U.K., 1969: exports to, £80m; imports from £42m. Trade with the U.S.A., 1969: exports to, $190m; imports from $160m.

Aid

AID

International aid is complex and far-reaching. The chief aid projects during 1969-70 were:

ALGERIA. The Soviet Union is providing £90m for the development of industrial projects.

ARGENTINA. The IADB is lending 20m dollars towards the cost of a gas pipeline; 175m DM is coming from the West German International Development Agency towards a nuclear power station.

BOLIVIA. The IDA is lending 7.4m dollars towards the Santa Isabel HEP plant supplying Oruro and Cochabamba; 23.3m dollars is being provided by the IBRD (International Bank for Reconstruction and Development) for a major pipeline from the Santa Cruz and Monteagudo areas for natural gas to Argentina; the IAB is lending 9.9m dollars for a pipeline from Monteagudo to Sucre in southern Bolivia; 20m dollars is being provided as stand-by credit from the IMF.

BRAZIL. The IADB is lending 26m dollars for expansion in beef production.

BRITISH AID. The U.K. made payments totalling £20m in 1969. The United Nations Conference on Trade and Development has called for 1% of the donor country's Gross National Product as a minimum amount to be transferred annually to poor countries. In 1969 British official and private disbursements totalled 0.82% of the GNP. Aid was given to 120 countries in 1968. India (£40.6m) was the chief recipient, then Kenya (£9.7m), Pakistan (£9.8m) and Malawi (£7.6m). In the same year recipient countries repaid £30m of previous loans and £26.6m in loan interest. At the end of 1968 the outstanding amount was £1.073m.

CHILE. The IADB is lending 10m dollars and USAID is providing 48m dollars for drought relief.

COLOMBIA. The IDB is providing 9m dollars for improving the drinking water system in Medellin.

CEYLON. Authorization, from the World Bank and the IDA, has been given for the first part of a 1,200m-dollar loan for the Mahaweli River Scheme.

COSTA RICA. The World Bank is providing 3m dollars for an agricultural credit designed to increase production of beef cattle, bananas, cotton and pineapples.

ECUADOR. The World Bank is lending 5.3m dollars to buy tuna boats; there are loans from the World Bank and the IDA for beef cattle production, and one from West Germany for an iron and steel plant.

EIRE. The World Bank is providing £6m to finance an HEP scheme in County Wicklow. This is Eire's first World Bank loan.

GHANA. World Bank finance is being given for the Accra-Kumasi Highway; large loans are coming from the U.S.A. and from West Germany.

ICELAND. 10m DM is coming from the Council for Europe Resettlement Fund for economic development, and much help from the Nordic countries.

INDIA. Aid for India is coming from West and East. Western aid is largely co-ordinated by the Aid-India Consortium, chief members being the U.S.A., the U.K., West Germany, Japan; £45m is coming from the U.K., £26m of this for the import of British spares, components and food, £1m for the family planning programme.

MALAYSIA. The Asian Development Bank has lent money to develop the palm oil industry; the World Bank is making two loans to raise agricultural productivity.

MEXICO. The World Bank is providing 1,000m dollars, with half that amount to extend the electricity supply; 34m dollars is coming from the IADB for irrigation.

NIGERIA. A loan from the U.S.A. is for completion of the Ibadan water supply, and one from Japan is for the import of Japanese goods; Rumania is providing a loan to establish a

Aid

timber industry; another from the Soviet Union (supposedly £85m) is to build an iron and steel complex; other loans are coming from the World Bank and the U.K.

PAKISTAN. The World Bank Aid to Pakistan Consortium is lending 450m dollars; a 16m-dollar credit from the IDA is to improve the country's rudimentary telecommunications services; two interest-free loans of £2.5m are coming from the U.K., partly to help finance the Tarbela Dam, and 8m dollars from the World Bank to expand gas transmission services; another £6m from the U.K. is for the purchase of British chemicals, pharmaceuticals, printing machinery and scientific equipment. A further £0.5m from the U.K. is an outright gift for the purchase of wheat and flour.

PAPUA–NEW GUINEA. The IDA has granted a loan of 4.5m Australian dollars for agricultural development, mainly in existing coconut estates and in stocking 150,000 acres for beef production.

PERU. The IMF is providing a 60m-dollar stand-by credit. 110m is coming from the IADB.

SIERRA LEONE. The World Bank is lending £1.75m for electrical expansion; British aid consists of a £1.8m loan towards the cost of a new road between Taiama and Bo, Southern Province; also £660,000 interest-free to be spent on British goods and services.

SINGAPORE. Aid has been given by the World Bank and the ADB for telecommunications and electric power distribution.

SOMALIA. The U.S.A. is lending 8.5m dollars for water supplies to Mogadishu; 3.5m dollars is coming from the U.N. Special Fund and the EEC for other water supplies.

SOUTH KOREA. The ADB and the IDA are providing 17m dollars for highway and railway projects; 10m dollars from the World Bank is to help finance the Korean Development Finance Corporation.

SUDAN. The U.K. is lending £1m towards irrigation dams on

the Nile and replacement of the Sennar Dam sluice gates.

THAILAND. Large amounts are being provided by the Asian Development Bank to help three major agricultural products: an integrated development programme initially for 24,000 acres on an irrigation scheme in the north-east; intensive studies of selected areas of the north believed to have high agricultural potential, and the establishment of a land bank.

TUNISIA. Considerable aid reflects confidence in the country's future. 15m dollars are coming from the World Bank and 5m from Sweden for a water supply to Tunis and the Sahel; 8.5m dollars from the World Bank is for the improvement of three ports; aid is coming from Italy for developing the port of Gabes; the World Bank is to finance the modernization of Tunisia's 1,200-mile rail system; another 6.2m dollars from the IMF is towards building a new international airport at Tunis.

TURKEY. Aid to Turkey was 250m dollars in 1969, 20m more than in 1968. Up to 1972 Turkey will rely heavily on foreign money for official projects. Most of the money, from the World Bank, the IMF and various nations, will be used for developing backward regions.

UNITED ARAB REPUBLIC. The U.N. is supplying £45m for food aid; 12m dollars from the World Bank is for extending the railway system and £30m for irrigation projects; another £380m is coming from various countries for development projects. British aid includes £62,500 (June 1, 1970) towards the cost of preserving the temples of Philae which would have been submerged in an artificial lake created by the construction of the Aswan High Dam.

VENEZUELA. Considerable money is being received from the World Bank and the U.S. Export-Import Bank for various projects; 85m dollars is coming from a group of American and Canadian banks to cover repayment of debts and 75m dollars from the IADB to finance a farm programme.

AUSTRALIA

2,968 sq. m. Pop. 12.5m. Australian geography, in the widest sense, is as interesting as ever, with significant developments in agriculture, mining and trade.

POPULATION. New South Wales is the most populous state with just over 4,600,000 people. Victoria has slightly more than 3,400,000, and Queensland's population is 1,750,000. South Australia has 1,150,000; Western Australia almost 1,000,000 and Tasmania 389,000 with 69,000 in the Northern Territory. The population of the Australian Capital Territory is slightly more than 125,000.

The Australian government hopes to attract another 350,000 British settlers between 1971 and 1975. The average annual intake between 1966-70 was 74,000.

AGRICULTURE AND PASTORALISM. Improved seasonal conditions contributed to a rise of about 17% in the value of the agricultural output in 1968-69. Production of wheat was a record 535m bushels, nearly double the figure for the previous year. However, a decrease in exports led to the accumulation of vast stocks and an acute marketing problem. The glut and lack of storage facilities resulted in the imposition of a production quota of 357m bushels in 1969-70 and only 288m bushels in 1970-71.

Drought. Western Australia and Queensland were badly affected by drought in 1970; the net rural income fell by 20%. In the 12 months ended May 1970 Queensland lost more than £A160m in rural production.

Meat. Meat has now become a major export product; its value reached 380m dollars in 1970, 42% higher than in 1968-69, with beef and veal the main contributors. Because of U.S. import restrictions Australian exporters have been directed to ship greater quantities to the expanding Japanese market.

Poultry. Australia's poultry industry is now one of the most modern in the world. Chicken slaughterings totalled 75m in 1968-69 and yielded 206m lb of chicken meat (52.5m and

127.5m lb in 1965-66). Once the sideline of farmers and horticulturists, this industry is now highly organized, integrated and scientifically conducted. The consumption of chicken meat in 1960 was 4 lb per person; in 1970 it was 18 lb. (In the U.S.A. it is 38 lb.) During 1968—69 more than 2m live chickens were exported.

Prawns. Australian prawn trawlers are now operating in what are believed to be the best prawn fields in the world off the southern coast of West Irian (formerly Dutch New Guinea).

Wool. The clip for 1969-70 was expected to be a record but prices reached a 10-year low because of rising world supply in the face of decreasing demand.

Mining. Mineral reserves are being greatly developed and exploited. In 1968-69 the output of iron ore was 53% higher and bauxite 38% higher than for the previous year. Sizable increases were also recorded in copper, tin, lead, zinc, silver and mineral sands concentrates. Nevertheless, mining and quarrying provide only 2% of the GNP. At least 50% of mineral exports go to Japan. Oil production is increasing. As recently as 1967 95% of Australia's requirements were imported. By the end of 1970 no less than 70% of total consumption was being met from indigenous sources, chiefly from the new Bass Strait fields. When the Halibut field in the strait reaches full production in 1971 it should supply 50% of Australia's needs.

Asbestos is being opencast-mined on a large scale at Barraba, northern New South Wales. A mill costing £A14m is being built on the site, which has deposits of 27m tons.

Ilmenite, a mineral used in steel processing, is being exported to Japan from North Stradbroke Island, Moreton Bay. In February 1970 a consortium of Japanese steel mills contracted to buy another 60m tons of iron ore over 11 years from the Mount Newman field in Western Australia. This order, worth nearly 500m dollars, is part of an arrangement to supply 203m tons from 1973.

Mount Isa Mines Ltd. is now the world's largest producer

of copper, silver, lead and zinc. The company is recruiting labour from Britain and Europe and is building a new town. Another new town, near Cape Lambert, Western Australia, will accommodate 12,000 people concerned with iron ore mining in the Robe River area.

Coal is booming as never before. In 1970 total black coal exports from New South Wales and Queensland exceeded 14m tons, equally divided between the two states. Moura opencast mine in central Queensland, operated by Theiss Peabody Mitsui Coal Co., produces 4m tons of the total.

The greatest boom has been in nickel. Deposits at Mount Windarra, Western Australia — the Poseidon boom — were responsible for one of the most astonishing events in the investment world, after a decade of other startling mineral discoveries in Western Australia.

A feature often overlooked in Australia's mineral development is the ancillary investment generated by the mineral development itself. In the case of nickel this is important in aiding growth in many sectors of the West Australian economy. For example, it provides A2m dollars freight business to the railways and building and construction contracts for Kwinana and Kambalda worth over A50m dollars. Nickel has also revitalized life in the goldfields region. A new town with every modern facility has been built at Kambalda when there was practically nothing before.

A new Australian iron product is Hinix, which contains 95% pure iron ore. It enables steel to be made directly in electric furnaces, bypassing the conventional two-stage pig-iron process. A plant to produce another metal agglomerate product, Hinet, is being built at Dampier at a cost of 80m dollars.

Yet another enormous plant is the one now being built near Port Warrender, in the Kimberleys region, to process 1.2m tons of alumina a year. One of the largest alumina plants in the world, it will cost 330m U.S. dollars.

MANUFACTURING. Expansion of factory activity continues; manufacturing now accounts for a third of Australia's national income. The chief growth areas are iron and steel, motor vehicles, chemicals and building materials. Victoria's first steelworks is being built near Hastings on Westernport Bay, where deep-water channels are being dredged to accommodate the largest iron ore ships. The works will be in operation by 1973 with an initial annual output of 2m tons of raw steel.

Chemicals. A £70m plant is being built at Gladstone, Queensland, to produce caustic soda from local salt.

AUSTRALIA AND JAPAN. The Australia-Japan association should not be under-estimated economically. In May 1970 a senior officer of the Australian Department of Trade said that the two countries would find themselves "out on a limb" unless they formed a closer relationship in the trade, economic, political and cultural spheres. Since the last edition of *New Geography* Japanese businessmen have begun joint ventures with Australians in developing the resources of Papua and New Guinea — fishing, tea, vanilla, pepper and other spices. In May 1970 the Japanese government announced a policy which will allow Japanese trust companies to invest £A100m on overseas exchanges.

Japan is continually placing enormous orders in Australia, such as that in mid-1970 for £A250m of retail products, consisting mainly of food, household goods, clothing and hardware.

Despite the overwhelming importance of trade with Japan, Australia's other trade connections are unimpaired. Those with New Zealand are particularly strong, with imports increasing. Timber imports, for instance, doubled in quantity from 1969 to 1970.

TRANSPORT. By the end of 1969 all mainland capital cities except Adelaide at last had a standard railway gauge link. Adelaide will be included by the end of 1971. Improved co-ordination between the six mainland government-owned railway networks is evident. Ingenious equipment enables rapid gauge-changing of freight cars. Much greater co-operation between rail and road transport has developed.

On December 4, 1969 the east-west standard gauge

Aviation

railway line from Sydney to Perth was completed at Broken Hill: this is one of the great steps towards overcoming Australia's transport problems.
Ports. The N.S.W. government is spending 75m dollars in developing historic Botany Bay as a second major port for Sydney and as a big industrial complex.
NEW TERRITORY. The Coral Sea Islands Territory has been created; it consists of scattered, virtually uninhabited islands off the Great Barrier Reef and will be administered from Norfolk Island.
  Trade with the U.K., 1969: exports to, £237m; imports from, £321m. Trade with the U.S.A., 1969: exports to, $700m; imports from, $800m. (See *Minerals.*)

AUSTRIA

32,376 sq. m. Pop. 7.35m. Austria's economic geography is interesting, with industrial production having increased by 11% in the 12 months up to August 1970. Pig iron and crude steel production increased by 13%. Despite the large numbers of immigrant workers most employers have had to resort to overtime working. Major projects put in hand in 1970 include an extension of oil refining capacity, petro-chemical plants (in Salzburg and Linz) and various regional projects, especially in the Salzburg area. The country is exporting more machinery, steel and electrical equipment, and its profits from tourism are high.
  Trade with the U.K., 1969: exports to, £64m; imports from, £71m. Trade with the U.S.A., 1969: exports to, $485m; imports from, $869m.

AVIATION

COST OF FLYING. Unlike practically every other service, air

travel is expected by the public to become progressively cheaper. Remarkably enough, this has happened and seems likely to continue. In 1946, for example, the return London-New York air fare was more than 1,000 dollars; this is equivalent to about 2,000 dollars in 1970. But it is now possible to cross the Atlantic both ways by the cheapest scheduled service for 300 dollars. Air fares are equal to or below many of those for surface travel.

The paradox in air transport is that if fares are to continue to come down the airlines must make unparalleled investment not only in new high-capacity aircraft but in sophisticated ground equipment to handle the resulting flood of passengers and freight. Compared with the 9m-dollar cost of the Boeing 707, the Boeing 747 and the Concorde will each cost about 25m dollars.

There is a large difference between the cost per ton-mile of transporting freight by air and by ship. The premium which has to be paid for the greater speed of air freighting may be reduced by the introduction of wide-bodied jets and by increasing containerization.

It has always been maintained that high-volume commodities, such as coal, grain and oil, will never be transported by air in the same quantities as they are at present carried overland or by sea. However, with the increasing size of aircraft it may be possible to carry a greater volume than once seemed feasible. Air cargo growth is dependent on increasing automation in ground handling which, at the moment, accounts for about half the operating costs of the freight industry. The IATA container standardization programme, intended to reduce these overheads, is introducing 17 standard-sized containers to replace the hundreds now in service.

High-capacity aircraft will be the most revolutionary factor in air travel over the next few years. Early in 1970 the first jumbo jet, the 500-passenger Boeing 747, began to bring down long-range costs. In the next few years airbus-type airliners such as the Lockheed TriStar, Douglas DC10 and the European A-300B should perform the same function over shorter ranges.

Aviation

Supersonic travel should become available by the mid-1970s, assuming all goes well with the Concorde and the Soviet Tu-144.

In 1950 world airlines, excluding the Soviet Union and China, flew 530m ton-miles; in 1957 1,125m; in 1967, 4,590m, and in 1970, 7,800m ton-miles. Projected figures for 1975 and 1980 are 19,200m and 43,150m ton-miles respectively.

AIRWAYS. These are the principal new routes of 1969-70:

Australia-Hawaii: continuing to Los Angeles and New York.

Belgium-Japan: a weekly service via Athens, Bombay, Bangkok, Manila.

Germany-Japan: a polar air cargo service from Frankfurt, via Paris and Anchorage to Tokio.

Japan-Indonesia: Tokio to Djakarta via Manila.

Netherlands-Philippines: from Amsterdam to Manila via Rome, Karachi, Bangkok.

Peru-Europe: twice-weekly from Lima to Madrid, Paris, London.

Portugal-Argentina: cargo jet service from Lisbon to Buenos Aires via Rio de Janiero, São Paulo and Montevideo.

U.K.: a city to city service between Luton/Southend to Leeds, Tees-side, Newcastle, Edinburgh, Aberdeen.

U.K.-Japan: London to Osaka via Anchorage and over the North Pole.

U.K.-U.S.: daily service between London and Minneapolis-St. Paul via Detroit.

Round-world service (TWA): calling at Honolulu, Guam, Okinawa, Bangkok, Bombay, Tel Aviv, Athens, Zurich, Frankfurt, New York, Los Angeles.

AIRPORTS. Before long major airports will be located at sea or in lakes. Land-based airports are becoming hopelessly jammed and land for new ones is scarce and expensive. Even when sufficient open space can be found public opinion is often too powerful for plans to be implemented. Many American cities are seriously considering expensive marine airports. These are the principal ones:

New Geography 1970-71

Chicago. The city badly needs a third jetport and one consisting of aluminium nodules and reached by helibus and hovercraft has been suggested. However, a more conventional billion-dollar airport, 35 ft. to 55 ft. below the level of Lake Michigan is more likely. It would be connected to the city by six miles of tunnel, causeway and bridge.

Cleveland. A jetport on Lake Erie, built on 1,050 acres of landfill and protected by breakwaters, dams and dykes. A mile offshore, it would be linked to the city by a 10-lane causeway.

New Orleans. A jetport is to be built above the shallow waters of Lake Pontchartrain.

New York. The probable solution is to move a greatly enlarged Kennedy Airport onto a nine-mile concrete island five miles off Long Beach.

B

BELGIUM

11,870 sq. m. Pop. 9.640m. Belgium has two main problems — shortage of labour and the strong separatist movements in the Flemish and Walloon provinces. The proposals of the government for a more decentralized system of administration may help. Despite social and industrial problems the nation's output reached record levels in 1970. For example, cement production in February was 100,000 tons greater than in the same month in 1969; textile production for 1970 was up 13% on 1969 and paper 5%. Agriculture, however, employs a steadily decreasing number of the population. Only 5% work on the land, a figure smaller than any other European country except the U.K., and this trend is likely to continue, though dairying is becoming more important.

In the western regions horticulture is thriving. Located near Western Europe's main industrial markets, it is likely that horticulture will remain an important part of the national economy. Total exports between August 1969 and August 1970 rose by 23% because of commercial expansion with France and West Germany. British sales to Belgium rose by 20% in 1969. The growth of the chemical industry could provide great trading potential. Competition from U.S. subsidiaries situated in Belgium is strong but Belgium is possibly more ready to trade with non-EEC countries than are her other community partners.

Farms in Belgium are generally small. When a farmer dies his land is divided among his sons. Much farming land has been lost because of the growth of Belgian cities, where about half the population lives and works in industry. Belgian industries, especially steel, engineering and chemicals, have been expanding so rapidly that there has been a shortage of labour. Wages have therefore increased and many farm-workers have taken up full-time work in factories. This has meant that "commuting" is particularly common in the Brussels region. Many commuters travel from Flanders and particularly from east Flanders. Though such a small percentage of the population is occupied full-time in farms, many keep their small farms and travel to work. If his farm is near a large city the part-time farmer may grow vegetables with the help of his wife, provided that she herself has not taken a town job. However, the small farmers' incomes are so low compared with factory wages that many will move to the suburbs.

Trade with the U.K., 1969: exports to, £183m; imports from, £288m. Trade with the U.S.A., 1969: exports to, $766m; imports from, $779m.

BOLIVIA

415,000 sq. m. Pop. 4.45m. The most important developments have been in power and mining. Large uranium deposits have been found at 1,000 miles south-east of La Paz. Alumino Minas Gerais, a subsidiary of Alcan, is going ahead with bauxite mining following confirmation of adequate reserves. A £4m tin smelter built at Vinto by a West German firm came into operation in June 1970. The uncertainty of tin prices has forced the government to encourage other export industries. In 1970 tin accounted for 53% of exports (55% in 1967).

In August 1970 the pipeline exporting gas to Argentina was completed; the gas is expected to bring in £2m annually. The trend for Bolivia to import from an increasing range of countries will probably be reversed under the influence of the Andean Group Agreement; this is expected to cause a reorientation of trade back into Latin America. The tendency towards economic integration also spread westwards when an agreement was signed by Argentina, Bolivia, Brazil, Paraguay and Uruguay to co-ordinate development in the River Plate Basin.

Trade with the U.K., 1969: exports to, £26m; imports from, £3m. Trade with the U.S.A., 1969: exports to, $135m; imports from, $89m.

BOTSWANA

275,000 sq.m. Pop. 600,000. The opening of the Agricultural Demonstrators' Training College at Content, five miles from Gaberones, the capital of Botswana, marks the halfway stage in the territory's £1m agricultural development scheme. £500,000 in capital costs are being provided by the United Kingdom Committee for the Freedom from Hunger Campaign and the remainder by the Botswana government aided by the U.K.

Like other developing countries, Botswana is fighting poverty, hunger, ignorance, illiteracy, disease and drought. During the past five years droughts have been particularly severe; there have been serious crop failures, heavy losses of cattle and consequent malnutrition. Until recently, the livestock industry was considered more important than arable farming. Nevertheless, it is now realized that the annual arable crop output, even at its present low level, is approximately equal to the output from the national cattle herd. In addition, efforts by the Ministry of Agriculture have shown that the use of new varieties of crops, more timely cultivations, more modern equipment and techniques, better seed, good fertilizers and insecticides can produce considerably increased yields even in Botswana's difficult climate.

Increased yields are a vital need. The territory is already a large importer of its basic food requirements and the population is rising at a rate of over 3% per annum. There are about 100,000 farmers in Botswana; UNESCO recommends a ratio of one agricultural demonstrator per 400 farmers. This means that 250 demonstrators are needed but at present there are only 100. More demonstrators are therefore essential. An increase in their numbers can produce a direct rise in agricultural production even within one season. During 1968-70 farmers within the Pupil Farmers' Scheme produced on average 6 bags per acre compared with 2½ bags produced by farmers outside the Scheme.

Even in a drought year there is some rain in Botswana, but most of the water runs to waste, often taking with it valuable soil; the grazing is exhausted as the veldt grasses are trampled to extinction and a well which should be the focus of life becomes a dry hole in the middle of a desert. A wider distribution of water would go a long way towards preventing this and allow proper use to be made of the land. This is why Christian Aid and Oxfam are providing, under the auspices of the Freedom from Hunger Campaign, £165,774 for the capital costs of the Soil Conservation and Farm Dam Building Unit in Botswana. The Unit is building small dams of 10 to 20m gallon capacity which catch the surface water and hold it. The object of the Unit is to build 35 small dams per year; these dams will be of sufficient capacity and depth to make water available throughout the year. The dams are being sited to fit into a comprehensive land use plan for each catchment area and thus ensure an even distribution of cattle. This policy is reinforced by grazing control.

With the help of British Broadcasting Corporation advisers Botswana has established a valuable and developing broadcasting system. Integrated into this system is a farm broadcasting service. With a total of little over 4,000 licensed receivers this service is already proving to be a useful arm of agricultural education. By means of radio, improved farming methods penetrate deeply amongst a widespread, largely illiterate population. The Freedom from Hunger Campaign has provided £11,500 to buy 1,000 radio receivers for distribution to chiefs, school teachers, agricultural demonstrators and other community leaders for use in group listening.

BRAZIL

3.3m sq. m. Pop. 89.1m. Major long-term aims announced by Brazil in June 1970 included raising the annual growth rate to 10%, doubling income per head to £400 by 1980 and gradually reducing the annual inflation rate to 10%. Agriculture, though not developing rapidly, nevertheless employs 50% of the labour force and earns about 80% of foreign exchange income. Production of practically all crops in 1969-70 showed substantial gains over the previous year and for 1970-71 output was forecast to rise by 20%. The major exception is coffee. Affected by drought, frost and coffee rust, the 1970-71 crop is estimated at 12m bags (15m in 1969-70, 17m 1968-69, and 23m 1967-68). Schemes for extensive re-planting of coffee bushes are in operation in several states, notably Parana and São Paulo. Agrarian reform is paramount and £1,100m will be spent between 1970-73.

Fishing is receiving attention: the 1969 catch of 500,000 tons is to increase to 900,000 in 1971. Major capital spending programmes are being carried out in the motor industry, notably by Italian, French and West German manufacturers. Indeed, foreign capital is vitally important in Brazil's development and 699 industrial projects were approved in 1970. Several major HEP schemes, largely financed by the World Bank, are the crux of industrial development, together with 3,000 miles of trunk roads and major improvements to railways and roads.

The creation of the Mineral Resources Surveying Bureau to make basic geological surveys should help the more rapid development of mineral resources. UNESCO and the Brazilian government are charting the Pantanal, the huge region of the Mato Grosso, which is flooded half the year. The co-director of the 2.5m-dollar project says that it will lead to "the building of a new world, capable of providing food for millions of people and will facilitate the migration into the interior of part of the population now concentrated along the coast". The object of the hydrological studies is to reclaim and develop the region, which offers excellent conditions for cattle-breeding and has iron and manganese deposits.

Trade with the U.K., 1969: exports to, £51m; imports from, £44m. Trade with the U.S.A., 1969: exports to, $670m; imports from, $705m.

BRITISH COMMONWEALTH

14m sq. m. approx. Pop. 1,000m. In view of the many British territories which have become independent an outline of the status of all British Commonwealth units is given here.

INDEPENDENT MEMBER COUNTRIES. The fully independent status of the member countries of the Commonwealth was given legal recognition by the Statute of Westminster in 1931. The countries whose membership dates from then are:

1 Britain
2 Canada
3 Australia
4 New Zealand

Since World War II nearly all the countries administered by the U.K. which could sustain sovereign status have achieved it. Most of them have remained within the Commonwealth, whose membership has grown to 28 countries. In all, over 30 British dependent territories, with a population of well over 750 million, have become independent during this period. These are:

5	India	1947
6	Pakistan	1947
7	Ceylon	1948
8	Ghana	1957
9	Malaysia (since 1963; formerly the Federation of Malaya)	1957
10	Nigeria	1960
11	Cyprus (date of membership; became independent in 1960)	1961

British Commonwealth

12	Sierra Leone	1961
13	Tanzania (since 1964; formerly Tanganyika and Zanzibar)	1961
14	Jamaica	1962
15	Trinidad and Tobago	1962
16	Uganda	1962
17	Kenya	1963
18	Malawi	1964
19	Malta	1964
20	Zambia	1964
21	The Gambia	1965
22	Singapore (part of Malaysia from 1963 to 1965)	1965
23	Guyana	1966
24	Botswana	1966
25	Lesotho	1966
26	Barbados	1966
27	Mauritius	1968
28	Swaziland	1968

ASSOCIATED STATES. The following Caribbean islands have become states in association with the U.K., which retains responsibility only for their external affairs and defence. An essential feature of this new non-colonial status is that it is voluntary and terminable at any time; there is a built-in option for independence, without further recourse to the British Parliament.

29 Antigua
30 Dominica
31 Grenada
32 St. Lucia
33 St. Kitts—Nevis—Anguilla

New Zealand has a similar arrangement with

34 The Cook Islands

DEPENDENCIES OF MEMBER COUNTRIES. Of the remaining British dependencies, few are rich in natural resources and a number consist of extremely scattered groups of islands. In Rhodesia, never directly administered by the U.K., a "declaration of independence" was made on November 11, 1965. Because of Hong Kong's special circumstances it is not possible to think of self-government in terms of an elected legislative council. In Fiji there are special problems arising from the racial composition of the population. Independence for British Honduras is being considered. *All the remaining dependencies combined have a total population of about 1m. and none of them individually has more than 150,000 people.* Any arrangements that are ultimately adopted involve organizing the relations of these small communities with the decision-making machinery in the territories themselves as their peoples move towards complete control of their internal affairs.

35 Rhodesia
36 Brunei (Protected State)
37 Hong Kong
38 Fiji
39 Pitcairn
40 Tonga (Protected State)
41 British Solomon Islands Protectorate
42 Gilbert and Ellice Islands
43 New Hebrides (Anglo-French Condominium)
44 Cayman Islands
45 Montserrat
46 St. Vincent
47 Turks and Caicos Islands
48 British Virgin Islands
49 British Honduras
50 Bahamas
51 Bermuda
52 Seychelles
53 British Indian Ocean Territory
54 Falkland Islands (and Dependencies)
55 British Antarctic Territory
56 St. Helena
57 Tristan da Cunha } Dependencies of St. Helena
58 Ascension Island

Bulgaria

59 Gibraltar

Australia and New Zealand also have dependencies:
Australia.
60 New Guinea (Trusteeship Territory)
61 Papua
62 Norfolk Island
63 Christmas Island
64 Cocos Islands
65 Australian Antarctic Territory
New Zealand.
66 Niue
67 Tokelau Islands
68 Ross Dependency

Western Samoa and Nauru. The former trust territories of Western Samoa (administered by New Zealand) and Nauru (administered by Australia, designated as the administering authority jointly with Britain and New Zealand) have both become independent (Western Samoa in 1962 and Nauru in 1968). No decision has been reached on the form that their relationship with the Commonwealth might take.

69 Western Samoa
70 Nauru

BULGARIA

43,000 sq.m. Pop. 8.4m. Bulgaria is particularly dependent on the Soviet Union, which is providing a major part of the finance for industrial development under the current five-year plan. Links between the two countries are stronger than ever. Trade with the Soviet Union is to expand to 1,800m roubles (60% of the total in 1970). Agreements cover the supply of raw materials — mainly oil and iron. A new joint cellulose and paper combine is being built at Arkangelsk in northern Russia and Bulgaria is supplying components for the Fiat car plant at Togliattrigrad. Integration with the Soviet Union is also to be the foundation of a radical change in power supplies. Bulgaria is excessively dependent on coal and water but by the end of 1971 it will switch over to oil, methane and nuclear power.

Experimentally, there have been complex mergers of state, co-operative and collective farms to form huge units covering every stage of food production from the raw material to processing and marketing. The tourist industry is an increasingly important part of the economy.

Agriculture, although accounting for 60% of exports, is receiving a much smaller share of new investment and now employs a third of the working population compared with two-thirds 15 years ago. Nevertheless, efforts are being made to improve productivity. In addition, state farms are to be further reorganized into large collectives averaging 40,000 hectares; the success of this move is in doubt because it has proved difficult to manage farms only a sixth of this size. Horticulture is receiving a high proportion of investment funds and following the installation of a large acreage of glasshouses, Bulgaria is now one of Europe's largest suppliers of tomatoes. Sales of horticultural produce have been most profitable in West Germany despite EEC barriers, and Bulgaria is emerging as a serious competitor to Italy and the Netherlands.

Among Western trading partners Italy is the only country with which there was any increase in trade and, with a marked decline in transactions with West Germany in 1969, Italy became Bulgaria's principal trading partner in the West. The Soviet Union is financing a pipeline across Rumania to bring methane to Bulgaria's chemical complex near Varna.

Trade with the U.K., 1969: exports to, £7.3m; imports from, £5.1m. Trade with the U.S.A., 1969: exports to, $40m; imports from, $30m.

C

CANADA

3.9m sq. m. Pop. 20.9m. Probably the most acute problem facing the Canadian government is that its attempts to reduce the overheating of the economy bear equally harshly on all parts of the country, regardless of local conditions. This applies particularly to Quebec Province which was economically stagnant in 1969 before the 1970 economic repressions. The Maritime Provinces and Manitoba fear that financial measures will make the economic situation more difficult, while Saskatchewan is probably worst hit of all. Two of the province's most important products, wheat and potash, suffer from an excess world production. The most prosperous provinces, Alberta, British Columbia and Ontario, suffered the worst inflation in 1970 and were unaffected by measures to control it. The Federal government is holding out great inducements to attract industry to the depressed areas.

In agriculture, the government took drastic steps in mid-1970 to solve the wheat crisis. In spite of a reduction of 4.4m acres by farmers during 1969, on their own initiative, the year's crop was 5% higher than in 1968 and the fourth largest on record. With export demand falling, huge stocks have been built up and the impact on farming incomes has had repercussions on the whole economy. At the end of 1969 the Russians contracted to buy wheat worth 200m dollars but even this disposed of only one-eighth of the surplus. The aim was to sow only 18½m acres in 1970 and farmers were being encouraged to transfer to other types of farming, particularly forage crops.

In the year ending June 30, 1970, the car industry for the first time reached a production of 1m cars produced in any

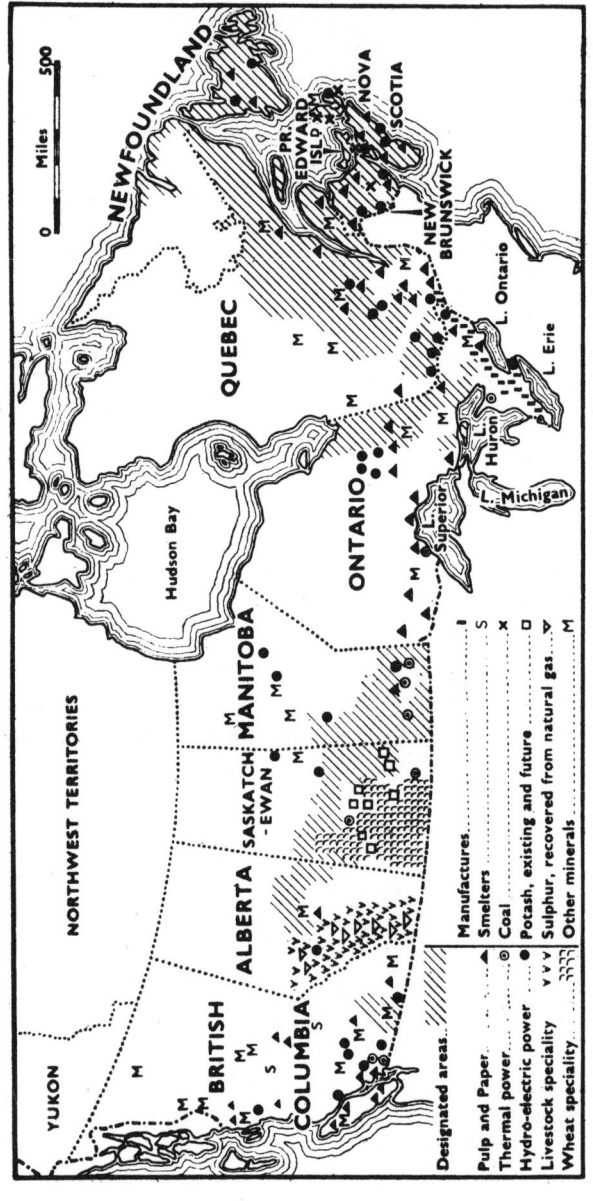

Mining and agriculture in Canada, showing designated areas for expansion

Canada

12 months. The Canadian paper industry has made an impressive recovery with world demand exceeding production for the first time in three years.

OIL. The oil industry faces uncertain conditions. There is doubt about the continued strength of its export markets, and the impact of the far northern petroleum discoveries has yet to be felt. In 1969 production rose by 7.5% and a similar gain may be achieved for 1970. The Canadian domestic market grows at the rate of between 3 to 4% a year. Demand for natural gas has continued to grow rapidly — last year production rose by 12% and exports to the U.S.A. by 21%. The new trans-Canada pipeline means that the industry is fully equipped to meet demand from the eastern states of both Canada and America.

CANADIAN-JAPANESE TRADE. However, Canada is not holding her own in world export trade. The U.K. remains Canada's second most important trading partner (after the U.S.A.) but Japan is rapidly expanding its share of Canadian trade, importing increasing amounts of forestry, mining and agricultural products.

The extent of Japanese commercial involvement with Canada and particularly with British Columbia should not be under-estimated.

Japanese technology has astonished some Canadians. The Minister for Lands and Forests, when touring the Honshu Pulp and Paper Company, found hardwoods — oak, birch, willow and cottonwood — being used in paper manufacture. These woods are considered waste in British Columbia. The Japanese have now built a pulp mill in British Columbia using the "waste" hardwoods and their bark.

Coal mining in British Columbia had been in the doldrums for years, with more than a million tons a year and no prospective sales, when the Japanese steel industry offered to buy 45m tons a year over 15 years for £270m. But there were some tough conditions. The Japanese were building 57,000-ton coal carriers, and they needed vast new port facilities if they were to load at full capacity. They wanted the Port of Vancouver, already the busiest in Canada, to build extensions to accommodate the new vessels, with a 50-acre coal assembly area and a three-mile causeway for road and rail traffic. The cost was over £17m in the first stage. The British Columbia Energy Board surveyed an area 20 miles from Vancouver at Roberts Bank and the agreement was signed.

This coal agreement is one of the most interesting developments in the eventful history of Japan's commercial courtship of British Columbia. This vast province, with its small population, is doubling its exports to Japan in four years.

British Columbia's mines shipped 25% of the total production to Japan in 1969, and the forest industry increased its sales to Japan by 200% in two years.

The figure of 50m dollars of Japanese capital invested in British Columbia will grow beyond 300m dollars in a few years — when it will be greater than the amount invested by Japan in the U.S.A.

In 1969, 11,000 Japanese cars were sold in Canada, compared with sales of 35,000 throughout the U.S.A. Into Vancouver steamed the first Japanese auto-carrier. Two wide gangways were lowered to the dock, and the neat little cars began rolling down, driven by crew members. They had been washed and polished in Tokio, unlike the grease-covered vehicles that arrive from Europe. The carrier unloaded 1,200 cars in five hours and loaded grain for the return trip.

Trade with the U.K., 1969: exports to, £504m; imports from, £308.7m — 9% and 6% respectively of the totals. It is interesting to note that in 1938 50% of Canada's imports came from Britain and in 1964, 10%. Trade with the U.S.A., 1969: exports to, $8,925m; imports from $7,936. (See *Great Lakes*.)

CANARY ISLANDS

(7) 2,807 sq. m. Pop. 1.1m. The Canary Islands are rapidly being overtaken by modern cosmopolitan development, with the number of tourists growing by 60% annually. Construction is rapid on Tenerife, Gran Canaria and La Palma, financed mainly by British, Belgian, German, Spanish and Swedish interests. Air traffic is now so important that international airports have been built at Las Palmas and Tenerife. The Canary Islands are an important and growing market for British goods.

CAYMAN ISLANDS

Grand Cayman, Cayman Brac and Little Cayman: 76, 14 and 10 sq. m. respectively. Pop. 11,600. The agricultural potential of these islands is not great because much of the land is mangrove swamp but standards are being raised; the growing tourist industry will help to increase agricultural production. The Pioneer Industrial Encouragement Law, passed in 1968, has already resulted in tile manufacture and printing. Lack of pipe-borne water is a disadvantage but surveys in 1970 show that there is adequate underground water.

The islands have the highest per capita income in the Caribbean — £400 annually. Two-thirds of the islands' trade is with the U.S.A. The cost of transhipment charges of British goods in Jamaica is one of the reasons for the predominance of the U.S.A. in the import trade of the islands, though cheaper air transport is expected to give British goods an advantage. Tourism is the most important source of earnings, as these figures show: 1964, 4,834 visitors; 1967, 10,278; 1968, 14,627; 1969, 20,110; estimated figure for 1970, 25,000.

New Geography 1970-71

CENTRAL AMERICA

Economic growth in Central America continues at a comparatively high rate, despite the region's dependence on primary products. Over 90% of foreign exchange earnings come from agricultural products, especially coffee, cotton and bananas. Regional trade in foodstuffs has, however, decreased in importance because few of the economies are complementary in the production of food. A rapid expansion in intra-CACM trade has been based on the growth of manufacturing industries; many new industries have grown up, including chemicals, pharmaceuticals, plastics, and assembly of vehicles. The future depends on the development projects — road systems, port facilities, irrigation and power supplies. Substantial loans have been made by the World Bank, the Inter-American Development Bank and the Central American Bank for Economic Integration.

CEYLON

25,332 sq. m. Pop. 12m. Depressed prices for tea and coconut products were mainly responsible for the highest trade deficit on record in 1969. Still, there are ambitious schemes for irrigation and industry. Tea still accounts for 60% of Ceylon's foreign earnings. In 1969 rubber had one of its best years in recent times with earnings up about 30%. An important contract was signed with Poland in March 1970 for 13,700 tons of sheet rubber.

Much of the effort of the former government between 1965 and 1970 was devoted to rice production. Crop yields rose in the three years to 1968 from 50m to 65m bushels and would have risen further but for the floods at the end of 1969. Even so Ceylon's import requirements have been halved with the aid of irrigation and reclamation projects. The Mahaweli River diversion scheme will bring water to 900,000 acres of the arid north-central province. The first

Chile

stage alone will save a quarter of the nation's rice import bill; the entire scheme will take 30 years for completion.

The Japanese have invested in a variety of enterprises including electricity distribution, telecommunications, car assembly and electronics, and pearling. Israeli assistance has developed the ceramics industry. The building of the Pegasus Reef Hotel is one of the major parts of Ceylon's tourist programme.

Ceylon is dependent on its overseas trade in traditional markets and commodities; a quarter of all exports go to the U.K. However, the need to diversify markets, plus the continued closure of the Suez Canal, has forced Ceylon to find outlets in Asia, especially in China and Japan.

Trade with the U.K., 1969: exports to, £33m; imports from, £29m. Trade with the U.S.A., 1969: exports to, $30m; imports from, $75m.

CHILE

300,000 sq. m. Pop. 9.5m. Following the 1969 drought Chile has had sharp economic reverses. Agricultural output fell and industry was hampered by shortages of water and HEP. The total cost of the drought is put at 50m escudos. More than 700,000 cattle and 400,000 sheep died and wheat and beans, both staple foods, were badly hit.

Controversy over copper has been incessant. It remains the nation's most important industry and earner of foreign exchange and accounts for about three-quarters of exports; however, the government wants to "Chileanize" it and to double output by 1973. Foreign mining companies object to semi-nationalization. The U.K. is Chile's leading market for copper, with imports of £30m annually.

Trade with the U.K., 1969: exports to, £40m; imports from, £9m. Trade with the U.S.A., 1969: exports to, $300m; imports from, $276m.

New Geography 1970-71
CITIES

This necessarily brief account can begin by noting that by the end of this century the population of the U.S.A. alone will swell by 100m people. Most of them will crowd into the nation's urban areas, which already house 70% of all Americans on a minuscule 1% of the land. To an increasing number of urbanologists a part solution to the problem, which finds echoes in all continents, is to start from the beginning by building "new towns" — completely planned communities that could support up to 1m people. The optimum size could be 100,000 to 250,000. A new town can be a satellite city close to an already developed metropolitan area or a wholly new urban centre erected on virgin land in much the way that Chandigargh, Canberra and Brasilia were built.

The concept is not unique to the U.S.A. There are more than two dozen "garden cities" in Britain, housing 1.25m people. The French plan is to build six new towns near Paris before the twenty-first century. The Netherlands, Sweden and Russia have already built a number of new towns. Tapiola, Finland, an urban "Shangri-la" six miles from Helsinki, is the new town that comes closest to meeting many planners' ideal. Its main shopping centre is a paved plaza; nearby are a theatre, hotel and swimming pool. No house is more than 250 yards from a shopping or amusement centre and people walk to do their shopping and so there is no car problem.

Though roughly 100 communities described by their developers as new towns have been built or are now being built in the U.S.A., few approach Cumbernauld in Scotland or Welwyn Garden City, England. Too often the American new towns prove to be little more than well-planned upper and middle class suburbs that provide few jobs for residents and no homes for lower-income workers.

At Westlake, California, a new community developed by the American-Hawaiian Steamship Co., 38 miles north-west of Los Angeles, the price of homes is prohibitive — up to

Cities

£50,000 — and only 20% of the people who work in the local trading estate industrial park live in the town.

The Housing and Urban Development Department has received 26 applications to build new towns, the most ambitious of which is for Park Forest South, 28 miles south of Chicago. Wolf van Eckhardt, a leading urbanologist, urges the need for 350 new towns in two decades to accommodate 35m people.

Estimating that by the year 2000, 5000m people out of a world population of 7000m will be living in cities, and that the total population will reach 20,000m by the end of the twenty-first century, Dr. Constantinos A. Doxiadis, Greek town-planner and head of the Athens Centre for Ekistics, sees it as inevitable that the whole planet will merge into one single world-city.

This world-city, ecumenopolis, is the ultimate stage following the rapid growth of "megalopoli", such as the east coast of the United States, the Tokio-Osaka complex, Greater London, and others elsewhere in the world.

If the inevitable ecumenopolis "is built along today's lines, according to present day trends," says Dr. Doxiadis, "it will be a city doomed to destruction." He lays down the elements of a "human-engineered" world-city: small town-like cells of 30,000 to 50,000 people; roadways; food transport tubes and utilities moved underground; and tentacles of nature everywhere inter-penetrating population centres.

Dr. Athelstan Spilhaus, Director of Research at New York University, and a noted urbanist, urges the building of cities of 250,000 people along the lines of the Minnesota Experimental City — MXC. "Suppose that the world population, if we do little about population control, reaches 15 billion by 2070. And let us assume that our technology permits us to build cities on any solid land, from Antarctica to the tropics, from desert to rain forest. The area of all the continents is about 2.3 billion acres. Thus, if we built cities of controlled size, dispersed throughout the world, there would be 60,000 cities of 250,000 people each and each city would be surrounded by 40,000 acres or 64 sq. m. of open land. The alternative of allowing the present big cities to grow unplanned or to accelerate their growth through so-called urban renewal would mean that vast tracts of the earth's surface would be uninhabited and the urban complexes would be intolerable." (*Bell Magazine,* October, 1969.)

CLIMATE

If power generation continues to increase at the present rate, there is a danger that man will overheat the earth, according to two Soviet scientists, Professors G.P. Kalinin and V.D. Bykov of Moscow University. They say that "power is generated and consumed by industry at such an accelerating rate that, even in the near future, this will seriously affect the earth's heat budget".If generated power increases annually at 10%, in 100 years it will have an effect comparable to that of solar radiation. Water resources accordingly become particularly important since a large increase in water consumption (thus, evaporation) would lead to a corresponding cooling effect. One way more water could be made available for human consumption, the Soviet scientists say, is by diverting ocean water into the Dead Sea, the Qattara Depression and other enclosed basins in hot regions of Africa and Eurasia, where it would evaporate and then return to the earth as rain.

According to recent studies by J.O. Fletcher of the Rand Corporation, Santa Monica, California, man may be changing the planet's climate whether he wants to or not. Among the human-generated factors that are affecting climate are heat production, smog, aircraft vapour trails, and increased carbon dioxide content in the atmosphere as a result of the burning of fossil fuels. The carbon dioxide content has gone up by 10% to 15% in the twentieth century, creating a "greenhouse effect" that prevents heat from escaping out to space, and consequently warms the earth.

Mr. Fletcher says that "the purposeful management of global climatic resources will eventually become necessary".

He notes that "man already has the technological capability to carry out many climate-influencing schemes". Such schemes include the removal of ice from the Arctic Ocean, the damming of the Bering Strait to stop or reverse the present northward flow of cold Pacific water through it, the deflecting of the Gulf Stream and its Pacific counterpart, the Kuro Siwa (Kuroshio) Current, and the damming of the Congo to create, with the help of the Ubangi River, two enormous inland seas covering 10% of Africa.

COCOA

Although the FAO and other authorities noted in 1968 that a cocoa shortage was unlikely there has in fact been one. In 1969 the FAO predicted a shortage of 107,720 tons following a harvest of 1.4m tons. Nobody had realized that stock reserves had dwindled so alarmingly.

COLOMBIA

461,606 sq. m. Pop. 21m. Coffee provided nearly 70% of export earnings in 1969 (90% in 1965) but minerals are being developed more intensively. Oil is the most thoroughly exploited and a Trans-Andean pipeline is greatly expanding the effective "local" market of the existing oil fields.

The most significant industrial development has been in Cartagena, (pop. 300,000). Cartagena has a thriving industrial complex, Mamonal. Its 18 major companies produce 56m dollars' worth of goods a year — 64% of the total production of Bolivar, the north Colombian state.

Much progress is evident in the production of cotton, timber, cacao and soya beans but less in secondary industry. Population pressure is becoming a problem. The national increase is 3% but the rate of growth in the cities, by birth and by drift, is as high as 18%.

Trade with the U.K., 1969: exports to, £9m; imports from, £11m. Trade with the U.S.A., 1969: exports to, $190m: imports from, $100m.

COLOMBO PLAN

Most of the countries of South and South-east Asia, assisted by the Colombo Plan, have had growth rates of 5% or better but the four with slower rates — Afghanistan, India, Indonesia and Vietnam — contain over two-thirds of the region's total population. It seems probable that seven of the countries will have achieved a greater than 5% annual average increase for the entire 1960-70 decade in spite of their many difficulties. They are South Korea, Iran, Singapore, Thailand, Pakistan, Malaysia and the Philippines.

The major impediments to more rapid and sustained growth include high population increases, low levels of domestic savings, insufficient supply of trained manpower, and inadequate foreign exchange earnings. During 1969 the Colombo Plan member countries made major payments to the under-developed ones. In American dollars, the amounts were: U.S.A., 1,864m; Australia, 33.2m; Canada, 134.5m; Japan, 290.94m; New Zealand, 3.02m; the U.K., 125.29m. The core of the Colombo Plan is probably provision of technical assistance; during 1969, 1,702 Asian students were financed in the U.K.

COMMON MARKETS

This is a summary of the principal common markets and their evolution. The member countries of each group are listed in order of population size.
EEC European Economic Community: West Germany, Italy, France, Netherlands, Belgium, Luxembourg.

Common Markets

EFTA European Free Trade Association: the U.K., Portugal, Sweden, Austria, Switzerland, Denmark, Norway, Finland, (associate but for all practical purposes full member) Iceland.
COMECON Council for Mutual Economic Aid: Soviet Union, Poland, Rumania, East Germany, Czechoslovakia, Hungary, Bulgaria, Mongolia.
LAFTA Latin American Free Trade Association: Brazil, Mexico, Argentina, Colombia, Peru, Venezuela, *Chile, Ecuador, Bolivia, Uruguay, Paraguay.
CACM Central American Common Market: Guatemala, El Salvador, Honduras, Nicaragua, Costa Rica.
EAC East African Community: Kenya, Uganda, Tanzania.

Other groups are in the process of formation. In West Africa 12 countries are to form a common market and four central African countries have formed a customs and economic union. The Caribbean has a form of common market (CARIFTA) as have the Arab countries and the Arab Gulf Emirates.

The EEC came into being on January 1, 1958, based on the Rome Treaty signed on the previous March between Belgium, France, West Germany, Luxembourg, Italy and the Netherlands. A full customs union was completed in July, 1968. The original idea was an eventual political union, but French policies make this at best a distant prospect. Association agreements have been signed with Turkey, Greece and Spain, and with a number of African states.

The EFTA convention was signed in 1960. It established a free trade area between Austria, Denmark, Norway, Portugal, Sweden, Switzerland and the United Kingdom. Finland became an associate member during the following year. Iceland joined in 1970. Internal tariffs on most industrial goods have been abolished, but the convention does not cover agriculture, nor does it envisage the setting up of a common external tariff. The objectives of EFTA thus differ in scope from those of the EEC.

Argentina, Chile, Brazil, Mexico, Paraguay, Peru and Uruguay joined together to form LAFTA in 1961. Colombia and Ecuador acceded later in the same year, followed in 1967 by Venezuela and Bolivia. Progress towards free trade and co-ordinated regional development has been slow over the last three years because member countries have been reluctant to accept tariff reductions which would increase competition with domestic industries.

The CACM was established in 1960 by El Salvador, Guatemala, Honduras and Nicaragua; Costa Rica joined in 1962. It has made considerable progress towards freeing intra-regional trade, adopting a common external tariff and stimulating industrial investment. The aim is a customs and economic union.

In 1949 COMECON was set up "to strengthen economic collaboration of the socialist countries and to co-ordinate their economic development". Its main aim was, in fact, to integrate the economies of Eastern Europe with that of the U.S.S.R. Founding members were Bulgaria, Czechoslovakia, Hungary, Poland, Rumania and the U.S.S.R.: Albania and East Germany joined soon afterwards. Albania subsequently left and Mongolia was admitted.

CONTRASTS. The member countries of two of the groups — LAFTA and CACM — have largely similar economic structures. However, LAFTA's intra-regional trade is dominated by Argentina, Chile and Brazil, and consists mainly of an exchange of agricultural products. The CACM's record of growth has been more encouraging, with trade between members increasing nearly five-fold in over five years, and at the same time a substantial increase in trade in manufactured products has been recorded.

It was becoming evident that COMECON was increasing its external trade while maintaining internal trade at a fairly constant level but, during the 1968 Czech crisis, the Russians made it clear that they would not contemplate a further tightening of economic links between East and West.

The EEC and EFTA are both groups whose members compete with each other. The comparative size of the EEC's market and the high degree of industrialization in all member countries allow a greater potential growth than in EFTA, whose members rely heavily on specialization in production. However, in a number of fields there has been a slowing down in the progress previously achieved in the EEC.

CONTINENTAL DRIFT

Many geologists have thought that the unusually harsh landscape of the Afar triangle, north-east Ethiopia, is connected with the peculiar formations of the Great Rift Valley. Afar is at the meeting place of three great undersea rift systems, two of them leaving the Red Sea and the Gulf of Aden; geophysicists think that both bodies of water are gradually being widened into oceans at the rate of perhaps an inch a year as the lava pours out of the rifts. The Belgian geologist, Haroun Tazieff, contends that the Afar triangle is a section of the expanding floor of the Red Sea and that tens of thousands of years ago it was partly covered by seawater. Much of the rock that Tazieff's expeditions have gathered in the area is younger and heavier than typical land rocks and bears other similarities to specimens found on the ocean floor.

COOK ISLANDS

0.2 sq. km. Pop. 20,000. The construction of Raratonga international airport began in June 1970; it will be operational in June 1972 at a cost of 5.1m NZ dollars.

COPPER

Several new fields are in production, principally in Albania (Mirdite region), Australia (Mons Cupri, Western Australia),

New Geography 1970-71

South Africa (Tshipise, and Mutali, Transvaal), South Korea (Yongyang), U.S.A. (Casa Grande, Arizona); this last is a major field with reserves of 475m tons.

COSTA RICA

19,653 sq. m. Pop. 1.65m. The banana industry is developing so rapidly that it overtook coffee as the main foreign exchange earner in 1970. Production was 52m boxes (20m in 1967). Meat and sugar have become important earners of foreign exchange, mostly U.S. dollars. An American firm plans to invest 60m dollars in a bauxite plant to produce over 600,000 tons of semi-refined aluminium annually.

Trade with the U.K., 1969: exports to, £0.5m; imports from, £3m. Trade with the U.S.A., 1969: exports to, $101m; imports from $70m.

CUBA

44,178 sq. m. Pop. 8.2m. The economy depends almost entirely on the sugar crop which constantly lags behind official expectations. The 1970 harvest target was 10m tons; the 1969 target was 9m tons and the actual crop made only 4.5m tons. Full mechanization of sugar harvesting is unlikely until 1975. The International Sugar Agreement of 1969 gave Cuba a basic export quota of 2.15m tons; this larger amount will increase foreign exchange earnings, since previously most Cuban sugar was disposed of by barter.

Some progress in agricultural diversification has been achieved, notably in poultry, cattle and citrus fruits. Rice and coffee have been introduced in some areas. The fishing fleet and dock service have been modernized and Cuban lobsters and fish have found a ready market in Europe. Minerals are certainly being exploited.

Cuba claims to have 40% of the world's nickel supplies and there is a world shortage of nickel, but lack of technical skills retards mining development. The Soviet Union continues to be Cuba's largest trading partner, accounting for 60% of Cuban imports and 50% of exports. It is interesting to note that Cuba's chief imports are harbour and transport equipment.

Trade with the U.K., 1969: exports to, £5.5m; imports from, £12m. Trade with the U.S.A. continues to be at a standstill.

CYPRUS

3,572 sq.m. Pop. 622,000. Economic conditions have been more stable. The 1969-70 citrus crop was high; exports of minerals have increased steadily. The most spectacular results are seen in tourism, with 82,000 visitors in 1969, principally from the U.K., the U.S.A., Greece, Lebanon and Israel. The U.K. supplies Cyprus with one-third of her imports; other main suppliers are Italy and West Germany. The U.K. also takes one-third of Cyprus' exports.

The Cypriots are making determined efforts to boost exports of citrus, grapes, wines and canned goods to new markets; trade missions visited Finland, Norway, Sweden and Austria in 1970.

Trade with the U.K., 1969: exports to, £14.5m; imports from, £16.8m. Trade with the U.S.A., 1969: exports to, $30m; imports from $18m.

CZECHOSLOVAKIA

49,000 sq. m. Pop. 14.4m. Not all Czechoslovakia's economic problems stem from its political difficulties. The long-term direction of economic development had assumed that there would be a continuing demand from other East European countries for such products as rolling mills, pipes, compressors, power stations and cars. However, COMECON countries are buying an increasing supply of these commodities from the West. Also, earlier plans to lessen Czechoslovakia's reliance on coal depended on ample supplies of alternative sources of energy such as oil, natural gas and nuclear power from the Soviet Union, which is now finding other markets more profitable.

Farm output has been poor, with a low potato harvest and inadequate supplies of meat. Shortages of labour — since 1968 there has been an outflow of much skilled labour — have led to a cutback in acreage. Since early 1969 the Czech and Slovak states have had separate control over many domestic matters which may help to rationalize labour.

The trade agreement with the Soviet Union in 1970 provides for an exchange of goods, including large shipments of Soviet oil, iron ore and cotton. Earnings from tourism have shown a marked decline; 4m tourists in 1968 instead of the expected 6m; (1969, 2.9m).

Trade with the U.K., 1969: exports to, £21.5m; imports from £18.2m. Trade with the U.S.A. 1969: exports to, $75m; imports from, $91.5m.

DENMARK

16,000 sq. m. Pop. 4.9m. Denmark is an interesting example of diversification in an already diversified industrial pattern. In the last two years industrial building and design, plastics, pharmaceuticals, office machinery and electronics have all prospered. Since 1963 the contribution of farm produce to the total value of exports has fallen from over a half to a third while industrial exports have been growing by 20% a year. This does not mean that farm produce is less important, for while sales to the EEC have fallen considerably those to EFTA have proportionately increased.

Denmark's application for membership of the EEC is based on the need to maintain its markets both in the EEC and in the U.K., its principal outlet for butter (95%), cheese, bacon and eggs. However, the country's close and expanding trade links with the Scandinavian countries raise several complications. Because of their tradition of political neutrality neither Sweden nor Finland has applied to join the EEC. But, with Sweden now Denmark's second trading partner after the U.K., difficulties would arise should the Danish government impose external tariff barriers.

Scandinavian links will also be tightened by Denmark's proposal to build an international airport costing at least £230m on Saltholm Island between Denmark and Southern Sweden, linked to Copenhagen by a tunnel and to Malmö by a bridge. The Danish government hopes for Swedish and Norwegian co-operation and has offered to share sovereignty of the island.

Although Saltholm is the key to the region's future development, it is still only one of a number of factors. The population of the Oresund area, about 2,650,000 Danes and Swedes, will total nearly 4m by the year 2000, according to studies made by the Oresund Council.

The Copenhagen of the year 2000 will spread over much of north-east Zealand, inland to Roskilde, 32 kilometres to the west, and a good stretch south along the coast. Planners hope that the metropolitan area can retain much of its farmland appearance by spreading out population areas and incorporating existing farms and woodland into the overall plan.

The tentative city blueprint for the future, largely dependent on the airport plans, involves construction of new housing on much of the western third of Amager, where dispersed towns could provide housing for up to half a million additional residents.

Under a £10m container shipping service, inaugurated in November 1969, Denmark will deliver bacon and butter to the U.K. and return with British cars, tractors, agricultural equipment and caravans.

Trade with the U.K., 1969: exports to, £239m; imports from, £163m. Trade with the U.S.A., 1969: exports to, $207m; imports from $105m.

DUBAI

One of the seven Trucial States. 32,000 sq. m. Pop. 40,000. American, Japanese and European oil firms are engaged in oil exploration and in 1969 production was started from the Fateh field, which includes unique innovations in oil storage techniques. Two floating storage tanks with a joint capacity of 645,000 bbl have been built from converted tanker hulls and an underwater vessel with a capacity of 500,000 bbl, the first of its type in the world, has been anchored to the Gulf floor. These developments permit tankers to load directly from the production area, avoiding the use of shallow coastal waters and also saving the cost of construction of submarine

Dubai

pipelines to the shore. Even if oil revenues continue to grow trading must be the basis of the Dubai economy; the principal trade is in gold smuggled to India. Dubai's entrepôt imports in 1969 amounted to £80m (£14m from the U.K.).

E

EARTHQUAKES

CALIFORNIA. On opposite sides of the 600-mile San Andreas fault, the coast strip of California is slowly but inexorably moving to the north-west while the remainder of the state is shifting towards the south-east. This mobility produces the earthquakes that suddenly jolt areas of California, occasionally with catastrophic results.

By carefully measuring movements along the San Andreas and nearby smaller faults, seismologist Renner Hofmann has predicted recent Californian earthquakes. A team led by Hofmann developed the quakecast method while investigating fault zones for the California Department of Water Resources, which is concerned about the effects of earth slippage and quakes on its vast system of pumping plants, dams and aqueducts. To measure the earth movements in the fault zones, they established over 90 fixed observation points along the faults.

Using a geodimeter, Hofmann aimed a beam of intense light from a site on one side of a fault at a reflector set up on the other side, between twelve and twenty miles away. By measuring the time required for the light to travel to the reflector and back to the geodimeter, he calculated the precise distance between the two points. By repeating the measurement annually, he was able to determine with precision the amount and direction of movement that had taken place since the last measurement.

At many observation points along the San Andreas fault, the scientists found that California's coastal strip was moving to the north-west at a rate of two inches per year. In some areas, however, friction between the sliding masses of rock

Earthquakes

caused the movement to slow and even to stop. "When the fault sticks," Hofmann says, "the movement is transferred to smaller, adjacent faults that can stand only a limited amount of movement. When these smaller faults reach their limit, the forces increase until the main fault breaks loose again. This sudden breaking loose is the earthquake."

JAPAN. The International Institute of Seismology and Earthquake Engineering, Tokio, has been carrying out intensive research in the last two years. It was set up under a five-year joint project between Japan and the U.N. Development Programme. Japanese scientists and engineers have largely solved the problems posed by earthquakes in a highly industrialized and economically advanced country situated in one of the most active seismic zones. Central Tokio today has several skyscrapers of 500 ft. and more, yet old laws forbade buildings taller than 120 ft. By July 1970 the Institute had trained 200 professionals from 32 developing countries; 60 countries lie within seismic zones.

Research into micro-earthquakes is being carried out at IISEE. Several hundred earthquakes are recorded daily in Japan, though only a very few are felt by the population. They are recorded by a network of 150 seismic stations. Movements of the earth's crust down to a few thousandths of a millimetre are simultaneously registered and timed with an accuracy of a hundredth of a second. This enables the locality to be pinpointed. Study of the recordings gives a picture of the strains which exist below the surface.

Another branch of study concerns the possibility of heading off an impending natural disaster with small, man-made earthquakes. Man has already caused earthquakes through ignorance, for instance by the construction of large reservoirs, or by the injection of waste waters into deep wells, or again by underground nuclear explosions. This knowledge of how to produce a minor earthquake could develop into a method of heading off major natural quakes. For example, if many small quakes could be generated in an area where seismologists were sure that increasing strains in the earth's crust were about to produce a large earthquake, enough of the strain might be relieved to keep the larger disturbance from occurring.

PERU. From May 31 to June 1, 1970, Peru suffered the worst earthquake in the recorded history of Latin America, with 50,000 people killed. The seaport of Chimbote was demolished, the departmental capital of Huaras practically destroyed and the tourist city of Yungay, at the foot of Mount Huascaran, virtually disappeared under a *huayco* — a wall of water, rock and mud. Only 3,000 of 41,000 people survived. The epicentre of the earthquake was in the Pacific 42 miles west of Chimbote.

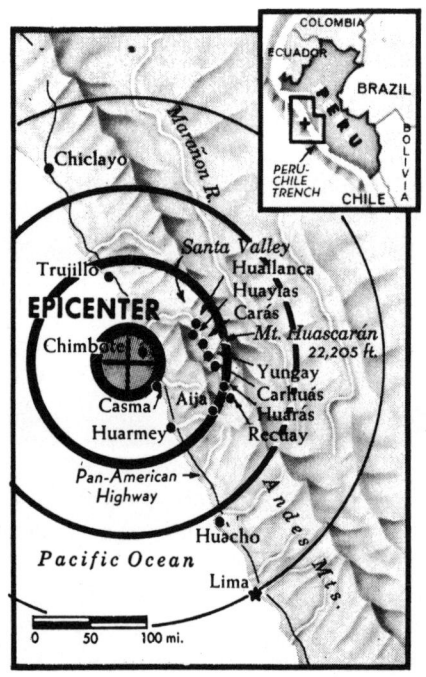

Diagram of the Peruvian earthquake.

Ecology

TURKEY. On March 28, 1969, a strong tremor affected several western provinces in Western Turkey along the Anatolian fault. The epicentre was near Alasehir in Manisa province, and about 1,100 people were killed.

YUGOSLAVIA. On October 27, 1969 an earthquake which damaged the industrial town of Banja Luka (50,000) in central Yugoslavia killed 20 people.
(See *Italy*.)

EAST GERMANY (German Democratic Republic)

41,479 sq. m. Pop. 17.2 m. The targets set under the 1965-70 development programme seem likely to be achieved. These include rises of 50% in investment, 40% in industrial production and building and 33% in agricultural output. The chemical industry, which accounts for 17% of total industrial production, and shipbuilding are especially prosperous. About 40% of East German trade is with the Soviet Union but transactions with the West are increasing. The importance of the trade fairs held in Leipzig in the spring and autumn of each year cannot be over-estimated. Each fair has about 10,000 exhibitors, including 300 British.

Trade with the U.K., 1969: exports to, £20m; imports from, £15m. Trade with the U.S.A., 1969: exports to, $94m; imports from $111m.

ECOLOGY

In his State of the Union Message, January 1970, the American President noted: "The great question of the 70s is: shall we surrender to our surroundings or shall we make our peace with nature and begin to make reparations for the damage we have done to our air, to our land and to our water?"

This is the business of ecology, an emerging geographic science. Ecology is the systems approach to nature, the study of how living organisms and the non-living environment function together as a whole or ecosystem.

The prominent ecologists are disturbed by mankind's blindness to his own utter dependency on all ecosystems such as oceans, coastal estuaries, forests and grasslands, all of which constitute the biosphere, the thin global envelope that sustains the only known life in the universe. The "domino theory" is applicable to human environment. DDT is an example. When farmers wipe out one pest with powerful chemicals they may soon find their crops afflicted with six pests that are resistant to the chemicals. DDT kills insect-eating birds that normally control the pests that now destroy the farmers' crops.

Ecologists also stress the crowding problem. Since 80% of the population is likely to live in cities occupying only 2% of the land the sheer density of people will strain the urban ecosystem. Ecologists are not hopeful that a "green revolution" can increase farm harvests sufficiently to feed twice as many people.

Modern technology is putting pressure on nature with tens of thousands of synthetic substances, many almost totally resistant to decay, which will poison man's fellow creatures as well as man himself. The burden includes smog fumes, aluminium cans that cannot rust, inorganic plastics that may last for decades, floating oil that can change the thermal reflectivity of oceans and radioactive wastes whose toxicity lingers for centuries. The earth has its own waste-disposal system but it has its limits. The winds that ventilate the earth are only six miles high; toxic garbage can kill the tiny organisms that normally clean rivers.

U.S. ecologist Paul Ehrlich says, "Each American child is 50 times more of a burden on the environment than each Indian child." Although the U.S. contains (1970) only 5.7% of the world's population it consumes 40% of the world's production of natural resources.

In 70 years of life the average American consumes: 26m

Ecology

gallons of water, 21,000 gallons of petrol, 10,000 lb of meat, 28,000 lb of milk and cream; 8,000 dollars' worth of school buildings, and 6,000 dollars' worth of clothing. (Figures from Washington University, St. Louis, Missouri in 1969.)

Every year Americans junk 7m cars, 100m tyres, 20m tons of paper, 28 billion bottles and 48 billion tins. The U.S.A. also produces 50% of the world's industrial pollution with the nation's 85m cars causing 60% of the air pollution in cities (*Time Magazine,* February 2, 1970).

However, the environment is being damaged in many other places. The smog in Tokio is so dense that often no sky is visible. Swiss surveys during 1969-70 show that Lakes Geneva, Constance and Neuchatel are polluted. Some Norwegian fiords have stinking cakes of solid wastes. The Rhine has become known as "Europe's sewer", but fish can now live in it following an improvement in purity during 1970.

Many ecologists are concerned about the effect of pollutants on phytoplankton. Near Marseilles two large aluminium refineries each day discharge 6,000 tons of red sediment into the Mediterranean. Though not toxic it blankets and kills all living things. Other ecologists think that various particles in the atmosphere are reflecting sunlight away from the earth, thus cooling the planet. About 31% of the world's surface is covered by low cloud and if this were increased to 36% through pollution the temperature would drop about 4°C — enough to start a return to the ice age. (When Krakatoa exploded in 1883 the temperature at the earth's surface was reduced for several years.)

There are unexpected geographical side effects to progress. For instance, the Aswan High Dam has stopped the flow of silt down the Nile which in the past offset the natural erosion of the land from the Nile delta. As a result downstream erosion may wash away as much productive land as is opened up by new irrigation systems around Lake Nasser. Without the nutrient-rich silt reaching the Mediterranean the Egyptian sardine catch declined from 18,000 tons in 1965 to 300 in 1969.

New Geography 1970-71

A promising start to ecological forecasting is being made in Colorado where the ecologist G. Van Dyne is running a key project under the International Biological Programme to discover how a grasslands ecosystem responds to various stresses. More than 80 scientists are gathering data for a computer-modelling scheme.

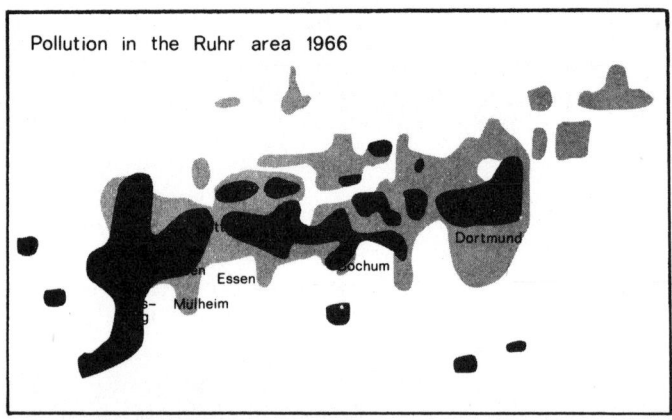

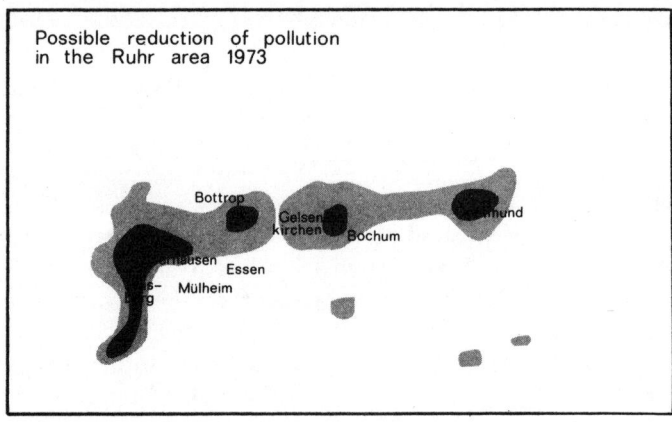

■ Heavy pollution
▨ Pollution
☐ Little or no pollution

Education

ECUADOR

226,000 sq. m. Pop. 5.7m. The nation's balance of payments problems stem largely from heavy dependence on agriculture, which employs more than half the working population. Plantation crops, particularly bananas, provide four-fifths of the country's foreign earnings. Because of increasing competition from Central America, growers have had to introduce new methods of packing, to look for new markets, e.g. Japan, and new crops, e.g. oil seeds. Shipments of rice, once a major export commodity, have been resumed and wheat-growing is being encouraged to reduce the need for imports. The fishing industry is growing and tourism is expanding at 10% a year.

The main future prospects for increasing Ecuador's foreign exchange earnings will probably depend on oil discoveries in the north-east which has reserves estimated at 1,500m bbl.

Trade with the U.K., 1969: exports to, £400,000; imports from, £3.2m. Trade with the U.S.A., 1969: exports to, $105.8m; imports from $76m.

EDUCATION

Education in Asia developed greatly in the 1960s. In 18 of UNESCO's 19 member states in the region, total school enrolment at all levels rose from 89.5m in 1969 to just over 150m by the end of 1970. Teaching staff increased from 2.7m to over 4.3m and the number of primary and secondary schools rose from 629,000 to 812,000. Data from a comprehensive review of educational progress in the region from 1950 to 1967, prepared by the UNESCO Regional Office for Education in Bangkok, show that in 1960, when the Karachi Plan for long-term educational development was drawn up, there were only nine countries in Asia with a primary school enrolment of more than 70%. The Karachi Plan called for at least seven years' universal free primary education in the region by 1980.

By early 1968, 13 countries had passed the 70% enrolment mark, and eight had more than 90%. Despite this rapid growth, the total was still nearly 15m short of the targets the Karachi Plan countries had set themselves.

More impressive were the increases at other levels. Secondary school enrolment jumped from a little over 17m to more than 32m. Higher education figures increased from 1.9m to 39m.

EIRE (Republic of Ireland)

26,600 sq. m. Pop. 2.911m. Predictably, the main domestic contribution to growth continues to be made by industry which achieved an increase of 10% during 1969. Metal, engineering and the chemical industries showed a pronounced upturn but most notable of all is the performance of the mining industry. Significant deposits of zinc, lead and silver are being exploited and Eire is rapidly becoming a major European producer. The increase is astonishing. In 1961 mineral exports brought in £16,000; in 1969 they made £11m.

While agricultural output continues to grow very slowly, labour productivity is increasing more rapidly as fewer people work on the land. Nevertheless, agriculture still provides employment for a third of the total labour force.

The industrial expansion programme is one of the most attractive in Europe because of tax incentives, exemptions and grants. As a result 212 foreign firms were established in Eire during 1960-70, providing employment for 50,000 people.

The £10m storage terminal at Bantry Bay received its first mammoth tanker – the 312,000-ton *Universe Ireland* – late in 1968. Since then Gulf Oil, owners of the terminal, have had six giant tankers working the Kuwait-Bantry run. Smaller vessels transfer the crude oil to Milford Haven, Stignaes (Denmark) and Rotterdam. Gulf Oil claims that the Kuwait-

Bantry shipment costs per ton equal the cost of taking fully laden 200,000-tonners direct to refinery.

Eire is trying to diversify its markets; in 1970 the U.K. took 70% of all exports. During 1969-70 a sharp increase in imports was particularly marked in wood, lumber and cork, chemicals, plastics, textile yarns and threads, iron and steel, and motor vehicles. Despite a deficit the government remains committed to a free trade policy and in mid-1969 implemented a 10% reduction in tariffs against British goods, as provided for in the Anglo-Irish Free Trade Area Agreement of 1965. In July 1970 Eire began negotiations to join the EEC.

"Growth points" are being developed at Shannon, Galway and Waterford in the form of industrial estates.

Irish trade with the U.K., 1969: exports to, £294m; imports from, £330m. Trade with the U.S.A., 1969: exports to, $40m; imports from, $50m.

EL SALVADOR

7,772 sq. m. Pop. 3.26m. The main problem facing El Salvador is that its export quota for coffee is fixed at a level that is consistently below the annual crop. But prospects for industrial development are encouraging; in the five years ending June 1970 no fewer than 500 plants worth 150m dollars were established.

El Salvador was able to take advantage of free trade in manufactures because of an efficient transport system, low-cost power and well-developed financial organization. Trucks, buses, tractors and agricultural machinery are being assembled. Other industries include textiles, fertilizers, furniture, brewing, oil refining, cement and packaging materials.

Trade with the U.K., 1969: exports to, £1.8m; imports from, £300,000. Trade with the U.S.A., 1969: exports to, $70m; imports from, $30m.

New Geography 1970-71

ETHIOPIA

395,000 sq. m. Pop. 23.9m. The most interesting aspect of Ethopia's geography is research into the 400,000-sq. m. Afar triangle at the juncture of the Red Sea and the Gulf of Aden. The Belgian vulcanologist Haroun Tazieff says that the mountainous area could be extremely prosperous from exploitation of the great fields of superheated water and steam just below the desert floor. This power could be used to develop aluminium, fertilizers and petro-chemicals.

Lying astride the strategic routes connecting the continent with Asia, Ethiopia occupies one of the most favourable agricultural areas in Africa, and its varied topography is reflected in its climate and vegetation. Economically, it is a primitive country, with an average income of only about £20 per head. Approximately 90% of the population is directly dependent upon agriculture. It is essentially a single commodity economy, coffee providing over 50% of total exports.

Despite this rather gloomy picture, the economy, particularly the agricultural sector, has great potential. About 70% of the total area of the country is grazing and cultivable land, timber and coffee forests, but less than a fifth is actually cultivated. Waste ground could be profitably irrigated.

The wide variety of soils, climate and altitudes permits production of diversified agricultural commodities in addition to coffee. These include cereals, oil seeds, pulses, livestock, hides and skins, timber, fibres, fresh vegetables and fruit, and, with more extensive use of the sizable unexploited acreage, production could be increased enormously. Significant improvements on present yields and quality are possible without large capital expenditure. Development along these lines would create an important source of foreign exchange and would encourage the growth of new processing industries.

In order to mobilize this agricultural potential, which is supported by equally hopeful prospects in the field of HEP, the implementation of the third five-year development plan is important. Concerted efforts are required to modernize farming methods, and to continue with comprehensive regional development schemes in key areas, such as the 50,000-acre irrigation project planned for the Middle Awash Valley.

The country is ideally situated and has the agricultural potential to provide the increasingly prosperous but arid Middle Eastern countries with vital foodstuffs. During World War II, Ethiopia was a major supplier of food grains to the Allied forces, and, as such, it became known as the "bread basket" of the Middle East. There is scope to achieve this in a permanent sense.

Trade with the U.K., 1969: exports to, £370,000; imports from, £265,000. Trade with the U.S.A., 1969: exports to $0.5m; imports from, $400,000.

EUROPEAN ECONOMIC COMMUNITY
(The Common Market)

The six member states are taking the first steps towards a common industrial policy, designed to make the most of the Common Market. The Ministerial Council has given broad directives to the planning officials in Brussels, which say in effect that industrialists in the Common Market must break with the old industrial systems tied to the nation-state and its rules. They must create new companies, exploit new inventions and find the necessary investment on a continent-wide basis, and generally do business as if they were a single community of 180m people.

Ultimately a company which wishes to spread itself throughout the big market should not have to fight its way through a mass of conflicting laws and other problems in the six member states but should be required only to obey one set of Common Market rules.

Only in this way, say the planners, will a sufficient number of companies be encouraged to make "trans-national" mergers with companies in other member states so as to create firms big enough to face up to the challenge of the American industrial giants now dominating a large part of the Common Market. The proposed common industrial policy is a recognition that member states must, in many sectors, work as closely together industrially as do the American states.

Advanced technological industries (nuclear power stations, computers, aviation and space equipment) would, under the proposed common industrial policy, be developed on a community instead of on a national basis, by the awarding of Community industrial development contracts.

Agreement between the Six is near on a European employment office in which representatives of employers and trade union organizations would be represented. Here special arrangements would be made for helping workers who are losing their jobs, owing to changing industrial patterns, to be retrained, preferably before they become unemployed, and to provide relief through a reformed European social fund.

EUROPEAN FREE TRADE ASSOCIATION (EFTA)

During the ten years of EFTA's existence, member countries have achieved a vigorous expansion of their trade with one another and with the world. Measured in terms of exports, EFTA countries' trade with the world grew faster from 1959 to 1969 than from 1950 to 1959, from an average annual rate of 6.5% to one of 7.8%. In value, total EFTA exports increased from 10 billion U.S. dollars in 1950 to 18 billion U.S. dollars in 1959 and 38 billion U.S. dollars in 1969.

Intra-EFTA exports followed a much more dynamic trend in the 1959-1969 period, reaching an average annual rate of growth of 11%, compared with 6.5% from 1950 to 1959. In value, intra-EFTA exports increased from 2 billion U.S. dollars in 1950 to 3.5 billion U.S. dollars in 1959 and 10 billion U.S. dollars in 1969.

The progress should be seen in the context of the development of world trade. Both in the 1950s and since the creation of EFTA, the rates at which the exports of the

European Free Trade Association

EFTA countries have grown have been less than those at which world trade has grown. One reason for this is that even at the beginning of the 1950s the trade they were doing was out of proportion to their size, so that any expansion they later achieved was proportionately less impressive. Their citizens amount to no more than 3% of the world's population, but they engage in 16% of the world's trade.

Although in both periods the growth in EFTA's trade has been less than the world average, the performance of its member countries has been better in the second period than in the first. In the 1950s the exports of several EFTA countries grew less rapidly than world trade. Since 1959 all with the exception of Denmark and Britain have increased their exports by more than the world average. The growth rates of total EFTA exports were, however, mainly influenced by the relatively low growth of British exports, since these represented almost half of the total. British exports increased at average annual rates of 5.2% in the first period and 6.2% in the second.

For EFTA countries other than Britain export growth rates were above the world average. They increased their combined exports to the world by an average of 8.3% in 1950-59 and by 9.7% in 1959-69. These are substantial growth rates by almost any standard.

At no time in the past 20 years has the trade of the EFTA countries with each other been more than a quarter of their total trade. For the six countries of the EEC, their trade with each other has never been less than a third of their total trade, and the share has risen in the past decade to become fairly close to half of the total. The creation of the Common Market gave a strong stimulus to trade between its members; the result has been that their trade with each other, which was already growing by nearly 12% a year in the 1950s increased by an annual average of about 16% between 1959 and 1969. Before the founding of EFTA, the annual growth of trade between its member countries was less than 7% but since then it has risen to 11%. The acceleration has evidently been greater than in the EEC.

New Geography 1970-71

EURO-TRADE CENTRES

Four multi-million pound skyscrapers are rising within 150 miles of each other in Amsterdam, Rotterdam, Brussels and Antwerp. All these cities are now firmly committed to matching the world trade centres of New York (for £240m) and Tokio. Both Dutch cities agree that it will be bad for Dutch prestige to have competing centres but Rotterdam, as the world's biggest port, cannot drop out if New York has a centre. Amsterdam's argument is that it is a more important centre than Rotterdam for financial and insurance interests. In Belgium, Antwerp as one of the great world ports insists that it needs a centre. Brussels has the ambitious plan of rebuilding part of the centre of the city.

EXPLORATION

Thor Heyerdahl reached Bridgetown, Barbados, on July 13, 1970 after crossing the Atlantic from Morocco in a papyrus boat. The object was to prove that the ancient Egyptians could have sailed to the Americas in similar craft. The 16-ton boat, *Ra 11*, was built in Morocco by four Aymara Indians from Lake Titicaca on the Peruvian-Bolivian border. The 3,900-mile journey took 57 days. (In 1969 Heyerdahl had *Ra I* built in Egypt by Chad tribesmen who still use papyrus boats on Lake Chad, but it failed to make the Atlantic crossing.)

In December 1970 the "Hudson 70" expedition completed its 48,000-mile circumnavigation of the American continents.

The British Trans-Arctic (four-man) expedition completed (May 22, 1969) its 464-day, 3,000-mile crossing of the Arctic.

The ice-breaker *S.S. Manhattan,* 115,000 tons, navigated the North-west Passage in September 1969. The voyage was westward via Davis Strait, Lancaster Sound, Prince of Wales Strait, Beaufort Sea to Port Barrow, Alaska.

F

FINLAND

130,165 sq. m. Pop. 4.725m. The latest statistical survey of January 1970 produced these revised figures for land use and population. Land use: inland waterways, 9.4%; forested, 71.3%; cultivated, 9.2%. Density of population: South Finland, 26 per sq. km; North Finland, 4 per sq. km. Capital and largest cities: Helsinki, 535,165; Tampere, 155,585; Turku, 154,710; Lahti, 89,443; Oulu, 86,709; Pori, 72,970; Kuopio, 64,793; Jyvaskyla, 58,072; Lappeenranta, 51,176; Vassa, 49,821.

The recovery in production in 1969 was led by the country's traditional forest industries which account for two-thirds of Finland's exports. The newer industries, such as electrical engineering and plastics, are becoming increasingly significant. Other industries which are steadily expanding are rubber, textiles, chemicals and metals. Several major investment projects are near completion, including Finland's first car assembly line, two steel rolling mills and several chemical projects. There is a drift from the land because of overproduction and marketing problems; areas under cultivation are being reduced.

British exports to Finland were 25% higher in 1969 than in 1968 and the U.K. has overtaken West Germany, Sweden and the U.S.S.R. to become Finland's largest supplier. The U.K. is now Finland's most important trade partner in both directions. In 1969 the U.K. spent £140m in Finland, mainly on paper, wood pulp and timber, and exported goods to a value of £85m to Finland. In 1970 British exports to Finland were expected to pass £100m for the first time — which makes the

Finns about the world's biggest buyers of British goods per head.

The biggest rise in British trade is in such goods as tractors, textile machinery and construction equipment, also woollens, telecommunications equipment and building materials. Two British companies won contracts in October 1969 for three steel mills.

Trade with the U.S.A., 1969: exports to, $90m; imports from $110m.

Regional pattern of Finnish exports.

	1960	1968
EFTA	35.1	40.0
United Kingdom	24.5	20.6
Sweden	4.9	10.9
Denmark	3.5	3.7
Norway	1.3	2.6
Switzerland	0.6	1.5
Austria	0.2	0.5
Portugal	0.1	0.2
EEC	28.2	24.5
West Germany	11.6	10.5
Netherlands	6.1	4.6
France	4.7	4.0
Italy	2.1	3.0
Belgium-Luxembourg	3.7	2.4
Eastern Bloc	19.5	19.2
(Soviet Union)	14.2	15.5
Other	17.2	16.3
(United States)	5.0	5.8
Grand Total:	100.0	100.0

FISHING

The world's fishery resources are more intensively exploited than at any previous period; they contribute roughly a tenth of the animal protein for world food supplies. The total catch has doubled since 1950 through the efforts of developing nations and the continued growth in catch from traditional fisheries. The freezer and factory ships which were first used in the north-west Atlantic are now operating in the central and south Atlantic.

In 1969 Portugal bought five large stern-trawlers to work the South African fishing grounds and ships from the West and East German fleets have been to eastern South America. The major impact in 1969-70 was made by the Spanish freezer fleet which brings back the largest catches from South Africa.

Larger catches resulted in world surpluses of frozen fish; prices, especially for cod, were depressed. Large quantities of white fish suitable for human consumption are being turned into fishmeal and flour for pig and poultry food.

One of the world's more immediate hopes for richer fishing is the mid-water trawl. The usual commercial trawl net is dragged along the bottom, but there is not much bottom left which has not been trawled many times. The FAO believes that there could be good prospects for a trawl which rides a considerable distance from the bottom.

By far the most practical idea for increasing supplies of fish protein is simply to use the great quantity of fish caught but not used. Many species, because they look ugly or have harsh-sounding names, will not be accepted by customers despite their excellent quality. The redfish was one, until it was christened "ocean perch".

Another possibility lies in krill, a shrimplike creature as long as a matchstick which feeds on plankton of the unexploited southern ocean. Krill occurs in enormous densely-packed shoals and is the main diet of the southern whales. Since whales have been decimated by unscrupulous killing the vast areas of krill have increased.

New Geography 1970-71

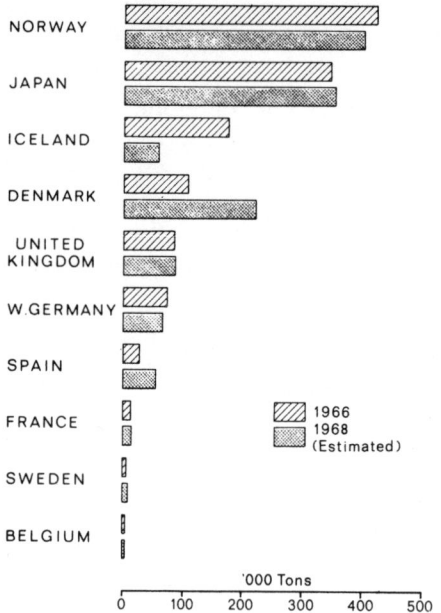

Fishmeal production in 1966 and 1968.

FISHING OFF U.S. COAST. The Russians constantly have 160 ships off the east coast of the U.S.A. while the Poles have 25 ships. At least 125 Japanese boats operate off Alaska. The U.S.A. does not share most other nations' hunger for fish as a source of protein, hence the American fishing industry has not kept pace with some of its competitors in technology or organization. The Americans resent the indiscriminate fishing of the foreign trawlers. For example, the Russians generally fish for herring but they do not throw back the cod. Foreign activity, generally within the law, could prove disastrous for some U.S. areas where fishing is a major industry. In the New England fishing states the local share dropped from 93% to 35% between 1964 and 1969.

FISH FARMING. In Britain research into fish farming reached the marketing stage in 1969. The sea-water fish farm at Loch Ailort, western Scottish Highlands, put its first crop on the British market. The farm is now concentrating on rainbow trout; reared in sea water the trout reach 5.5 lb in two years. In Britain, too, there is increasing work on intensive marine farming of plaice and sole.

CATFISH FARMING. The catfish is a repulsive-looking bottom scavenger that will eat nearly anything and thrives in some of the most polluted American rivers. Northern fishermen usually throw catfish away but tens of thousands of Americans, mostly in the South, consider its sweet white flesh a delicacy. This is especially so when it comes from catfish raised in the comparatively clean waters of a commercial pond.

In response to this appetite, a growing number of farmers are flooding their acreage and raising fish instead of conventional crops. In 1969, the nation's 4,000 catfish farmers sold 12m lb of their product, and the 1972 harvest is projected at 52m lb by the Interior Department's Bureau of Commercial Fisheries.

Switching to catfish makes sound financial sense. The fish require less care than crops and bring their growers a better price per pound than beef, pork or poultry. One of the first to discover the market was Edgar Farmer. In 1969 Farmer reaped 55,000 dollars from 500 acres of catfish ponds. They are far more profitable than the 1,300 acres he devotes to rice, soya beans and subsidized cotton. Like most catfish raisers, Farmer can sell all he produces. The United Fruit Co. hopes to raise catfish in Central American ponds.

The fish farmers get aid from Washington, where pond-raised catfish are regarded as one answer to a rising American demand for all types of fish products. The Agriculture Department's Soil Conservation Service, for example, offers free technical advice on the construction of ponds for catfish farming or flood-control purposes.

A variety of new products, services and jobs is growing up around the thriving catfish industry. Manufacturers have developed special catfish foods. Several firms are experimenting with pumps, mechanical feeders and harvesters, and there is a race to develop the best machine to behead, skin and eviscerate catfish.

Arkansas has opened the nation's first catfish-processing plant, a co-operative that will package 900,000 lb of fish in 1971. Restaurant chains specializing in farm-grown catfish are opening up in Tennessee, Arkansas and Mississippi.

FISH FARMING AND WATER POLLUTION. Fish farming is helping to provide an answer to water pollution. Polish scientists of the Water Biology Laboratory in Cracow are successfully experimenting with ways of converting non-toxic industrial wastes, rich in organic compounds, into fertilizer for fish culture. This has increased fish production five-fold. Good results have also been obtained at the Research Institute of Fisheries and Hydrobiology in Bodnany, where effluents from starch factories and waste water from poultry farms were used. Both substances produced life-sustaining plankton in ponds, which resulted in a remarkable increase in fish production.

FLOODS

RUMANIA. Serious flooding of the Danube devastated 3,000 sq. m. of the country in June 1970, killing 500 people and leaving 75,000 homeless. The floods were the worst recorded in central Europe.

SOUTH KOREA. Severe floods in the southern coastal areas on September 15, 1969 left 60,000 homeless and killed 300.

TUNISIA. More than 500 people died in October 1969 and 120,000 were made homeless when floods affected ten of the country's 13 departments.

FOOD

THE "NEW AGRICULTURAL REVOLUTION". Until recently all too few practical measures had been taken to tackle the problem of producing more food of the kind that was needed in the places it was needed most. At last a general upgrading of agricultural priorities is evident, including significant contributions to agricultural research. These are the principal examples.

India. The area planted with new varieties of wheat, rice, millet and sorghum increased from about 23,000 acres in 1965-66 to nearly 4.5m acres in 1969. India harvested 95.5m tons in 1967-68 and expects to achieve self-sufficiency in 1970-71. (It probably will, but greater difficulties are those of administration and distribution.)

Mexico. This country had for years imported half the wheat it consumed. After an extensive wheat research programme conducted by the Rockefeller Foundation Mexico became self sufficient in 1966 and in 1969 exported 1m tons.

Pakistan. Having imported large quantities of Mexican seed wheat, Pakistan harvested a record 5.5m tons in 1969 and in 1970 expected to produce twice as much food grain as in 1965.

Philippines. At Los Banos research sponsored jointly by the Rockefeller and Ford Foundations developed new varieties of rice, the IR 5 and the IR 8 which increase yields up to 8.5 tons an acre — 15 times the average yield of traditional varieties. Between 1966 and 1969 the Philippines changed from a rice-deficit country to a rice-surplus one.

Thailand. In 1962 American agronomists planted improved varieties of Guatemalan corn. Corn had never before been grown in Thailand but in 1969 Thailand had an export crop of 104m dollars, the world's fourth largest corn export. The same crop is being grown in Indonesia.

Extended to other critical food areas the results of these research efforts have produced a revolution in deficient regions — though this should not be taken as an indication that the crisis is passed. However, some examples are interesting.

In October 1969 the Director-General of the FAO, Addeke Boerma, said, "I believe that the long lag in food production which plagued the last decade may be coming to an end."

The FAO has made agricultural predictions for the next 30 years, based on a two-year study of U.S. agriculture completed early in 1970. The chief points are these:

1. Wheat harvests will jump to 300 bushels an acre — ten times the present maximum yield.
2. Corn output will reach 500 bushels per acre; today's average is 75 bushels.
3. A single cow will produce as many as 1,000 calves in its lifetime, compared with the present ten, through the use of hormones which keep the entire cycle of ovulation and pregnancy in cows and other domestic animals under exact control. Embryos will be transferred from special "breeder" animals to ordinary "incubator" animals.
4. Milk production will rise from 8,000 lb per cow to 30,000. Synthetic milk will also be manufactured from carrot tops and pea pods.
5. Farming will become automated and computerized, with tilling of the soil, planting and harvesting crops and regulating the growing process controlled from a centre equipped with computers, radar and remote control devices.
6. In the U.S.A. in July 1970 no fewer than 30,000 agricultural research projects were under way. The average U.S. farmer now produces enough food to feed 40 people — four times the number he could feed in 1940. In the next 30 years, says the FAO, productivity will increase another four-fold.

PROTEIN FROM OIL. A fruitful field of potential industry, government co-operation involves one of the most widely discussed developments in the world food industry, a process developed by a British petroleum company at its French refinery for producing protein from crude oil. The final product, a yellowish, odourless powder is similar to fishmeal in composition. It is not yet suitable for direct human consumption but it is suitable for feeding to animals and poultry which in turn convert it into meat, milk and eggs.

High-protein foods, no matter how "good" for people, are not catching on. Traditions regarding food are strong and, in developing countries, new foods delivered in a different form or package are looked on with suspicion. Most people ignore the meaning of the word "protein", which has no commercial appeal. Other people shun high-protein products for social reasons, regarding them as "the food of the poor". In Ethiopia some obstacles have been overcome by the nutritionists, who called their product *Faffa*, meaning "grow big and strong" in the local language. But in many other countries, where illiteracy is as high as 85%, people cannot even read the name of the product.

CONVENIENCE FOODS. Convenience foods — frozen and packaged products — have been dominant in the U.S.A. for several years but only relatively developed in other nations. For instance, per capita consumption in the U.S.A. for 1969 was 75 lb, in the U.K. 12 lb, in Sweden 23 lb, in Switzerland 16.4 lb, and in Denmark 12.6 lb.

However, British convenience food research has brought to vegetable growing a degree of stability and productivity never before known. Pea yields, for instance, have risen by more than 40%; spinach and broad beans have increased even more. Poultry output doubled between 1960 and 1970.

THE GLOBAL GLUT. Once uniquely American, the farm glut has become international. Overabundance is common in the developed nations that can afford to subsidize farming. It is a costly bounty that threatens to stimulate further protectionism and provoke trade-damaging price wars behind the barricades of new border taxes, import quotas and additional grain subsidies. While almost half of the world's people are malnourished, there is sufficient food to feed them today.

The problems are manifold in the Common Market

countries. A policy combining protection and unrealistic price supports without production quotas has yielded a surfeit of foodstuffs. Excess sugar stocks were 1m tons in 1969 and are expected to grow by more than 300,000 tons annually. In Italy, landowners have destroyed crops of fruit and vegetables, and the Ministry of Agriculture did not know what to do with 150,000 tons of ripening surplus oranges, more than 10% of the annual harvest.

One threat to trade relations between the U.S.A. and the Common Market is the Market's surplus butter, 600,000 metric tons in July 1970. With storehouses filled and the world market clotted, leaders of the Common Market's agricultural section are trying to persuade consumers to switch from margarine to butter. One proposed solution, which included a tax of at least 60 dollars a ton on the food oils used in margarine, would slash by one-third the U.S.A.'s 500m dollar annual soya bean exports to the Common Market. The tax plan was shelved after the U.S.A. threatened retaliation — by raising tariffs on imported European cars.

Beyond Western Europe and the U.S.A., there is an almost global glut of grains. Major advances in farming have coincided with successive years of beneficent weather to produce a bumper crop of wheat. The total stock in 1969 in wheat producing nations was 51m metric tons, or almost the same amount of wheat as has been exported annually in world trade.

Price-cutting has started as the five major wheat exporters — France, the U.S.A., Canada, Australia and Argentina — unload stockpiles below the price minimums set by the International Grains Agreement in 1967. France opened negotiations with Red China. Not wanting to be left holding a surplus, the U.S.A. followed by underselling grain to Germany and Britain.

Even the Russians, saddled with their own surplus, seem disinclined to accept the final 150m bushels of wheat that they had ordered from Canada in 1966 as part of one of the largest grain sales ever concluded.

FOOD AND AGRICULTURE ORGANIZATION

The FAO's 119 member nations, in November 1969, created the FAO Indicative World Plan for Agricultural Development. The global plan embodies the results of five regional studies on the Near East, South America, Africa south of the Sahara, Asia and the Far East.

The IWP concludes that five key objectives must be achieved if agriculture in the developing world is to grow at a rate necessary to meet the challenges of population growth over the next 15 years. They are:

1. Securing the staple food supplies required by a population growing at 2.5% to 3% annually.
2. Improving the quality of diet.
3. Earning and saving the foreign exchange that is crucial to overall development.
4. Providing employment in agriculture and related industries.
5. Increasing productivity through intensification of land and water use.

The plan suggests that the bulk of investment, expenditure on inputs and allocation of human resources should be concentrated on crop production. The four priorities are:

1. A breakthrough in cereal production, the main staple of human nutrition and the principal source of concentrated livestock food.
2. An improvement in the nutritive value of diet, firstly through a greater contribution of cereals to the protein supply and secondly through a faster rate of growth in the production of other food. Demand for pulses, vegetable oils, fruit and vegetables is expected to rise more rapidly than that for cereals.
3. Increasing efficiency in the production and processing of export crops and reducing dependency on too narrow a range of crops by diversification.
4. Creating additional income and employment by a more intensive use of physical resources and modern technology.

The key medium-term objective to achieving a staple

food supply is a rise in cereal production from about 230m tons in 1962 in the developing countries surveyed to about 500m by 1985. To combat malnutrition IWP proposes a broad-based programme. In the short-term emphasis is placed on animals with a fast reproductive rate — pigs and poultry, instead of cattle. The annual increase would need to be 10%. This would be supplemented by measures to increase output of vegetable protein by growing more leguminous crops such as peas and beans.

In the longer term, the IWP proposes development of higher yielding pulse varieties, the build-up of ruminant livestock inventories, the improvement of oceanic fishing practices and increases in the output of inland fisheries.

The Plan's objectives for higher livestock production would require 110m tons of grain by 1985 compared with an estimated 31m tons in 1962 (the base year for the study).

To enable developing countries to earn and save more foreign exchange the IWP proposes a fairly substantial increase in the growth of their exports and a sharp drop in the rate of their imports. Net exports would have to rise from 6,200m dollars to 14,600m dollars on the basis of constant 1962 prices.

An increase from 562m hectares cultivated in developing regions in 1962 to 660m hectares in 1985 is proposed. The bulk of increased cultivation would come from grasslands, some from forested areas and only 10% from wastelands. The major additions are proposed in Africa south of the Sahara, Latin America and in parts of Asia and the Near East. It is proposed to increase the irrigated harvested area from 72m to 139m hectares between 1962 and 1985. This would mean that 27% of the total harvested area would be irrigated by 1985.

The IWP estimates that the value of annual recurrent expenditure for seed feed, fertilizers, and the like would have to be more than three times higher in 1985 than in 1962 to meet IWP objectives. Some important changes of emphasis are predicted. Food aid, for example, would shift from massive supplies of staple cereals towards high-protein foods and particularly milk products.

FRANCE

212,700 sq. m. Pop. 50.3m. France's main long-term objective is industrial competitiveness and to this end powerful industrial combines are being encouraged. For instance, in the textile industry ten firms now account for a third of the turnover. Mergers and combines exist in aviation, steel and vehicles.

Agriculture is undergoing significant changes. In 1970 it employed about 16% of the working population, a drastic reduction from the 61% of 1951. Further reductions are expected. The aim of the new Common Market farm finance system is to reduce and eventually eliminate national budgets for agriculture and to have one central fund in their place.

For 1970 the government forecast that exports would rise by 13.6% but imports by only 3%. There is intense competition for French trade among American, British and West German producers.

The changing geography of France is well illustrated from the plans for development of the lower Seine valley and the Marseilles area.

Before the end of the century the population of the lower Seine valley, 1.145m in 1969, is expected to reach 2.5m. The estuary zone of Le Havre, greater Rouen and the area between Evreux and Vernon will show the greatest population increase. Development of new port facilities in the Le Havre estuary zone will include the building of an industrial estate and artificial island port on 8000 hectares of land between Le Havre and Tancarville. The port will handle the largest oil tankers.

Rouen, with its two existing satellite towns at Elbeuf and Barentin-Pavilly, and Evreux are to be enlarged, and two new urban centres created at Bourg-Achard and Vaudreuil. New universities are to be established first at Le Havre and later at Evreux and Vaudreuil and all administrative and commercial activities will be focused on Rouen, which is to become a much more prominent regional centre. Road and rail links throughout the region are to be improved, and a site held in reserve at Lieurey for the possible installation of a third

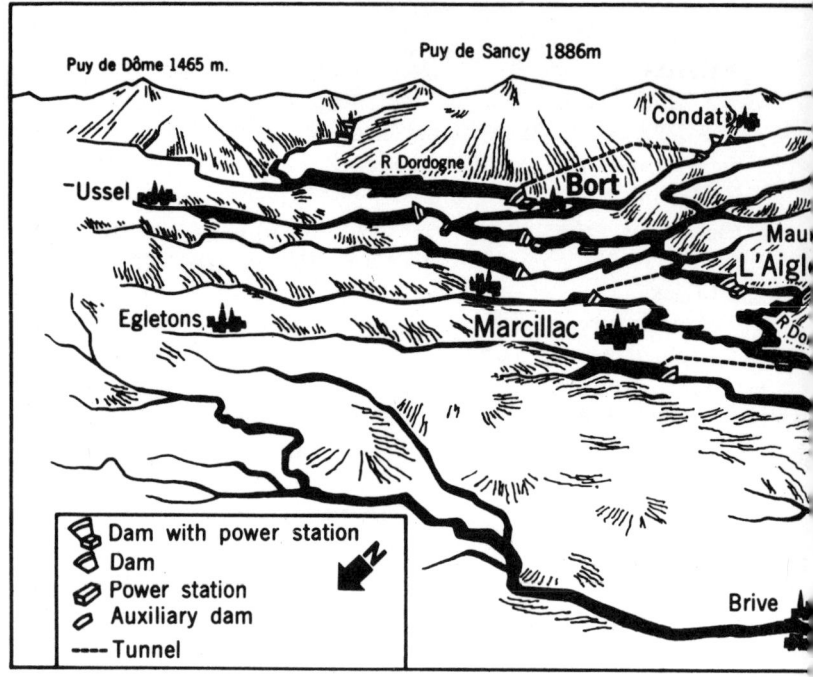

Power stations of the Dordogne.

international airport, when facilities at Orly and Roissy-en-France reach saturation.

Planning in the Marseilles area has to cater for an even greater projected population growth. From 1.35m in 1969, the number of inhabitants in the region is expected to increase to 3.2m by the year 2000. Heavy industrial development will be necessary to provide employment and it is estimated that 21,000 additional jobs will have to be created each year. An industrial and port area is to be developed at Fos and new metallurgical factories are to be set up by the Wendel-Sidelor group. New urban centres at Vitrolles, Martigues, Istres, Miramas, Saint-Chamas and Port-Saint-Louis will house the workers employed in the Fos industrial complex, but Marseilles will be maintained as the regional centre and is expected to have a population of 1.3m by 1985.

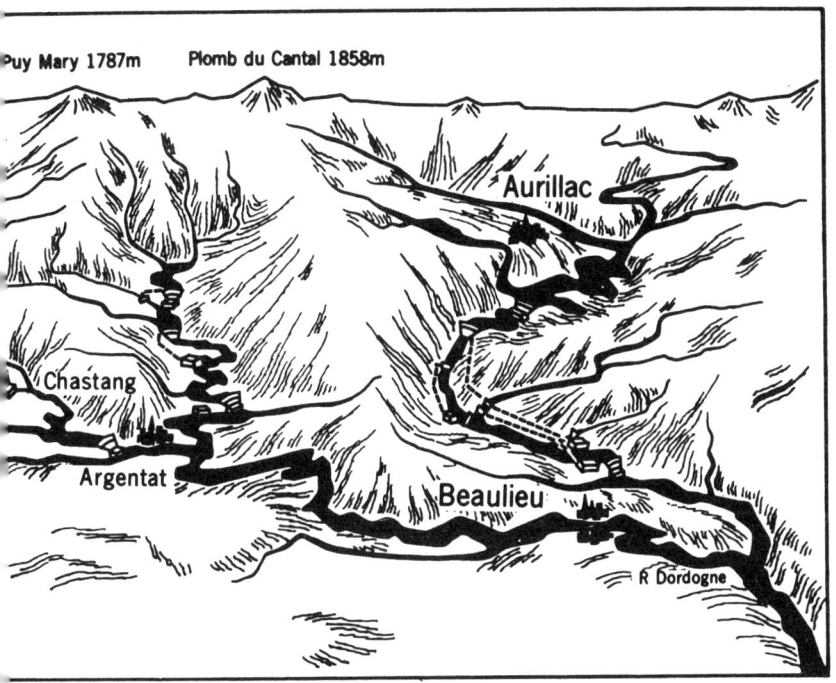

To prevent further degradation of the countryside the Marseilles plan aims to separate densely populated urban areas with intensive green belts. Mountain areas such as Alpilles, Sainte-Baume and Sainte-Victoire will be protected. Present railways are to be extended, a metro built in Marseilles and coastal hovercraft services developed. Provision is also to be made for moorings for up to 100,000 yachts and pleasure craft; additional tourist accommodation will be prepared in the coastal area.

Both plans provide for orderly development and controlled growth, and could become significant examples of successful development planning.

Trade with the U.K., 1969: exports to, £325m; imports from, £315m. Trade with the U.S.A., 1969: exports to, $842m; imports from, $1,069m.

FUELS

The pattern of changes in energy supplies has been characterized by a succession of wave-like movements. Each new fuel that has become important has gradually lost its share of the market as new sources of energy have appeared and expanded. This seems to have been true since muscle power was the sole source of energy. Each new fuel, however dominant its position, is likely to be superseded by new discoveries and new technologies.

The resources to meet world demand consist partly of reserves of fossil fuels known or believed to exist, and partly of resources producing such energy forms as HEP and nuclear energy for which the term reserves is inappropriate.

The often asked question: "How large are reserves of fossil fuels?" may be answered variously. The total reserves found and measured; the proportion of these likely to be economically recoverable; the estimated total of reserves discovered but not measured in detail; and the quantity inferred to exist on a geological basis must all be considered. In any case figures of reserves should be taken with caution. Additional reserves undoubtedly exist, costs will change, technology will affect the degree of recoverability. There is no doubt that the total demand for energy will be met in the next few decades. In fact, it is very likely that some reserves of conventional fuels will never be tapped as other fuels supplant them. But nuclear energy is the only new source that is currently expected to make a large contribution to satisfying energy needs during the next 20 years or so. The fast-breeder reactors that should come into commercial operation in about 1976 will eventually breed as much fuel as they consume. In 1970 the total world energy demand grew by about 5%. In 1975 the world will have 300 nuclear power stations with a generating capacity of 150,000 megawatts compared with 20,000 at the end of 1969.

In a survey of fuel the EEC Power Commission forecasts that the Common Market will be importing half the 1970 total world oil production within 20 years. The Commission

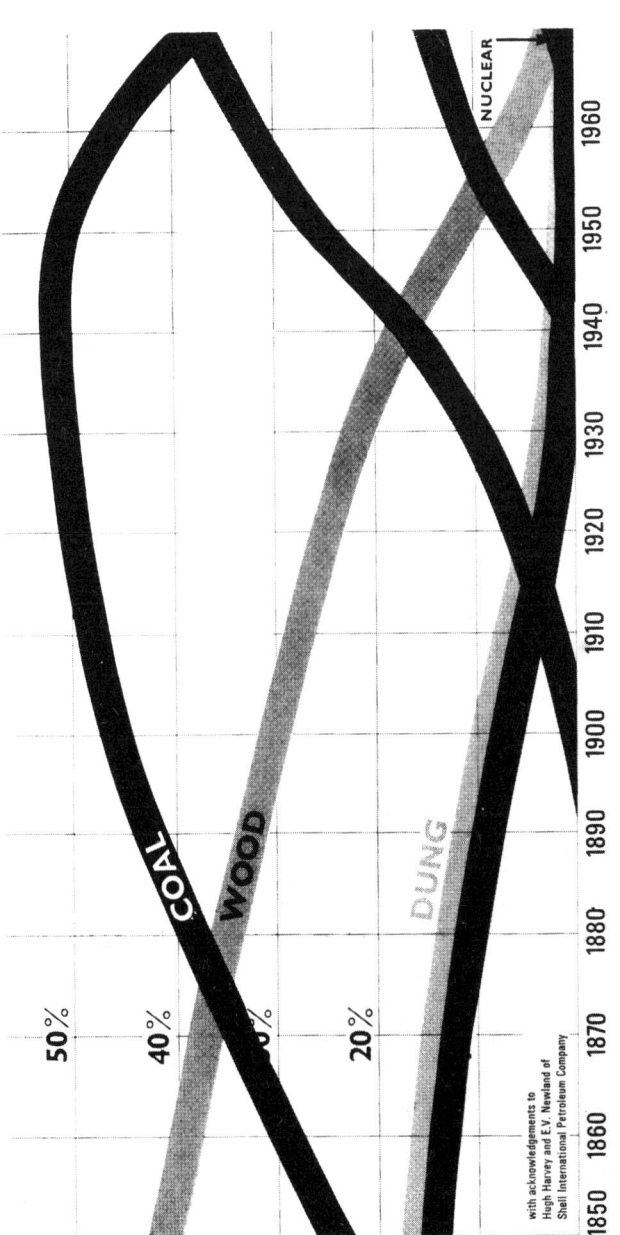

Shares in world consumption of fuels

has a record of accurate projection. The calculations underline the importance of the North Sea finds in 1969-70. The EEC analysis predicts the further running-down of Europe's coal industry; by 1979 natural gas will have replaced it as the second energy source. Crude oil continues to strengthen its position and should increase its share of total energy sources from 63% (1970) to 70% by 1975. By 1980 this would mean a demand of 710m tons and by 1990 Europe could be seeking 1,000m tons. (Britain would need another 300m tons, for the projection does not take into account Britain's possible entry into the EEC.)

The calculations also omit the potential of North Sea finds. But the Norwegian oil find in May 1970 — the "Ekofisk" strike — promises 300,000 bbl a day. This is about 15m tons a year — the equivalent of about 14% of Britain's 1970 needs or about 3% of Western Europe's needs.

The Power Commission also estimates that the EEC nuclear energy supply will treble by 1975 and maintain this rate of expansion. By 1990 it could account for about 11% of total energy requirements. Coal's share is expected to drop from 21.5% to less than 10% in the 1970s. Up to 1980 the biggest demand increases will be for methane. (See Charts.)

GEOMORPHOLOGY

THE AFRICAN RIFT. Studies of the earth's structure on a global basis, an outcome of the oceanographic results of the period 1966–70, have led to immense interest among geographers in the African rift system. Geographers, geologists and geophysicists of several nations were active in field research during 1969–70.

The system may well turn out to be a key zone in interpreting the processes that have shaped the continents and oceans.

Many oceanographers and geophysicists have drawn attention to the probability that the Red Sea-Gulf of Aden "elbow" is an incipient ocean, having most of the characteristics that the very early Atlantic Ocean must once have possessed. Every new piece of work supports this conclusion and it is reasonable to suppose that the African rift system is a still earlier phase in the break up of a land mass. It is even suggested that seismic activity south-west and south of Lake Tanganyika may herald the development of a further southward extension of the rift and thus constitute the earliest phase of all.

The combination of bathymetry and magnetic surveying has established that the ocean ridges, the sites along which run the central rifts, are also those where new material is being added to the ocean crust. The ocean floor flows away on either side in a near-symmetrical fashion forcing the continents apart at rates of from one to eight cm a year, finally becoming re-assimilated into the upper part of the

New Geography 1970-71

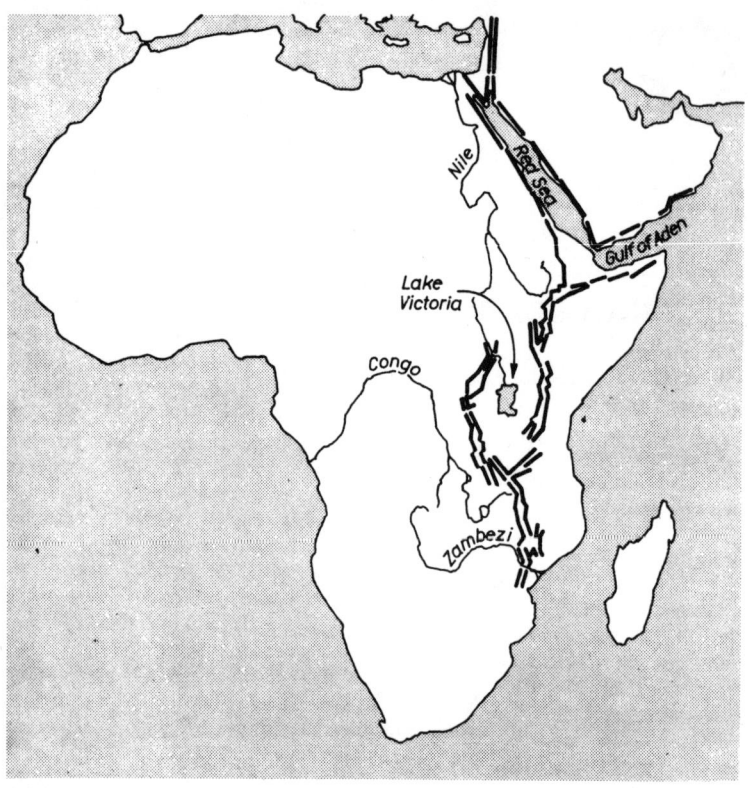

The Great African Rift Valley. The bold lines show its principal division from the north-west Mediterranean to south of the Zambezi.

earth's mantle along the lines of ocean troughs and continental margins.

In the past two years recognition that this gigantic conveyor belt really exists, coupled to other extensive geophysical evidence has led theorists to abandon the older idea of continental drift — the theory that the earth's major land masses ploughed through the allegedly viscous crust of the oceans in response to underlying drag forces. Scientists now think predominantly in terms of "plate tectonics".

Geomorphology

Basically the idea is that both oceans and continents consist of rigid crustal plates — six major and several minor ones; these plates are constantly changing shape with material being added along the rift system and subtracted at the other boundaries; a relatively shallow and underlying counterflow compensates for the outward displacement of the sea-floor plates from their ridges. This theory differs from its predecessors in regarding each part of the evolving map of the globe as dependent upon all the other parts — the continents do not simply drift independently.

Far from being a simple trough, bounded by a pair of faults, the African rift system consists of a whole series of faults. Despite this irregularity the 1800 miles of the African system proper never vary much from a remarkably uniform width of between 40 and 60 miles — from the southern termination at the Lower Zambezi, through its eastern and western branches around Lake Victoria, up to its northern end in Ethiopia.

The close association of volcanic activity with the rifts is obviously one reflection of the deep-seated processes beneath; but only in some places — northern Tanzania, for instance — is there a direct link between specific periods of faulting and vulcanicity.

The main formation of the rift trough dates back (according to Professor B.C. King of Bedford College, London) 25m years while the general trend of the rift and many of its faults could be linked to very ancient Pre-Cambrian structures.

THE ATLANTIC "RIFT". Interest is also growing among marine geologists and geophysicists in international co-operative research in the enigmas now raised by the western coast of Africa. It is here, according to current theories, that the primordial supercontinent, Pangaea, began to open about 200m years ago along a rift that was to become the Atlantic Ocean. What is now the Atlantic seaboard of the United States was split off from the western hump of Africa.

The continental margin of North America is perhaps the

best known in the world to marine geologists, while that of the western coast of Africa is certainly among the least known. This knowledge gap can best be closed, scientists believe, by investigations involving not only the world's leading oceanographic nations but also the developing countries along the coast.

This was the trend of opinion at a symposium in April 1970 organized by SCOR, the Scientific Committee on Oceanic Research of the International Council of Scientific Unions. SCOR serves as scientific adviser to UNESCO's Intergovernmental Oceanographic Commission, which has already co-ordinated a number of co-operative investigations at sea.

The subject was the "Geology of the East Atlantic Continental Margin", taking in the coast of the Atlantic from Novaya Zemlya, the Soviet archipelago in the far north, to Cape Agulhas on the southern tip of Africa. The symposium brought out that exploration of the northern and the southern tips of the East Atlantic shoreline is well under way. But more work is needed along the edges of the tectonic plates and the line running from Gibraltar to the Azores along the edge of one plate. South of this line, it is believed that the sea floor is spreading 30 millimetres more a year than to the north. Further to the south and around the hump that starts with Morocco, there is the Y-junction where Europe, America and Africa may have been joined in Pangaea. One of the world's best-equipped research vessels, the 2,100-ton *Atlantic 11* operated by Woods Hole Oceanographic Institution on Cape Cod, will work in this and other areas off Africa.

SAHARA-SOUTH POLE. The hottest part of the world today was once the coldest, according to a team of leading earth scientists who visited south-eastern Algeria in 1970. They claim that, without doubt, the territory that was the earth's south polar region in the Upper Ordovician period (450m years ago) moved to become what is now the central Sahara. The flattened topography of the area and great parallel grooves running hundreds of miles across ancient rock showed the results of continental glaciation — the kind that occurs only under a polar ice cap. The ice groovings show that the glaciers were moving from south to north. The hypothesis is confirmed by radioactive dating and fossil evidence.

The ancient South Pole arrived in the Sahara by a sliding action of the earth's crust round the globe. The earth's axis itself did not shift — it has remained stationary throughout the earth's history.

The Sahara findings and conclusions fit in with the large body of recent geological evidence that the earth's crust is a series of vast plates that slide over a fluid zone. A further likelihood is that what is now Antarctica was probably near the equator in the Ordovician period, because sediments have been obtained from Antarctica showing rich coral deposits.

GHANA

91,753 sq.m. Pop. 8.4m. The central problem facing the Ghana economy is the difficulty of encouraging growth in the face of the excessive burden of external debt and restricted foreign exchange earnings. There is a desperate need for more intensive training of cocoa farmers and greater subsidies are needed to fight disease and pests. The 1969–70 cocoa crop reached 376,000 tons (386,000 tons 1967–68).

Exports of timber are beginning to bring in more money but transport problems and heavy rains hampered progress in 1970. Gold was Ghana's second largest foreign currency earner in 1969, the 727,100 oz being valued at NC18.18m.

Reserves of 200m tons of bauxite have been found. The chief workings are at Kanayerobo in the western region; production exceeded 350,000 tons in 1969. Diamond dredging is in operation in the Birrim Basin, and eight international companies are prospecting for offshore oil. During 1969–70 Ghana signed major trade agreements with the Soviet Union and Canada. Numerous new factories have been opened, chiefly an oil palm mill at Asraku and a cement factory. Work began in October 1969 on the highway to link Accra, Kumasi and Takoradi.

With the formation of Volta Lake — a result of the building of the Volta Dam — inland fishing is now becoming important and 3,500 tons were landed in 1969.

Resettlement of the 80,000 people evacuated from the Volta area has been completed and with the aid of the U.N./FAO World Food Programme a 440,000-acre farming project is under way.

Trade with the U.K., 1969: exports to, £35m; imports from, £33.2m. Trade with the U.S.A., 1969: exports to, $100m; imports from $71m.

GLACIERS

Glaciologists from many countries are studying glacial fluctuations. Some of the most important work is being carried out in the Soviet Union by Grigori Avsyuk, assistant director of the Institute of Geography and president of the Soviet Commission on Glaciology, and Vladimir Kotlykov, director of glaciology studies at the Institute of Geography. Pointing out that ice covers 11% of the earth's total land area, the Soviet specialists say that glaciers are a major answer to the world water shortage. About 80% of the world's fresh water — between 24m and 27m cubic kilometres — is locked up in glaciers. The total volume is equal to the water flow of all the world's rivers for 700 years. Enough fresh water for man's present needs could be obtained by liquefying only a part of this enormous mass of solid water. Even a relatively small iceberg — 2 km long, ½ km wide and 150 metres thick — contains enough water to supply each person in a city of 8m inhabitants with 1,000 litres of water a day for a month.

The glaciers of the Tien Shan mountains and the Pamirs in Central Asia contain about 2,000 cubic kilometres of ice; this is nearly twice the amount of water currently used for irrigation throughout the world. Glacier-melting experiments in the Soviet Union have been successful. The more difficult problem is spreading the melting water. Soviet glaciologists are working on plans to retain the snow on mountain sides with screens, stockpiling snow in the foothills and producing artificial avalanches to melt the glaciers more rapidly.

GRAVEL

The production of sand, gravel and aggregates more than doubled from 1960–70 and will probably double again before 1975 to become the U.K.'s largest extraction industry. It will possibly overtake coal mining. These are the chief raw materials used in the construction industry. In 1958 the output was 62m tons; 1968, 130m tons.

The boom has been caused by the radical changes in construction techniques, using reinforced concrete instead of steel girders. Each ton of concrete requires 17 cwt of sand gravel; a mile of motorway consumes 100,000 tons. By 1980, 47m tons per year will be used.

Marine-dredged aggregate is developing. It is obtained mainly from the Mersey, the Bristol and English Channels and off the Isle of Wight. The major aggregate supplies come from more than 1,350 pits but the labour force is relatively small — about 12,000.

GREAT LAKES

Against the background of an announcement in May 1970 that the Canadian Government had banned the sale of certain fish caught in the Great Lakes because of their high mercury content, the U.S. National Research Council confirmed that the International Field Year for the Great Lakes is to take place during 1972.

New Geography 1970-71

The IFYGL is a comprehensive programme of scientific studies of Lake Ontario, its drainage basin and the weather over them. It is a joint United States—Canadian undertaking, and part of the two countries' national programme for the UNESCO-sponsored International Hydrological Decade. Data will be collected by scientists from both countries, and then shared through data centres established at Detroit, Michigan, and Burlington, Ontario.

The Field Year (the study of data will actually continue for seven years) will directly benefit not only science, but the 35m North Americans who now live on the shores of the Great Lakes and the 70m expected to live there by the end of the century.

People even further afield may benefit, for Lake Ontario may be considered as representative of all large lakes, and many of the natural processes to be observed there are found in similar bodies of water from neighbouring Lake Erie to Lake Baikal in Siberia.

GREECE

41,328 sq.m. Pop. 8.8m. Industry continues to advance at a faster rate than agriculture, led by a boom in construction. Progress in metals, chemicals and rubber has been better than average and the development programme since 1967 appears to have diversified the economy away from food, tobacco and beverage industries. The share of manufactured goods in the total export trade has risen from about a fifth in 1967 to over a third in 1969.

New industrial estates at Ptolemais, Volos and Salonika will develop these areas. Salonika, where both agricultural and industrial development is taking place, is being called the "Milano of Greece". This is an optimistic description, but the potential exists.

Greece could become self-sufficient in food but at present imports large quantities, including £40m of meat and £16m of canned milk annually. There is some switching of cereal production from wheat into foodstuffs suitable for animal feed. The government is trying to discourage the production of certain grades of tobacco and to improve citrus fruit acreage.

Increased remittances from Greek workers overseas and greater receipts from tourism — because of improved political stability — are covering part of the trade deficit.

Trade with the U.K., 1969: exports to, £12m; imports from, £41m. Trade with the U.S.A., 1969: exports to, $37m; imports from $49.4m.

GUATEMALA

42,042 sq.m. Pop. 4.86m. Rising agricultural production — coffee, cotton, bananas — has stimulated industry, which consists primarily of small firms processing coffee, sugar, meat, vegetable oils and other foodstuffs. Textiles are more important but the effects of CACM competition are being felt. However, the production of tyres, plastics and pharmaceuticals is growing in importance.

International Nickel is engaged in a 125m-dollar venture to extract nickel from laterite ores and process it for export. Sulphur is being commercially extracted and several oil concessions were granted during 1969–70. The first steps have been taken to exploit vast reserves of mahogany, cedar and pine. The outlook for Guatemala is good; it is already in first place in CACM trade.

Trade with the U.K., 1969: exports to, £1.2m; imports from, £4m. Trade with the U.S.A., 1969: exports to, $31m; imports from, $44.1m.

H

HONDURAS

43,227 sq.m. Pop. 2.41m. Efforts to diversify agriculture have met with great success. On the north coast there have been wide-spread plantings of pineapple, grapefruit and other citrus fruits. Production of sugar cane and tobacco has increased sharply and oil farms are now being extended. Improved crops of corn, beans and sorghum are expected from the use of high yielding seed. Livestock farming is becoming increasingly important and the fishing industry continues to expand. New factories are producing plastics, paints, textiles, pharmaceuticals and industrial gases. The food processing industries of sugar milling, fruit canning and the manufacture of edible oils are also expanding.

There is increasing investment in heavy industry and exploitation of natural resources. Texaco has built a large refinery at Puerto Cortes producing over 10,000 bbl a day. Seven oil companies have leased the entire Caribbean coastline and others are exploring the western part of the country. Deposits of 10m tons of high grade iron ore are reported in the Agalteca region. A pulp and paper complex costing 71m dollars will be in operation in 1971 to exploit the extensive hardwood and pine forests.

Between 1962 and 1970 foreign trade with Honduras tripled. Trade with the U.K., 1969: exports to, £0.5m; imports from, £1.2m. Trade with the U.S.A., 1969: exports to, $101m; imports from, $94. .

HONG KONG

398 sq.m. Pop. 4m. This remarkably prosperous British Crown Colony continues to develop and its exports are increasing rapidly. The textile industry remains the mainstay of the economy, accounting for 50% of exports and nearly 40% of the industrial work force. The Colony is the world's largest exporter of cotton garments.

The construction boom of 1970 was the result of increased demands by industrialists for new factories to meet their export requirements and by international companies which are making Hong Kong their base for South-east Asian operations. For instance, during 1969–70 220 American firms moved from Japan to Hong Kong, mostly because of low taxation. Much of the investment comes from West Germany, the U.S.A. and Japan, especially in electronics and other light industries. The U.K. remains the chief foreign participator but its interest is mainly in the traditional service industries such as banking and shipping. (Communist China owns ten banks in Hong Kong.) The proliferation of small businesses is a feature of the Hong Kong economy; only 130 of the 13,500 registered premises employ more than 500 workers. There is also a multitude of unregistered factories.

The U.S.A. takes about two-fifths of the Colony's sales; British purchases continue to decline and now account for only 14% of Hong Kong's exports (16% in 1967).

The innate skill of its workers enables Hong Kong to diversify as opportunities occur. For instance in 1958, the first year of transistor radio manufacture, Hong Kong earned only £800,000; in 1969 the figure was £53m.

The Colony's main suppliers are China and Japan; Hong Kong is traditionally dependent on China for half its food in terms of value, though since 1968 Japan has become the more important supplier. China earns nearly half its foreign exchange — 500m dollars annually — trading through and with Hong Kong. Trade with the U.K., 1969: exports to, £125m; imports from, £89m. Trade with the U.S.A., 1969: exports to, $639.8m; imports from, $203m.

New Geography 1970-71

HUNGARY

36,000 sq.m. Pop. 10.3m. The Danube Thermal Power Plant, begun in 1960, came on stream in June 1969 and is to supply a third of Hungary's electric power. A refinery has been built to provide fuel, but Hungary will have to import about two-thirds of the crude oil supplies, mainly from the Soviet Union. It is interesting to note that in 1965 coal provided two-thirds of Hungary's power; by 1973 barely a third of power will be coal-produced.

In 1969 agricultural output expanded by 6% and a record grain crop provided an export surplus of 600,000 tons of wheat, a rare occurrence for Hungary. But there is a serious lack of granaries and of cold storage plant for fruit — the 1969 crop was double that of 1968. Tourism, too, was up by 25% in 1969.

Hungarian trade is primarily with COMECON countries — the Soviet Union accounts for 35% of the total — but exchanges with the West are proceeding rapidly. A series of five-year trading agreements have been signed with several Western countries. Hungary is the only Eastern bloc country with which the U.K. generally has a favourable balance of trade.

Trade with the U.K., 1969: exports to, £9.4m; imports from, £13.3m. Trade with the U.S.A., 1969: exports to, $40m; imports from, $31m.

HURRICANES

PAKISTAN. The Ganges Delta area of East Pakistan was the scene of this century's worst natural disaster on November 24, 1970. A tremendous cyclone devastated an area of 3,000 sq.m., leaving 500,000 Pakistanis dead. Winds of 120 mph produced waves 20 ft. high, which destroyed 90% of the buildings and the rice crop. Millions of sheep, cattle and goats were killed and the fishing fleet destroyed.

Scores of islands in the delta were completely depopulated. Virtually all the 3m people of the delta have suffered from the disaster. Foreign aid was rapid and generous but Pakistani maladministration seriously hampered relief efforts.

QUEENSLAND. Cyclone Ada struck north-east Queensland in January 1970, badly damaging Great Barrier Reef tourist islands. In a 24-hour period Cairns recorded ten inches of rain.

TEXAS. Several areas of the Gulf of Mexico, particularly Texas, were badly damaged by Hurricane Celia in August 1970. At least 200 people were killed, mainly in Corpus Christi, Texas, (pop. 200,000).

HYDRO-ELECTRIC POWER

The biggest HEP project on the European continent outside the Soviet Union is virtually complete on the Iron Gates section of the Danube where the river breaks through the Carpathian and Balkan Mountain ranges. The dam, over half a mile long, links Rumania and Yugoslavia at Gura Vaii and Sip, respectively. The water behind the dam forms an 80-sq.m. lake. The dam brings impressive benefits. At least four times as much commerce can be transported on the Danube — raising capacity to 50m tons. A barge convoy, which in 1969 needed 120 hours to navigate the difficult passage, can now cover the distance in 31 hours. Seagoing craft up to 5,000 tons will be able to reach Belgrade.

The HEP capacity is 2050 megawatts. The Soviet Union is said to have given £16.5m towards equipment for the dam. Roads and railways have had to be "lifted" onto mountain slopes, involving the building of seven tunnels and dozens of bridges. In all 150 miles of road and 17 miles of railway have had to be re-routed and 13 river ports rebuilt.

New Geography 1970-71
HYDROLOGY

A slowing of the earth's rotation and an increase in the degree to which it "wobbles" on its axis could result from projects to reverse the flow of great river systems, according to research hydrologists assessing the first half of the International Hydrological Decade — 1964—74. Referring specifically to proposals in North America and the Soviet Union to send the big rivers flowing south to populous areas, Dr. R.L. Nace (U.S.A.) claims that such plans could brake the spin of the earth by moving weight from the pole out to the equator. He also sees a change in the heat balance of the regions affected.

Hydrologists attending the "half way" conference (Paris, December 1969) agreed that in water, as in other matters, the poor are getting poorer. Modern agriculture in developed countries maintains soil but this is not so with subsistence farming in the Third World. There irreversible damage is being done to water resources by overgrazing which strips the soil of its protective power. Development itself can harm the hydrological cycle; good agricultural land is being ruined by drainage from newly-built roads.

In developed countries the problem is not that soil is bare but that it is too well covered. As a result, rainwater does not seep into the ground but runs away. In one area near Washington D.C. river run-off has risen seven-fold with the appearance of a big suburban community. In northern France it is estimated that a million metric tons of water are lost each year for every square kilometre of built-up land. Effects include an increase in flash floods because rain water does not permeate into the ground and a lowering of the water table results. (This could affect such countries as Belgium and Denmark, which obtain 90% of their water from subterranean sources, and the Netherlands and West Germany which draw 75% of their water from the same source.)

Surprisingly little is known of the hydrological cycle; it was only in 1967, for example, that a big Amazon flood was accuratcly measured for the first time. Hydrologists are

Hydrology

demanding more research on the problems of small regions scheduled for development. Better evaluation of floods is one such problem. Tunisia has warned that calculation of the probability of great floods must be seriously revised following the Tunisian floods of 1969. Floods once believed likely only every century actually occur every decade.

West Germany spends more money per head on hydrological matters than any other nation — a total of 4,000m DM annually. The Ruhr Association and the Ruhr Barrage Union alone spent 140m DM in 1969. With ground water supplies diminishing major cities in North Rhine's Westphalia area such as Cologne, Dusseldorf and Duisberg are already drawing on the Rhine for most of their drinking water. Since the Rhine is heavily polluted this calls for expensive purification. Lake Constance is increasingly becoming the main water reservoir for Central Europe, with Stuttgart the main consumer — 4,000 litres a second. (See *United States.*)

I

ICELAND

40,500 sq.m. Pop. 203,400. Iceland became a full member of EFTA in March, 1970. This will significantly help its trade, especially after two years of depression following virtual collapse of the fishing industry, the mainstay of the economy. Nevertheless, fish and fish products contributed 90% of the nation's export earnings in 1969. EFTA membership will extend the fish market.

Agricultural production is rising but an increasing surplus cannot be sold. Farms are run mainly on a co-operative basis, a method adopted because of the extensive migration of population to the towns and to work in the fishing industry.

Interestingly, vegetables and fruit, such as bananas, grapes and oranges are now grown under glasshouses using geothermal heat. Plans to tap geothermal heat and HEP could lead to the development of several independent industries, notably copper and oil-refining.

In 1969 these enterprises commenced production: a seaweed factory at Reykholar; an aluminium plant near Reykjavik; the extraction of diatomite, a filtering agent, from deposits in northern Iceland, the largest in Europe.

The five Nordic countries — Denmark, Finland, Iceland, Norway and Sweden — have set up a fund of 14m dollars to foster development of industry in Iceland. The fund will support the development of Iceland's export industry and will also be used to strengthen the competitive ability of its domestic industry.

The U.K. has become Iceland's second largest buyer, after the U.S.A., and second largest supplier, after West Germany. Trade with the U.K., 1969: exports to, £5m; imports from £6.7m. Trade with the U.S.A., 1969: exports to, $30m; imports from, $15.1m.

INDIA

1.2m sq.m. Pop. Between 535–550m. The fourth five-year plan 1970-75 aims at an annual growth rate of 5.5% coupled with a 50% reduction of foreign aid by 1974. Substantial increases in output are projected, particularly in metal manufactures, heavy chemicals and petro-chemicals. However, expansion depends on overseas capital and foreign investment is low; Malaysia, with only 2% of India's population, received double the amount of investment.

India's troubles are the result of the enormous population increase — 15m annually — grossly inefficient administration and strikes. The jute and the tea industries have had damaging strikes. Tea, too, has been ailing because of increased competition from East Africa and the world glut. Still, tea and jute exports accounted for 27% of the total in 1969, though the U.K., the principal market, buys less.

On the credit side, Indian agriculture has been improving, particularly in wheat and rice production. The nation will, in fact, be self-sufficient in wheat within two years but hoarding and inefficient distribution result in many millions still being hungry.

Trade with the U.K., 1969: exports to, £140m; imports from, £82m. Trade with the U.S.A., 1969: exports to, $316m; imports from, $715m. (See *Agriculture.*)

INDONESIA

887,000 sq.m. Pop. 113.5m. The five-year plan which began in April 1969 has had an appreciable effect in stimulating exports and investment. The inflation rate for 1969 was 10% — compared with 115% in 1968 and 85% in 1967. The drastic reduction is the result of a better food position and increased revenue from oil.

Agriculture employs 74% of the population and despite

rises in output food imports are vast — costing £100m in 1969. In an endeavour to reach self-sufficiency in rice better fertilizers and high-yielding seeds are being used, the acreage is being extended to 9m hectares and irrigation is being developed. The target for 1974 is 15m tons of rice (10.5m in 1969).

Industrial production is expected to rise 90% during the five-year plan, mostly in textiles, light industries and food processing. Mining, which expanded its output by 10% in 1969, offers great promise, with Japan buying much oil. Japan and the U.S.A. are the two major customers and suppliers.

Trade with the U.K., 1969: exports to, £7m; imports from £9m. This is 3% of the market. Trade with the U.S.A., 1969: exports to, $280m; imports from, $275m.

IRAN

628,000 sq.m. Pop 27.7m With tremendous unexploited reserves and an ever-increasing revenue from oil Iran's economy is expanding at 10% annually. The biggest oil producer, a consortium of Western oil companies, is investing 28m dollars, partly in a new refinery at Teheran and construction of a pipeline to the Turkish port of Iskenderun; with a capacity of more than 1m bbl a day the line will cut transport costs by 35%.

To support the manufacturing industry a steel mill is being built at Isfahan and an aluminium smelter at Arak. The motor industry is one of the fastest growing; about 50% of Iranian cars are made in Iran. Also developing rapidly are rubber, pharmaceutical products, paper, glass and electricity.

Iran is rich in minerals and important deposits of copper, chromium, lead, zinc and high-grade iron ore have been discovered. Production may be hampered by shortage of water. Inadequate communications will cause difficulties until Bandar 'Abbas is developed as the major metal port of

Iraq

Iran. More than £14m is being spent on airport modernization.

Good harvests and generous loans from the Agricultural Bank have made it possible for production to keep ahead of the 3% annual population increase. Irrigation is constantly adding to the farming land and Iran has another 100m acres which could be cultivated; the present area is 15m acres. One new venture which may be important is the re-introduction of legal opium cultivation. In 1930 opium was Iran's principal cash crop. Because luxury goods carry high tariffs a thriving smuggling trade from the Gulf States has developed.

Eastern Europe provides the largest market for Iran's goods; trade with the Soviet Union, already large, should increase with the steady improvement of rail links. West Germany provides the largest proportion of Iran's imports. The U.K. follows Japan as the third largest supplier.

Trade with the U.K., 1969: exports to, £102m; imports from, £86m. Trade with the U.S.A., 1969: exports to, $72m; imports from, $27m.

IRAQ

172,000 sq.m. Pop. 8.8m. The North Rumaila oilfield is becoming Iraq's major field after only a year in production; by 1973 it should be producing half the nation's present quantity of crude oil. Development includes the laying of a 16-in. pipeline to the port of Fao on the Arabian Gulf.

There is increasing emphasis on the production of petrochemicals: ammonia, urea, ammonium sulphate and sulphuric acid are being produced for export. The government has set up a state-owned company to exploit Iraq's rich sulphur deposits; the Mishraq field has a productive capacity of 1m tons annually — about 4% of world production.

Several projects aimed at raising agricultural output are in hand, principally the irrigation of 600,000 acres along the Tigris and a dam at Rawah on the Upper Euphrates. A great fertilizer factory at Basra commenced production in July 1970. There is increasing emphasis on poultry and dairy farming, especially in the north. In Mosul state 80,000 acres are being brought under sugar beet, cotton and grains. Iraq is the largest Middle East consumer of sugar, hence the plans for sugar beet production.

Iraq is an expanding market but the British share has been declining, coincidental with the rise in importance of the Soviet Union and other Eastern bloc countries. Trade with the U.K., 1969: exports to, £40m; imports from, £16m. Trade with the U.S.A., 1969: exports to, $60m; imports from $32.4m.

IRRIGATION

The German Research Association is carrying out extensive and intensive irrigation investigation. Teams of experts from various German universities are working in Tunisia, Morocco, Saudi Arabia, Iran, Turkey and other countries on how specific types of irrigation affect cultivation and harvesting, how the available water can be put to the best possible use and what rotation of crops and socio-economic influences will ensure success.

AUSTRALIA. Plastic film is in frequent use in Australia to prevent evaporation and loss of water in dams and storages, but what is believed to be the longest polythene film-lined irrigation channel in Australia has been completed near Trangie, New South Wales. One mile in length it has an average width of about 12 ft., and a depth of four ft. The method has proved highly successful in ensuring effective watering of sorghum.

ETHIOPIA. With help from the Victorian (Australia) Water Supply Commission and the FAO, Ethiopia is developing an irrigation area which will produce cotton, sugar, bananas and citrus fruits, as well as grain to feed cattle. (See also *Irrigation* in general index.)

ISRAEL

25,992 sq.m. (including occupied Arab territory). Pop. 2.889m. The general picture of Israel is one of prosperity but government spending, of which defence costs form the greater part, amounted to 55% of Israel's GNP in 1970. Israel counts on aid and loans from foreign governments plus the sale of 250m dollars in Israeli bonds to private citizens abroad. The country also hopes to increase sales of the two chief exports — citrus fruits and industrial diamonds.

Israel is hoping to make money with its underground pipeline which stretches 159 miles from Eilat on the Gulf of Aqaba to Ashkelon on the Mediterranean. The 42-in. line is Israel's largest single construction job; it cost 67m dollars and can convey 133m bbl of oil a year. With the Suez Canal closed indefinitely some oil companies might prefer to use the pipeline than to ship around the Cape of Good Hope. Israel also has the largest refining capacity in the Middle East and by 1973 should be exporting more than 14m bbl a year.

The Diamond Exchange at Ramat Gan is turning Israel into a major trading centre for precious stones. The country is now in second place after Belgium both in exports and the number of workers engaged. Tourists are an important source of revenue, having increased from 328,000 in 1966 to 600,000 in 1969. The greater proportion came from the U.S.A. — 36%; Britain provided 13%.

American companies are now starting to use Israel as a manufacturing and export base for trade with European countries, Asia and Africa. The Israelis have invested £300,000 in Kallia, Judea, former Jordanian territory. In quickly developed irrigation areas they are growing corn, melons and tomatoes and an area has been set apart for hydroponics. (See *New Geography 1966–67*.)

Cotton is the only crop which has continued to expand at a rapid rate, while tobacco, groundnuts and sugar beet appear to have reached their peak. Israel's main suppliers are the U.S.A., the U.K. and West Germany; the main buyers: the U.S.A., Canada, Rumania and the U.K.

New Geography 1970-71

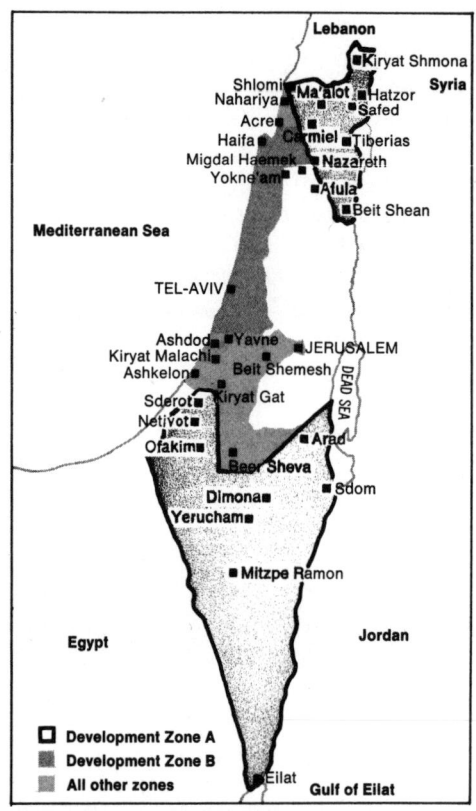

Priority Development Areas in
Israel

Trade with the U.K., 1969: exports to, £45m; imports from, £88m. Trade with the U.S.A., 1969: exports to, $290m; imports from, $301m.

ITALY

131,000 sq.m. (116,000 excluding Sicily and Sardinia). Pop. 54.1m. The emphasis for 1970–72 is on heavy industry, particularly chemical and power plant facilities, and on further development in the *Mezzogiorno* (southern area). As a result, the movement of workers from agricultural areas in the south to the industrial north is showing signs of slowing. The movement of industry to the south is an answer to the increasing congestion of the north.

The traditionally dominant axis of the urban and industrial geography of Italy is Milan-Turin. Its ramifications penetrate the whole region and tend to create a megalopolis of the north. A counterbalance is needed in the south; a Rome-Naples axis could serve to balance the northern megalopolis and constitute a new point of attack for southern problems, or, even better, a starting point for a southern programme to deal with big-city problems.

The Milan-Turin axis has brought about, through its dynamic character, a process of gradual diffusion of industrial activity and urbanization which penetrates through central and northern Italy. Similarly, a Rome-Naples axis, having acquired an effective metropolitan dynamism, should be able to do the same in the southern regions.

Large areas of the *Mezzogiorno* will go out of agriculture. The poor mountains and many of the hill lands will be turned over to forestry — thus improving the catchment area for water for irrigation — and to tourism which will play an increasing role. The new projects will perhaps support a third of the existing population. In the hill areas, holdings will become larger as farmers leave and those who remain will be able to obtain a fair living.

The bulk of agricultural production must, however, come from the plains, about 1.2m acres of which are either already irrigated or planned for irrigation, with prospects of remaining very profitable.

Industrial development is vital to the development of agriculture. When the new steelworks at Taranto opened and offered 4,000 jobs there were 40,000 applicants. Between 1965 and 1971 the plan was to find 700,000 new jobs in the south — a large figure by any standards.

Viewed in the light of progress already achieved the prospects for the success of future industrialization programmes are bright, especially when intervention to date by the *Cassa per il Mezzogiorno* (Fund for Southern Italy) has enabled industrial investment totalling 4,000m lire, providing employment for about 500,000 people.

Planned are organic engineering, chemical and foodstuffs projects, sectors particularly suitable for development in southern Italy. Also forming part of this general strategy is the vertical integration of existing basic industries. For example, the Taranto Steel Centre is to widen its range of production.

The basic objective of state intervention in the south is to achieve greater diversification, to facilitate the establishment of integrated and complementary projects, and thereby gradually to create a stable and self-sufficient economy for the whole of southern Italy. The recently created 100,000m lire fund for applied scientific research in Italy, with special consideration for the requirements of the south, will help.

While establishment in the south of industries providing basic products has eliminated deficiencies, there are still not enough labour-intensive manufacturing industry projects, which would enable a more suitable solution of the employment problem.

The difficulties in some areas are daunting. Two million Calabrese have the lowest income a head of any region — 327,000 lire (about £211), half the national average and one-third that of the Milanese. Life expectancy is three years less and infant mortality double that of Lombardy. Agricultural yields are about one-half to one-third less and emigration is 30,000 a year. There are only four companies with over 500 employees in Calabria.

The Caltanissetta-Enna-Agrigento triangle is the poorest area in Sicily although a statistical anomaly shows the per capita income to be 280,000 lire (about £188), as 3,000

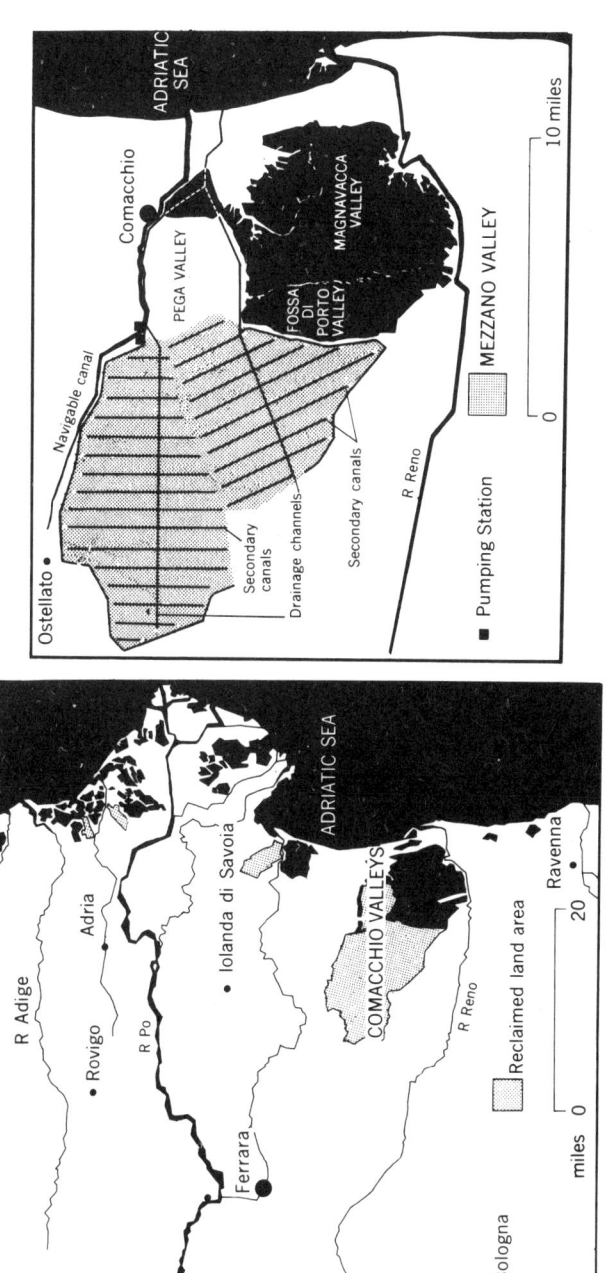

Drainage system in the Mezzano Valley

well-paid workers at the Gela complex boost the average for 300,000 other workers who make an average £89. In the last decade, 200,000 of the area's one million people emigrated.

Natural disasters add to the difficulties. The Sicilian earthquake of 1968 caused huge damage and left 80,000 homeless. Adequate funds were appropriated but as a result of ineptitude and bureaucracy the victims are still living in squalid encampments of unheated metal huts. No money has been spent on reconstruction.

The Agency for the Colonization of the Po Delta *(Ente per la Colonizzazione del Delta Padano)* is achieving good results. The area where the Agency carries out its work is between Venice, Ferrara, Ravenna and the Adriatic Sea. On the map (See page 124) there is a place named Iolanda di Savoia. This was one of the first areas where farmers were settled. Drainage canals were improved, and roads and farmhouses were built for the new settlers. The soils of the delta are alluvial and generally very fertile. There are some areas of peaty soil which are particularly suitable for rice cultivation. Basin irrigation is used. At present the biggest project being carried out by the Agency is the reclamation of lands bordering the Comacchio lagoon — a large inlet near Ferrara. The building of embankments and pumping stations; the digging of drainage cannals and ditches; and the construction of roads are providing much needed work in the area. Shelter belts of trees have also to be planted along the canals to give some protection from drying winds. Rainfall is low in the delta and part of the Agency's work is to provide fresh irrigation water for the farmers who will settle on the new lands.

Trade with the U.K., 1969: exports to, £240m; imports from, £182m. Trade with the U.S.A., 1969: exports to, to, $1,102m; imports from, $1,114m.

J

JAPAN

182,700 sq.m. Pop. 102m. The Ministry of International Trade and Industry made five confident forecasts for 1970 and at the time of printing of this book they seemed likely to be fulfilled.

(1) Production of iron and steel would reach 100m tons, ranking Japan third after the U.S.A. and the Soviet Union.

(2) Japan would outstrip the Soviet Union in machine tool output.

(3) It would outdistance France not only in production of motor vehicles but in exports, second only after the U.S.A.

(4) Japan would rank equal with the U.S.A. as a manufacturer of colour television sets.

(5) The production of man-made fibres would reach 1m tons.

Business firms operating in Japan under total or partly foreign ownership have been increasing. American interests predominate among the so-called "world enterprises" or giant Western organizations, such as American General Electric.

Looking ahead, it seems inevitable that Japan will play an important role in the development of Asia as the influence of Britain and probably the U.S.A. declines in relative terms. Japan will be the dominant power in the area. The likely pattern of economic relations that may evolve is one of an exchange of the primary commodities and materials which Japan lacks for manufactured goods and equipment and, more significantly, capital. Japan's trade with South-east Asia has already grown to 30% of the total.

The Japanese are making steel in Malaysia, drilling for oil

New Geography 1970-71

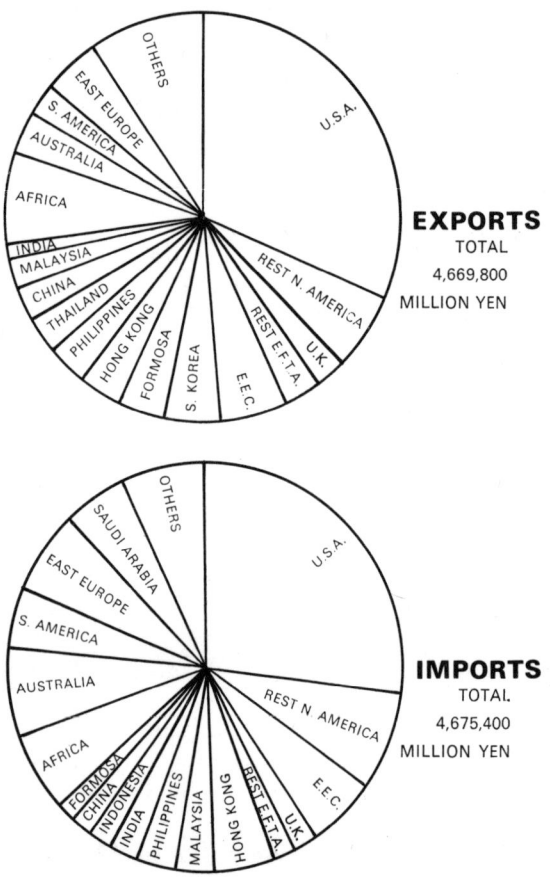

Distribution of Japanese trade in 1969

off Indonesia, building cars in the Philippines and assembling television sets in Taiwan. Other Asians are uneasy at the speed, size and cost of the Japanese invasion. They tend to play down or overlook Japan's growing aid to the area. Tokio is paying out 1.5 billion dollars in war reparations, has given 220m dollars to the Asian Development Bank and has lent

Japan

100m dollars to the World Bank. Japan's foreign aid — 1.4 billion dollars in 1970 — is second only to the U.S. figure of 1.8 billion dollars. However, the figure that most concerns Asians is Tokio's huge trade balance. In 1969 Japan sold cars, trucks and other machinery worth 4.6 billion dollars to East Asia but spent only half as much for the purchase of timber, maize and other raw materials.

Between 1958 and 1968 the output of cars increased at the remarkable average rate of 390% a year and, in the space of a decade, Japan has forged ahead of experienced manufacturing nations such as the U.K., France and Italy. In 1969 the production of passenger cars was 4.9m. Not only has a large and sophisticated domestic market been created, but Japan's automobile manufacturers have penetrated the domestic markets of American and European companies and have established overseas assembly plants.

Each day Japan exports 44m dollars' worth of goods — in almost equal thirds to the U.S.A., Asia and the rest of the world. Few nations can match Japan's prices — not because of cheap labour, which is no longer particularly cheap, but because of efficient production and shipping techniques. The Japanese, for instance, can deliver finished oil pipeline to Alaska at a total cost that is less than the freight charges alone from Pittsburgh. Between 1955 and 1970 Japan's share of world trade tripled to 7%; the U.S. share declined a little to 18%. Some economists predict that by 1980 each country will have 15%.

Japan has relaxed its anti-monopoly laws to encourage the formation of much larger industrial units capable of competing with the largest firms in the world. An important example is the union of the Yawat and Fuji steel companies to become the Nippon Steel Corporation. It is already second only to the United States Steel Corporation and is expected to become the world's largest steel producer within a few years.

Japan is importing 1m tons of wood chips from Australia each year, an extension of similar trade with British Columbia and Alaska.

New Geography 1970-71

In the summer of 1970 the Kawasaki Municipal Government began a project to create an island off the Kawasaki coast in Tokio Bay. The five-year project costing a total of 70,000m yen, is to make the city a better trade port, and to move industrial factories onto the reclaimed island from the city.

An artificial island of about 4,140,000 square metres will be reclaimed 700 metres from the city. A foreign trade wharf and an internal trade wharf, loading zones, warehouses and other port facilities will be built there. The foreign trade wharf will have 20 berths, each capable of accommodating a 15,000-ton vessel, and the internal trade wharf will be provided with 11 berths, each handling a 5,000-ton ship, and six berths each taking in a 700-ton ship. On the artificial island a 1,564,000 square metre lot will be set aside for the re-location of factories. The projected reclaimed island is to be linked by undersea tunnels to Kawasaki City, which has a population of nearly one million.

Kawasaki Port, situated between Tokio and Yokohama, annually handles 77m tons of cargo, the second largest after Yokohama Port. It is anticipated that the volume will rise to more than 90m tons around 1975.

URBANIZATION. More than in most countries urbanization has overwhelmed Japan. In 1950 60% of the population was tied to the farm and Japan still had to import rice. In 1970, as a result of agricultural advances, only 18% of the Japanese people are needed to feed the country and produce a surplus. The dispossessed farmers cram the cities. The Tokaido Corridor, the slender 366-mile coastal belt running along the Pacific from Tokio to Kobe, was a renowned beauty area. It now has 50% of the population and is smog-covered. The over-population of Tokio (11.4m) is particularly acute since earthquake research indicates that if another 1923-type earthquake were to hit Japan about 3m people would die.

Trade with the U.K., 1969: exports to, £106m; imports from, £125m. (Britain sent 17 trade missions to Japan in 1970.) Trade with the U.S.A., 1969: exports to, $4,098m; imports from, $2,931m. (See *Earthquakes, Tunnels.*)

KENYA

224,960 sq.m. Pop. 10.51m. Despite unemployment Kenya maintains its economic progress. The lateness of rains in 1969 and 1970 reduced food supplies but did not hamper economic progress. Collective ranches with incentives to modernize beef production are receiving enthusiastic response. Extensive research is finding ways to diversify agricultural production in order to break away from rigid patterns of output, especially where traditional crops are threatened by surplus (tea) or synthetics (cotton).

Kenya is trying to establish such industries as agricultural and food processing equipment, sisal and cotton manufacturing equipment, chemicals, plastics, paper, asbestos and glass. In 1969 the first phase of the Kindaruma HEP project, Tana River, was completed.

The East African Community has concluded negotiations with the EEC on a new association agreement. The EEC has suspended customs duties on most East African products and in return has been granted tariff preferences on some of their own products.

The changes in farming structure are interesting and far reaching. Formerly, the most productive areas of Kenya were European owned. Individual and national prosperity was based on large mixed farms, on cattle ranches and on coffee, tea, sisal and other plantations. These great farming enterprises produced almost all Kenya's exports and thus paid for almost all its imports. In 1970 2.2m of the 7m acres formerly held by Europeans were being worked by Africans. This has helped to ease Kenya's land hunger but has brought the problem of decreased production.

Four-fifths of the land of highest potential is occupied by small-scale African farms. The traditional land tenure systems have been altered. Fragmented land strips have been consolidated and communal land use is giving way to private ownership. The smallholders are now producing half Kenya's marketed output, partly as a result of the work of the 30 Farmers' Training Centres.

The Mwea irrigation scheme supporting 16,000 people is particularly prosperous. Here Kenya has grown its second rice crop. With 80% of its area arid and virtually useless for agriculture or pastoralism Kenya needs many more Mwea schemes.

The tourist trade is flourishing, with nearly 300,000 visitors in 1970. Several new game parks and reserves have been opened.

Trade with the U.K., in 1969: exports to, £28.8m; imports from, £50m. Trade with the U.S.A., 1969: exports to, $25.4; imports from, $31m.

KUWAIT

6,000 sq.m. Pop. 495,000. An interesting situation has developed in Kuwait's geography, with the economy progressing at a slower rate because of government restrictions on immigrants. The expatriate population, previously over half the total, was sharply reduced in 1969–70. This led to a dramatic fall in local purchasing power and the accumulation of large stocks of unsold imports. These problems have been aggravated by the state's shrinking role as an entrepôt for the Upper Gulf area, as other countries of the region, notably Iraq and Saudi Arabia, have reduced taxation on direct imports from outside the Gulf zone. Also, delays have occurred in establishing a free zone in Kuwait itself.

With oil marketing difficulties resulting from the Suez Canal closure Kuwait has an agreement with the Soviet

Kuwait

Union: the Soviet Union sells oil to Kuwait's customers in Scandinavia while Kuwait sells to Soviet markets in Pakistan, India and Japan.

Major water development and telecommunications projects are in hand, including a pipeline to bring water from Iraq. The fishing industry is growing following purchase of 20 seine trawlers from the Soviet Union. Other moves in the diversification programme are factories making cement, car batteries, detergents, ceramics and glass.

Trade with the U.K., 1969: exports to, £160m; imports from, £28m. Trade with the U.S.A., 1969: exports to, $94m; imports from, $80m.

L

LABOUR

Among the economic and social problems created by the world population explosion in the developing countries, one of the most critical and most immediate is that of unemployment. In some parts of the world, local and international projects to create full employment have had spectacular results. But given the enormity of the problem, even these must be regarded as insignificant. The ILO gives an alarming picture of world employment at present and its likely evolution in the near future. In the decade 1970–80 the labour force of the developing countries is expected to grow by about 226m, from 1,012m to 1,238m – an increase of 22%. For the industrial countries during the same period the estimated rate of increase is about 11% or 56m. Between 1960–70 the labour force grew by 20m a year!

In absolute figures (if not in terms of percentages of population) the highest growth rate will be registered in South and East Asia where the total labour force will jump from 804m to more than 970m. In Africa, 32m will be added (23% increase) and in Latin America some 30m (about 32%).

According to the ILO projections, the world's labour force under the age of 20 is expected to increase from 230m workers in 1970 to about 245m in 1980, and the 20-24 age group from 211m to nearly 264m. Thus, in spite of the expected decline in the proportion of young people in active employment as a result of the extension of education, the net increase in the world's labour force under age 25 will amount to 68m additional workers, of whom virtually all (64.5m) will be found in the developing countries.

The trend is a decrease in manpower engaged in agri-

Labour

culture, although the percentage is still very high in the developing countries — nearly three times that of the industrial countries. In absolute figures, the number of agricultural workers in the developing world is expected to increase by 80m during the next decade. These people are usually uneducated, untrained and, more often than not, unemployed. At the same time, a general scarcity of skilled manpower and migration from the rural areas aggravates the problem of under-employment in the towns.

The problem, then, is to provide means of subsistence for workers now unemployed. The number in the developing countries alone is expected to reach 76m by 1971. Also to be considered are the 282m who will be seeking employment for the first time during the coming decade. Faced with this problem, the ILO made employment the main theme for its fiftieth anniversary and for its strategy for the 1970s.

The report on the World Employment Programme points out that, up to now, insufficient attention has been given in the development plans to the expansion of employment in the countries of the Third World. Three spheres are particularly favourable for expansion of employment in the Third World: rural development, public works and the development of small industries and rural crafts.

Rural development provides a variety of employment opportunities for unskilled labour through the construction of irrigation and drainage systems and secondary road networks, general environmental improvement, extension of cultivated areas and the use of labour-intensive farming methods. Small industries and crafts, particularly those concerned with the processing of agricultural products on the spot or the manufacture of simple consumer goods, should be set up and developed. The project in the Comilla District of East Pakistan is an example worth citing: its civil engineering programme in rural areas accounted for 129m working days or, calculated on the basis of 300 working days per year, 430,000 man years.

With industrialization, the accent should again be on labour-intensive projects, and authorities should concentrate

HOST COUNTRY	AUSTRIA	FRANCE	FED. REP. OF GERMANY	SWITZERLAND	BELGIUM	NETHERLANDS	SWEDEN	U.K.	Total
Country of origin									
Europe:									
Greece	380	10,000**	140,310	8,000	6,400	2,050	5,920	4,000*	177,060
Italy	1,430	700,000	268,800	510,000	68,160	7,500	5,420	35,000	1,594,310
Malta	—	—	—	—	—	—	—	33,000	33,000
Portugal	—	300,000	17,800	—	2,110	2,350	—	4,000**	326,260
Spain	350	640,120	118,030	81,000	25,680	13,700	3,190	30,000	912,070
Yugoslavia	45,480	40,000	97,720	11,000	8,000	1,450	13,420	2,000*	219,070
Middle East:									
Cyprus	—	—	—	—	—	—	—	60,000*	60,000
Turkey	6,500	5,500	131,310	7,000	7,270	10,700	—	1,500**	169,780
Asia:									
Hong Kong	—	—	—	—	—	—	—	17,000	17,000
India	—	990	3,070	—	—	—	1	230,000	234,060
Malaysia	—	—	—	—	—	—	—	16,000	16,000
Pakistan	—	180	420	—	—	—	—	125,600	125,600
Singapore	—	—	—	—	—	—	—	18,000	18,000
America:									
West Indies	—	—	—	—	—	—	—	445,000	445,000
Africa:									
Algeria	—	600,000	1,480	—	1,710	—	—	—	603,190
Morocco	—	100,000	5,820**	—	13,370	12,520	—	—	131,710
Tunisia	—	60,000	760**	700	430	—	—	—	61,890
Total	54,140	2,456,790	783,520	617,700	133,130	50,270	27,950	1,020,500	5,144,000

N.B. — *Figures for Belgium comprise only migrant workers registered with the Belgian Social Security.*
* 1965 figures.
** 1966 figures.

Table of Migrant Labour

Labour

their efforts on production of industrial consumer goods for the rural population, such as cotton cloth, certain processed foods, utensils, ceramic products and furniture; and producer goods, such as ploughs, harrows, bricks and wheelbarrows.

Most developing countries suffer from a lack of skilled labour and of high-level personnel and technicians in both rural and urban zones. Moreover, a high percentage of the labour in these countries, particularly of women workers, is illiterate. Experience shows, however, that to learn a skill demands basic general knowledge and the development of the necessary faculties for comprehension of what is being taught. Workers must also be enabled to adapt themselves later on to new techniques or new skills as may be dictated by economic and technological developments.

Often villagers arrive in towns in greater numbers than can be absorbed by existing industries and unemployment reaches critical levels.

Thorkil Kristensen, former secretary-general of the Organization of European Community Development and now director of the newly established Development Research Institute, Copenhagen, says that rural depopulation could be checked by more progressive agriculture, such as the production of higher yielding rice or wheat and the bringing in of improved tools rather than complicated machinery. He suggests, too, great extension of poultry farming and stock rearing, activities little developed in many countries, which have the advantage of not being subject to seasonal variations.

OVER FIVE MILLION MIGRANT WORKERS IN 8 EUROPEAN COUNTRIES. The United Nations has prepared figures on the migration of people across frontiers, but no up-to-date statistics exist giving a world picture of the migration of workers per se. The table presented here is limited to migrant workers in eight European countries in 1967 and is based on a fuller study prepared by the Churches Committee on Migrant Workers in Western Europe. Establishing statistics on migrant workers is fraught with difficulties

New Geography 1970-71

since the definition and classification of what a migrant worker is differs widely from country to country. This table is therefore an approximation.

LEBANON

4,300 sq.m. Pop. 2.6m. There is to be intensive development of roads, railways and irrigation, despite increasing defence costs. Depending so profoundly on tourism, shipping and banking, Lebanon is particularly vulnerable to pressures resulting from the Israeli-Arab conflict. Prolonged peace is necessary to achieve the target of 4.4m visitors by 1974.

Only 11% of Lebanon's land is suitable for farming and with poor harvests of apples, wheat, soya beans and olives the nation has had a difficult two years, relieved only by rising industrial exports — all light consumer goods.

Beirut has greatly developed as an entrepot following the closure of the Suez Canal. In 1969 the volume of entrepot goods increased by 9% and in 1970 by 12%.

Trade with the U.K., 1969: exports to, £4m; imports from, £22m. Trade with the U.S.A., 1969: exports to, $15.2m; imports from $37m.

LIBERIA

48,000 sq.m. Pop. 1.2m. This sparsely populated country is socially backward but economically progressive. In 1969 the great Mount Coffee HEP scheme, 18 miles from Monrovia, and the ambitious Monrovia Water System came into operation.

The oldest African republic, Liberia has an impressive range of industries. They include: production of edible oils, soluble coffee, aluminium ware, wool garments, glass, pharmaceuticals, pineapple canning, plywood, rice growing

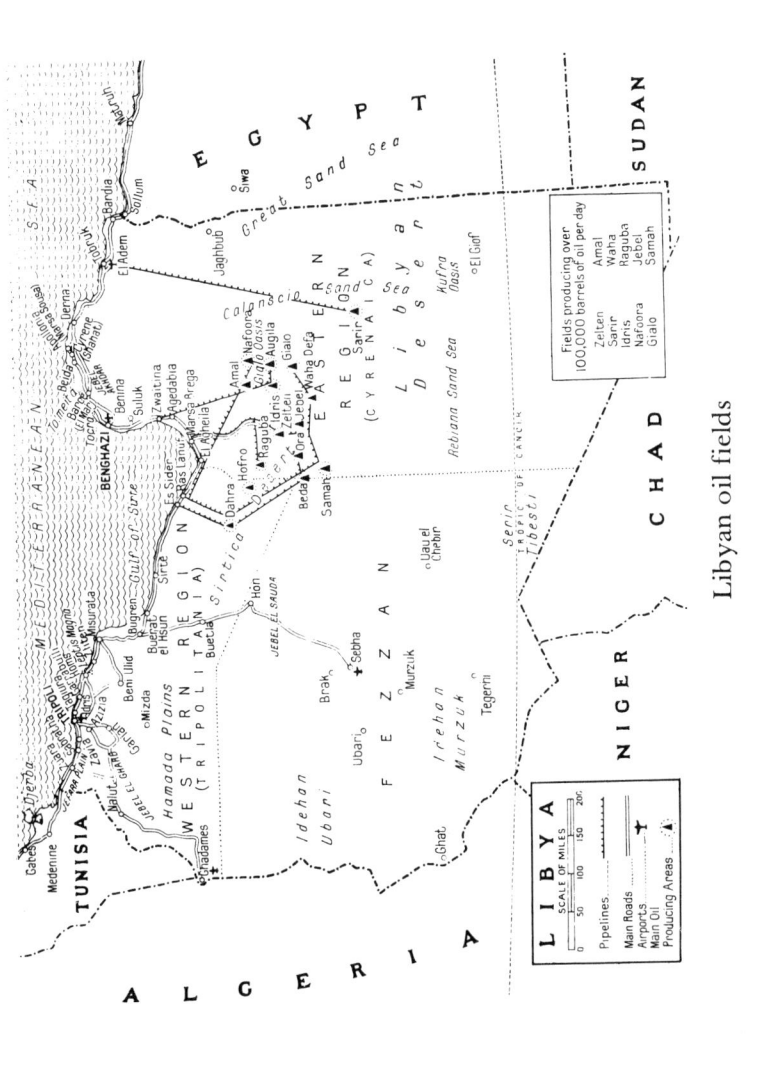

Libyan oil fields

and milling, confectionery, clothing, jute bags and gold jewellery.

Monrovia port is being developed and a new one is under construction at Buchanan so that the country's vast production of iron ore may be more readily shipped. Nil in 1960, iron ore output was 3m tons in 1960 and 21m in 1970. It accounts for 70% of foreign trade.

At one time the Liberian merchant marine — consisting of shipping from nearly every country in the world registered under the Liberian flag as a matter of great economy — produced much valuable foreign exchange. Today it supplies only a small part of the nation's wealth. Timber is increasing in value as roads are built into the jungle. Rubber, which had declined, is recovering; in 1970 Liberia was ninth in output, 62,000 metric tons.

Trade with the U.K., 1969: exports to, £9.1m; imports from, £3m. Trade with the U.S.A., 1969: exports to, $42.3m; imports from, $30m.

LIBYA

680,000 sq.m. Pop. 1.86m. Groundnuts have become the most consistently successful export crop, with a production of 4,985 tons in 1970. Many of the 5m olive trees planted by the pre-war Italian colonists are now reaching maturity but there is a shortage of labour to harvest the fruit. Tomato production, too, has increased greatly and 120,000 tons annually are processed in the western region. Other vegetables have become more abundant with the agricultural development of Siwa and Kufra oases, where oil companies have successfully drilled for water as part of their oil concessions. At the end of 1970 30 oilfields were in production, producing 3m bbl a day.

The National Agricultural Settlement Authority is successfully opening up new areas for farming, especially in converting areas of the fertile Green Mountains from semi-

Libya

nomadic shifting cultivation and grazing to mechanized cereal farming and orcharding. On the coastal plains of Tripoli major reclamation schemes should provide much new land.

Trade with the U.K., 1969: exports to, £190m; imports from, £31.5m. Trade with the U.S.A., 1969: exports to, $211m; imports from, $101m.

MALAWI

45,745 sq.m. Pop. 4.3m. Malawi's economy depends primarily on agriculture and farming returns were poor in 1968–69 — the groundnut and tobacco crops being particularly affected — but the country's progress is nevertheless good. Secondary industries in 1970 were working to capacity, especially in textiles and clothing, consumer goods and engineering. A notable trend has been closer relations with South Africa in commercial (and diplomatic) spheres. Malawi is the first Black African state to establish diplomatic relations with South Africa which, in turn, has provided a £6.4m loan for the first stage of developing the Lilongwe area and another £6.4m for building the vital rail-link to Nacula in Mozambique. This provides Malawi with a second sea outlet as an alternative to Beira. Britain is by far Malawi's principal trading partner.

Trade for 1969: exports to the U.K., £11m; imports from, £8.4m. Trade with the U.S.A., 1969: exports to, $12m; imports from, $9m.

MALAYSIA

128,703 sq.m. Pop. 10.5m (comprising Malaya, 51,000 sq.m. and 8.9m; Sabah, 29,000 sq.m. and 620,000; Sarawak, 48,000 sq.m. and 950,000). Despite racial and political disturbances, rubber and tin have given Malaysia high export figures. A chief reason for the racial rivalries is the high rate of unemployment with Malays comprising the majority of the 200,000 unemployed. "Cottage" industries are being encouraged to help solve the problem.

The palm oil industry is aiming to expand output to about 2m tons by 1980 (300,000 tons in 1970). The U.S.A. is Malaysia's chief buyer but Japan's share of total trade is increasing, and Japan recently overtook the U.K. as Malaysia's chief supplier. The Japanese, too, are co-operating with Malaysia to fish for tuna from Penang Island. Fishing advances, generally, have greatly increased the catch.

Trade with the U.K., 1969: exports to, £42m; imports from, £60m. Trade with the U.S.A., 1969: exports to, $180m; imports from, $160.7m.

MALTA

122 sq.m. Pop. 325,000. With the completion in 1969 of the industrial estates at Msierah, Marsa and Mriehel the country should be able to progress industrially. When the next such estate, at Buleben, is completed, another 95 factories will be in operation. The range of products is impressive and includes suede, fur and leather goods, spectacle frames, precision tools, plastics, toys and furniture. The Malta Drydocks, the largest industrial complex in Malta and the main source of employment, passed into government ownership in 1968. The yards are diversifying into the building of pontoons, barges, motor-yachts, cabin cruisers and factory construction.

Malta is trying to phase its tourist intake over all seasons to provide year-long employment; the island is being publicized as an ideal conference centre during the off-season months. The target for 1972 is 250,000 tourists (38,380 in 1964, 136,995 in 1968).

Trade with the U.K., 1969: exports to, £5m; imports from, £22.5m. Trade with the U.S.A., 1969: exports to, $12m; imports from, $16m.

New Geography 1970-71

MAPS

Recent experiments by the British Directorate of Overseas Surveys have been connected with the production of photo-maps. In these maps vegetation tones in air photographs are separated photographically and provided in different colours while water and man-made features are enhanced by conventional methods. This kind of map is particularly suited to low-lying areas. Photomaps clearly show features of swamps, vegetation cover and cultivation patterns which cannot be adequately depicted by symbols and lines. Detail submerged by shallow water is also visible.

The Directorate's work often provides a basis for development plans in developing countries. It assesses flood areas when HEP schemes are proposed and produces maps to assist red locust control, to prepare rice cultivation schemes and timber plantations, and to help in town planning. Perhaps few geographers realize the scope of the Directorate's work. It employs 500 trained staff in its three main divisions — field survey, mapping and land resource investigation. About 50 surveyors work permanently overseas in the Caribbean, West Africa, Central Africa and the Far East.

MAURITIUS

720 sq.m. Pop. 830,000. This island has become an object of interest to the great powers. The closing of the Suez Canal in 1967 turned Mauritius into a regular port of call on the round-Africa routes. Soviet warships are frequent visitors, the U.S.A. has a space rescue and recovery station, and the Chinese are politically and economically active. The U.K. still supports the price of sugar, which makes up 98% of the island's exports. No less than 45% of the island was planted with sugar in 1969.

Mauritius now has eight tea factories, including one of the most up-to-date in the world and tea exports in 1969 were nearly 2m kilos. Much of the tea goes to South Africa, which displaced the U.K. as chief buyer in 1968. Joint Japanese-Mauritian fishing operations are extremely successful with a harvest of 300,000 tons in 1970.

At present most tourists come from the neighbouring islands of Reunion and Madagascar but efforts to attract people from Africa are being successful through the work of the new (1969) Indian Ocean Tourist Alliance, designed to promote the tourist trade of Mauritius, Reunion, Madagascar and the Comores Islands. Mauritius had 18,000 tourists in 1969.

With a thriving industrial estate at Port Louis, new irrigation schemes, an HEP station and a new thermal station Mauritius can remain prosperous if its sugar crop is consistently sold and if the population increase can be checked.

Trade with the U.K., 1969: exports to, £30m; imports from, £7m. Trade with the U.S.A., 1969: exports to, $4.1m; imports from, $9.2m.

METHANE

It is now estimated that reserves of natural gas are more than sufficient to replace manufactured gas completely in the U.K. and by 1975 should supply 15% of the nation's energy needs. The area available for exploration off the coast is 100,000 sq.m. By the end of 1969 licences had been granted for 54,000 sq.m. (The first supplies came ashore in March 1967 at Easington, Yorkshire.) The operation of converting all gas appliances in the country to methane will take about ten years but by the spring of 1970 all Area Gas Boards were connected to the methane gas transmission system.

MEXICO

758,000 sq.m. Pop. 48.3m. The nation's manufacturing industry has been expanding vigorously at over 8% per year, and by as much as 12% in artificial fibres, cement, paper, chemicals, aluminium and fertilizers.

Despite the spread of industry, primary production remains of great importance. Agriculture, forestry and fishing still employ over half the labour force and provide nearly 50% of exports. Greater irrigation and more expert use of fertilizers are increasing farm output, especially of sugar.

Foreign sales rose by 14% in 1970, with the U.S.A. taking 65% of all exports, and supplying 60% of Mexico's imports.

The country's most serious problem is that the working population is growing by 500,000 a year while the creation of new jobs barely reaches 200,000. An interesting aspect of American investment has been the setting up, along the Mexican northern border, of subsidiaries of California-based companies. American capital has been attracted by the existence of cheap and dexterous labour, proximity to the U.S. market and political stability, which has led to some firms setting up plants in preference to the Far East. Such products as computer components, textiles and camera parts are manufactured.

Trade with the U.K., 1969: exports to, £22m; imports from, £31m. Trade with the U.S.A., 1969: exports to, $893m; imports from, $1,334m.

MINERALS

NICKEL. From 1960 to 1970 nickel consumption in the non-Communist world rose by over 80% to reach about 830m lb in 1968 and an estimated 900m lb in 1970. Since 1966 nickel consumption has outstripped production, the deficit being largely made up from accumulated stocks. The shortage was aggravated by the loss of considerable Canadian

Minerals

production owing to labour troubles. Canada normally produces 50% of the world's nickel. In London the price per ton rose from £902 in 1967 to £1,220 in 1969.

The Western Australian shield lands are the site of an unprecedented boom. Thousands of claims have been staked. About 150 Australian companies are competing with firms from North America, the U.K., Europe and Japan. Most exploration is centred on the pre-Cambrian shield in Western Australia where similar associations of basic and ultrabasic rocks to those of the Canadian Shield are found. This huge area, sometimes referred to as the "West Australian nickel province", stretches from Cue, Meekatharra and Wiluna in the north almost to Esperance in the south, a distance of more than 1,000 miles. Present exploration has largely been confined to the area around Kalgoorlie and the eastern goldfields.

Many extensions and new facilities are being developed on the field and by the end of 1969 treatment capacity reached 66,000 tons per four-week period (828,000 tons per year), thus more than doubling the Kambalda capacity in less than a year.

Australia's second nickel mine at Scotia has started production based on sulphide nickel reserves which are currently estimated at 1.25m tons. Plans are also being made to commence mining at Nepean near Coolgardie. Apart from the high grade ores of the shield lands, there are other significant deposits which in time may well become important nickel producers. Large deposits of low grade lateritic ore were located in the Blackstone Range near Wingellina in the 1950s. Since then exploration has revealed resources of 60m tons.

Two main deposits of lateritic ore have also been found in Queensland. The most important is at Greenvale, west of Ingham.

The question is often asked: will the boom end? The picture is optimistic. There can be little doubt that there will be more exciting nickel finds in Western Australia. It appears that economically exploitable ore bodies will be located within the area of present strikes between Mount Windarra and Widgiemooltha as systematic exploration of this area proceeds. The recent discovery at Mount Windarra has extended the known length of nickel occurrence to over 185 miles.

With an increasing amount of high grade ore available Australia should obtain a large share of the nickel export market, particularly with Japan. In 1968 nickel produced was worth $A 10.13 million. It is estimated that this will reach $A 60 million by 1971 and an anticipated $A 80.00 million by 1975, when nickel is likely to be the third most important mineral produced in Western Australia in terms of value, after iron ore and bauxite.

SULPHUR. Canada is now second only to the U.S.A. as a sulphur producer while the Libyan oil wells are also a major supplier. Because of industry's great demands for sulphur — used in synthetic rubber and many chemicals — vast complexes are being built, particularly at Amuay in Venezuela, Aruba in the Netherlands Antilles, Bayway in New Jersey and Benicia in California.

Sulphur production is also on the rise in other countries, notably in Belgium (Antwerp), West Germany, Canada and the U.K. (9,000 tons annually).

BAUXITE. Vast deposits (an estimated 150m tons) are to be exploited at San Isidro de El General, Argentina. Deposits have been discovered at Odo-Otun, western Nigeria.

COPPER. South Africa has opened two new mines in Transvaal, notably at Mutali where the deposit is 20m tons. South Korea is mining copper at Yongyang. The principal copper discovery is at Casa Grande, Arizona, where reserves are estimated at 472m tons.

GOLD. Several strikes have been made in north-east Japan. That in the Fukushima area is said to be very rich. Along 30 miles of the Burdekin delta, Queensland, gold mining operations are in progress for the first time.

GYPSUM. The largest world deposit — 25m tons — has been discovered in the Shark Bay region of Western Australia.

IRON ORE. The chief developments have been in further exploitation rather than in discovery. See index.

METHANE. The chief finds are: Algeria, 30 miles east of Ghardaia; Australia, Bonaparte Gulf; Canada, south-west Alberta, northern Alberta, Yukon; South Africa, Plettenberg Bay — this country's first commercial methane find; the Soviet Union, a 60-mile deposit on the Rural River near Orenburg.

PHOSPHATE. Australia has proven reserves of a billion tons around Duchess, Queensland, and another 250m tons at Lady Annie, further north.

POTASH. A tremendous deposit — said to be the world's largest — has been found at Holle St. Paul, in the Congo.

URANIUM. Bolivia reports important deposits at San Pablo de Napa, in the south-east. Canada has further reserves at Kitts, Labrador, and in Saskatchewan. The Netherlands has made its first major uranium find, in the south.

MINING

THE CHANGING PATTERN. The Ninth Commonwealth Mining and Metallurgical Congress, held in London in May, 1969, focused attention on the rapid progress the mining industry had made during 1965—69. Even on the basis of known mineral deposits, output will continue to increase rapidly over the next few years, but new and improved techniques now mean that large deposits may be discovered almost anywhere, though not all will prove commercially viable.

A basic problem for the mining industry is the vast cost of today's operations — costs that will continue to rise if only because the most accessible deposits are already being

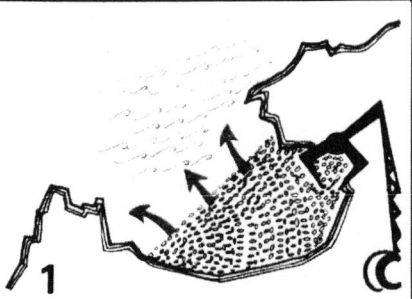

1. Nodules of titanium hydroxide, a "magnet" for uranium, are placed on the beach at low tide.

2. The rising tide covers the nodules. A barrage is placed across the bay to trap the seawater.

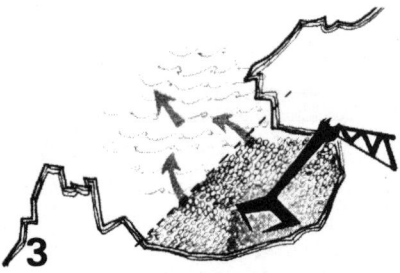

3. Two days later the barrage is removed. Nodules, on which uranium has combined with the titanium hydroxide, are recovered at low tide.

Mining seafloor uranium.

Mining

worked. Heavy expenditure is incurred in the use of intricate equipment to carry out ground and aerial surveys, and also to make some estimate of the quality and quantity of mineral available once a deposit has been discovered.

There is an increasing need to turn to deposits of lower grade ores, and this often involves more difficult mining operations. So that these may be commercially profitable, especially against a background of rising labour costs, scales of production and mines themselves are becoming much larger and capital intensive methods more widespread. In particular, the power and size of mining machinery and equipment have grown significantly while higher standards of engineering are being achieved. Even so, numerous technical problems still arise, especially with the terrain becoming increasingly difficult. The process of locating and recovering new mineral deposits is essential if supplies are to keep pace with rising industrial demand.

Demand for many minerals and refined metals grows substantially, and although there is a surplus of both tin and iron ore there is still a shortage of many other minerals which is keeping prices high. The rising demand for stainless steel, nickel's main outlet, means that despite increased output there is likely to be a further shortage of 75m lb of nickel in 1971. Conditions are also likely to remain tight for aluminium, where many large expansion schemes will not become effective until the early 1970s, as well as for lead, zinc and platinum. Moreover, within a few years known reserves of uranium will be insufficient to meet a world demand which is rising rapidly, chiefly as a result of its increasing use as a fuel for electric power generation, where it has the advantage of obviating air pollution.

The continual need to increase mineral supplies has led to extensive prospecting, especially in northern Canada and Australia and also beneath the sea. About seven-tenths of the world's surface is covered by water, but only a small proportion of the world's minerals are met from this source, the most important of these being salt, bromine and magnesium. There is clearly scope for exploiting mineral deposits under the sea, although so far this has usually proved to be a less profitable form of mining, chiefly because costs are high.

Progress is being made, particularly in dredging for deposits of such heavy minerals as tin, iron ore, diamonds and gold which lie on the sea bed in fairly shallow water, and also in extracting minerals, notably oil and gas, by drilling through the sea bed. Underground operations below the continental shelf are another form of mining. The basic difficulty here is one of access, and mining is usually confined to areas close to the coastline, often with tunnels from beneath the land surface. A substantial proportion of Japan's coal requirements are met from seams running under the sea, and some of the United Kingdom's coal and tin is also mined in this way. Other minerals which could be similarly extracted include phosphorite, oil shale, gypsum, potash, iron ore and bauxite.

MONGOLIA

1.75m sq.m. (approx). Pop. 1.22m. The Mongolian economy is dependent on animals to a degree unparalleled elsewhere. It has 23.5m cattle alone — more than 20 per head of population. Before the fairly recent introduction of agricultural co-operatives more than 200,000 nomadic families lived at subsistence level from their herds. The co-operatives — 300 in 1969 — have been largely responsible for making the country self-sufficient in food grains and giving it a surplus of wheat. State farms have increased to 35, with an average size of 250,000 acres. Because of the sparse population mechanization of agriculture is an absolute necessity; haymaking, for example, is 97% mechanized.

While agriculture is the mainstay of the economy it is wrong to think of Mongolia as only an agrarian state. About 40% of the GNP comes from industry. The country's rich natural resources and agricultural raw materials have made possible extensive mining and development of manufacturing industries. Coal is the most important mining industry (3m tons in 1969), but others are gold, oil, iron ore, salt and precious stones.

Light industry and food processing employ 40% of all industrial workers. Ulan Bator, the capital, has an industrial estate producing shoes, hides, building materials and consumer goods. The city of Darkhan is being developed as an industrial centre, and is expected to become one of Asia's most modern cities.

The UNDP has undertaken several projects in Mongolia. Principal ones are the training of farmers, technicians and engineers, the development of the livestock and dairying industry, and the food processing industry and expansion of leather and leather goods exports.

MONSOON

Indian weather scientists have drawn up an ambitious plan to study the anatomy of the monsoon. The investigation will last four years and will be the first organized effort to solve the riddle of the monsoon. (Almost one third of the world's land area and population depends on the monsoon for its crops.)

The primary cause of the monsoon is the difference in temperature over land and sea but nobody knows exactly when and where the formation of the monsoon begins or the exact air-sea interaction which helps the monsoon develop. The results of the investigation will aid an international monsoon study to be launched under the Global Atmospheric Research Programme in 1974.

New Geography 1970-71
MOROCCO

180,000 sq.m. Pop. 15m. Tourism is providing a lucrative source of foreign exchange. Morocco had 700,000 tourists in 1969, 50,000 of whom were Americans. But the greater part of foreign exchange is coming from phosphates — 12.5m tons were exported in 1970. Recent discoveries during the intensive hunt for minerals include a deposit of lead estimated at 10m tons.

Agriculture has not been so fortunate. Severe flooding in the Sebou Valley (January—February 1970) destroyed 10% of the citrus crop and affected production of grain, vegetables, sugar beet and wine.

Morocco's relations with its neighbours, Algeria and Mauritania, improved greatly in 1970 and increased stability in the region should have marked economic effects. Friendship with Mauritania should enable the two countries to act in concert in negotiations to settle the future of the Spanish Sahara region, over which Morocco and Mauritania claim sovereignty. This is a pressing problem for Morocco which fears the consequences on the world market of any exploitation of the area's vast phosphate deposits.

Morocco has signed agreements with Cuba and the Soviet Union and in September 1969 was permitted a "partial association agreement" with the EEC. France supplies 31% of its former protectorate's imports.

Trade with the U.K., 1969: exports to, £16m; imports from, £13m. Trade with the U.S.A., 1969: exports to, $58m; imports from, $49.6m.

THE NETHERLANDS

13,500 sq.m. Pop. 12.9m. Holland's trade is so prosperous that in 1969 and 1970 exports increased by 13.5% each year. During the period a remarkable growth of 28% was recorded in mining, largely because of the expanding methane output. Chemical production rose by 17% while that of metals increased by 14%. Productivity has led to a greater demand for labour, especially of foreign workers.

Western European countries take the greater proportion of Holland's exports, with West Germany the principal market. In 1969, however, exports to France increased by 31%. Exports to the U.K. rose only 7% indicating the effect that the Common Market is having of concentrating trade flows into intra-EEC trade.

Trade with the U.K., 1969: exports to, £409m; imports from, £295m. Trade with the U.S.A. 1969: exports to, $456m; imports from, $1,355m.

NEW ZEALAND

104,000 sq.m. Pop. 2.9m. New Zealand's economic future was changed in 1970 following the discovery of a vast methane field off the Taranaki coast. The cost of production will be high but the field does give New Zealand another source of power (it already has much HEP), thus eliminating the need for heavy investment in nuclear power stations which was previously planned. Furthermore, the country could save 50m dollars a year by refining petrol from the methane, and thereby eliminate imports. A petro-chemical industry would obviously follow. By the end of 1970 many international oil companies had begun searches for further oil in and around New Zealand.

Industrial production has doubled in New Zealand since 1958 and a boom in mineral production — copper, lead, zinc and many other minerals — is beginning. Aluminium and iron ore smelting are also rapidly developing. Forestry, fishing and tourism have been given high targets. Timber production, for instance, increased by 10% in 1970.

Despite the growth of industry, agriculture and pastoralism are still the mainstays of the nation's economy and in 1969 they were responsible for 90% of foreign exchange earnings. It is interesting to note that farm production increased 50% during 1960–70. In 1970 the country had 60m sheep. The renewed possibility of the U.K.'s entry into the EEC disturbs the New Zealand government but trade is flourishing in new directions, notably Japan and the U.S.A.

Britain's former supremacy in New Zealand markets is being eroded. But in April 1970 New Zealand exported to Britain 7m board feet of sawn timber, a major breakthrough into the British softwood market. The growing strength and diversity of New Zealand's exports can be seen by taking a sample month's trading. In February 1970 exports by manufacturers reached a value of 10.7m dollars, 0.5m more than in any previous month, 3.7m more than in February 1969 and 5m more than in 1968. Exports of processed fruit and vegetables exceeded 1m dollars for the first time in a single month. For the first time, too, the country is exporting coffee and cocoa preparations — 2m dollars' worth in the six months to August 1970.

During 1969–70 New Zealand had the worst drought since 1946. It so seriously affected dairy farming that many farmers dried off their herds and found other jobs.

Trade with the U.K., 1969: exports to, £199m; imports from, £100m. Trade with the U.S.A., 1969: exports to, $270m; imports from, $160m.

Nigeria

NICARAGUA

57,000 sq.m. Pop. 1.89m. To reduce dependence on the cotton crop the government is diversifying agriculture. Following the construction of an extensive rural water supply throughout the country between 1962–69, the production of vegetables, tomatoes, pineapples and other fruit is increasing. Further emphasis is being placed on fishing, exports of shrimps and lobsters rising by 21% in 1969. Gold, silver and copper are being mined in increasing quantities following an exhaustive geological study.

Trade with the U.K., 1969: exports to, £1.5m; imports from, £2.5m. Trade with the U.S.A., 1969: exports to, $85m; imports from, $61.7m.

NIGERIA

356,669 sq.m. Pop. 63.2m. The civil war with Biafra, now ended, placed great pressure on the economy but it showed remarkable resilience. Higher earnings from cocoa, groundnuts and tin and the resumption of oil production generally offset the declines in rubber and timber exports and the virtual cessation of palm produce exports. In 1970 Nigeria was the tenth largest producer of oil. It is noteworthy, too, that by 1969 Nigeria had become the sixth largest tin-producing nation. The smelting plant at Jos can handle the entire output — 14,000 tons of tin ore in 1969.

One of the most important priorities is road-building but dams, too, are vital developments. The Kainji Dam, opened in mid-1969, will satisfy Nigeria's power requirements throughout the 1970s. It means, too, that the whole of the Niger River almost to the border of the Niger Republic will be navigable all year. By controlling flooding the dam opens up once uncultivable land.

Several new industries have been commenced — the first paper mill, a cement factory, three textile factories, a canvas industry (at Kano).

Trade with the U.K., 1969: exports to, £60m; imports from, £70m. Trade with the U.S.A., 1969: exports to, $180m; imports from, $169.7m.

NILE

The Sudan, Kenya, Uganda, Tanzania and Egypt have combined to tackle overall regulation of the Nile. The building of dams and canals, begun in 1970, is complex and ambitious and will take five years to complete. In the first stage Lakes Victoria, Albert and Kiuga are to be converted for use as reservoirs. During the rainy season at least 200,000 million cubic metres of water are lost through seepage and evaporation. In the second stage the huge swamp areas of southern Sudan — steppe during the dry season and fever swamp in the wet — are to be drained. It is proposed to build a canal parallel to the Nile to contain and divert some of its waters. It will also be necessary to settle the nomadic tribesmen who live in the swampland.

NORWAY

125,183 sq.m. Pop. 3.9m. The pattern of industrial production is changing and although the transport and food industries are retaining their traditional pre-eminence, the iron and metal goods manufacturing industry has risen to third place, followed by the primary iron and metal industry. Wood processing, formerly the third largest, is now in fifth place while the chemical and electro-technical industries are rapidly becoming more significant.

Manufacturing industry now accounts for about a third of industrial employment and nearly half of total production though the nation still retains a basic dependence on the traditional resources of forests, fish and water.

Norway

The abundance of cheap HEP is causing sharp rises is metal production. Aluminium, for instance, rose by 35% in 1969 — to more than 600,000 tons. The new plant (1969) at Sunndalsora is the biggest in Europe. The industry is, however, facing difficulties. The bulk of Norway's aluminium output is exported and, with world capacity growing rapidly, international prices could come under serious pressure over the next few years, causing heavy losses. Moreover, Norway's cost advantage in using HEP may be diminishing. To safeguard the industry's future, links are being formed with foreign groups, thereby gaining technical and marketing expertise as well as securing a safe supply of raw materials. Partnership with foreign firms is also occurring in shipbuilding.

With the opening of a new copper mine at Tverrfjellet a copper processing plant is to be built; at present all Norwegian copper is sent to West Germany for processing.

Trade with the U.K., 1969: exports to, £180m; imports from, £145m. Trade with the U.S.A., 1969: exports to, $290m; imports from, $160m.

OCEANOGRAPHY

The United Nations now has a 42-nation Seabeds Committee which is preparing a set of principles to govern future exploration and exploitation of resources underlying the deep ocean floor.

The U.S. Deep Sea Drilling Project has been so successful that the Scripps Institution of Oceanography has obtained a three-year extension of the "deep ocean probe". Scripps was awarded in January 1970 an additional 22.2m dollars for a 36-month extension. This will cover 30 months of drilling with another six months for analysis. During the extension period the research ship *Glomar Challenger* will work in the Atlantic, Pacific and Indian Oceans and will also drill in the Mediterranean.

The Integrated Global Ocean Station System (IGOSS) seems to be producing useful information. Its purpose is to gather, transmit and process data from the oceans so that changing conditions can be predicted for users — such as fisheries and shipping — much as the weather is forecast by meteorologists. One of the main experiments has been the Soviet Union's 17 research buoys near the Canary Islands. The U.S.A. has similar buoys between Alaska and Hawaii; they transmit data several times daily to a shore station.

Oceanographers now know that currents are not fixed. The Woods Hole Institution put down a set of current meters 200 miles south of Bermuda in the central Sargasso Sea, at depths of 50 and 100 metres. For three months the current ran steadily north; in the fourth month it ran south (1969).

The U.S. National Institute of Oceanography has a new instrument which can take pictures of deep ocean ridges. On its first operational cruise in August 1969 it took the first pictures of such a ridge ever taken. It lies 4 km deep south of the Azores. A sonar tool, the instrument, known as *Gloria*, shows projections as black and depressions as white. The survey of the 90-mile feature was completed in 24 hours. The object of *Gloria* is to facilitate rapid large-scale surveys of major geological features in extremely deep ocean waters.

The Indian National Institute of Oceanography has been established at Panjim, Goa, by the Council of Scientific and Industrial Research. This action may be regarded as one of the long-range results of the International Indian Ocean Expedition, co-ordinated by UNESCO, since the site choice of Goa is based largely on the Expedition's findings of high fertility in the Arabian Sea. A fishing harbour is also being planned at Panjim, next to the 300-acre institute site. A research vessel, to be built abroad from Indian designs, is also projected.

OIL

The great oil strike of 1970 was that made by Phillips Petroleum Co. and its associates in the North Sea, 200 miles east of Scotland and 185 south-west of Norway, and 230 ft. under the surface. Labelled Ekofisk 2-X, the field, Phillips say, could produce 10,000 bbl of oil a day but other estimates put the figure for the entire area at 300,000 bbl a day. One of Phillips' partners, Petrofina S.A., a Belgian oil company, estimates that the field could contain 7.5 billion bbl. This would be four times greater than the known reserves in all Europe and would make the field equal in potential with Alaska's estimated reserves. The chief problem is the stormy nature of the area. Production of 200,000 bbl a day would require a pipeline. The most likely place to run the line would be to Phillips' refinery at Billingham, 220 miles away. Phillips estimates the cost of developing the Ekofisk field, including the pipeline, at 500m dollars.

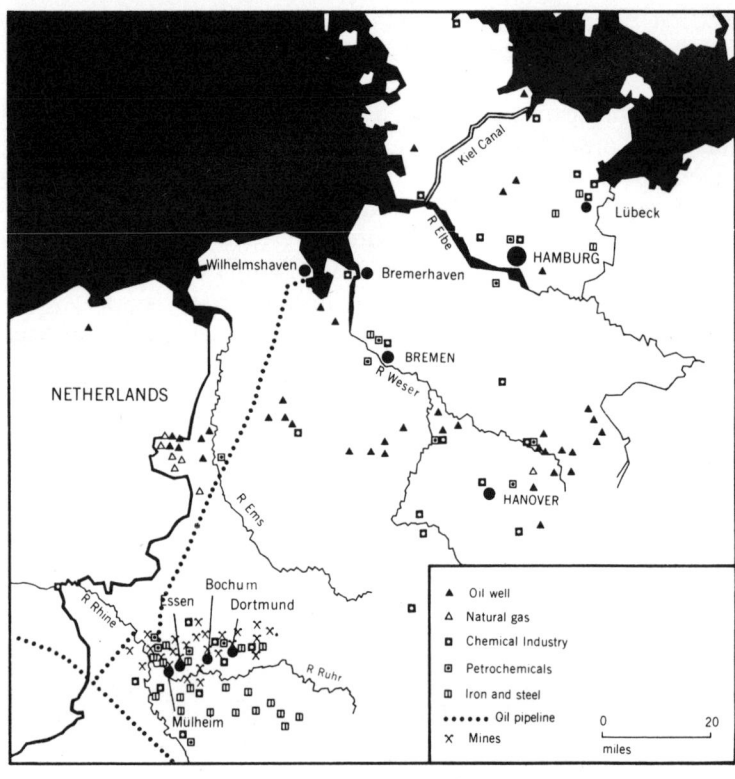

Principal oil and natural gas deposits in West Germany

Gulf Oil in partnership with the British National Coal Board began exploratory drilling in the Irish Sea off Lancashire in the summer of 1969.

WORLD'S OIL RESERVES. *How much oil will be needed?* In 1969 the world used about 1,974m tons of oil. This was 321m tons more than in 1966, and demand is expected to increase year by year. Oil (with natural gas) already supplies half the world's energy, and must make an even greater contribution as world demand rises.

Oil

Will there be enough oil? In 1938, when the annual production of oil was 290m tons, there were proven reserves totalling 4,830m tons. In 1962, production stood at 1,200m tons and reserves at 41,070m tons. In 1967 reserves were estimated at 56,800m tons, more than 31 times the amount used in 1967. The more oil has been taken out of the earth, the more there has been discovered for future use.

What are proven reserves? The oilmen make a cautious estimate of reserves by counting only those supplies of petroleum known to exist underground and to be recoverable economically by existing methods; these supplies are called proven reserves. Because of the geological conditions in which oil occurs, it is never possible to bring a large proportion up to the surface. On an average, only about 35% of the crude oil can be brought up economically.

Where are the greatest reserves? In the U.S.A., where 12,000m tons of oil have been taken out of the earth since 1859, reserves are comparatively low at about 5,200m tons, about ten times the annual production. The newer oilfields of the Middle East have produced less than 5,000m tons and have vast reserves of 33,900m tons, more than 20 times the annual production. There are also large reserves in the new African oilfields (5,600m tons), in the U.S.S.R. (4,900m tons), in the Caribbean area (2,800m tons), and in other areas. These are all proven reserves, and do not allow for expected improvements in recovery rates, or for further discoveries.

Are there any more oilfields to discover? Large quantities of crude oil still remain to be discovered. Geological knowledge and skills are improving constantly. New techniques of drilling will permit exploration to deeper levels and in areas not previously accessible, for instance Alaska. A high percentage of the world's potential oil-bearing regions has not yet been fully explored. With modern underwater techniques, a quarter or more of the new oil reserves may come from under the sea.

What other sources of oil are there? It is theoretically possible to produce liquid oils from natural gas, of which there are immense reserves. It is possible, but usually uneconomic, to make oil from coal. Oil-bearing shales contain about 5 to 10% of oil, which can be extracted by heat treatment; small-scale production is carried out in some countries. In the U.S.A., western Canada and eastern Venezuela large deposits of tar-saturated sands provide an enormous reserve that has been little exploited so far; a new method of extracting the oil at a competitive price has recently been evolved. All these considerations add to estimates of the world's ultimate resources of petroleum.

What is the long-term prospect? It has been calculated that by 2000 A.D. the world will be consuming energy at a rate at least four times as great as that of today. Oil and natural gas will probably continue to supply more than half; this means that the oil industry must find reserves nearly twice those that have been discovered over the past 100 years, but there is little doubt that these quantities exist. Coal's percentage share will continue to decline. Nuclear energy makes hardly any impact today but it will be the fuel of the future, and will provide about 11% of the world's requirements by 1985, and nearly 20% by the end of the century. Cheap and abundant nuclear energy may mean that petroleum will no longer be burned in large quantities as heavy fuel. Light fuels will still be needed, but petroleum will also be prized as a raw material, particularly as a source of chemicals. (See *Fuels.*)

P

PAKISTAN

West, 310,403 sq.m.; East, 55,126 sq.m. Pop. 112m. One of Pakistan's major difficulties is that about 22 families control two-thirds of industry, almost all insurance and four-fifths of banking. Steps to bring about a broader spread of industrial ownership have not succeeded but a new plan (July 1970) to encourage smaller industrialists may have better results. Several large projects are under way, notably three steel mills — one at Chittagong, East Pakistan, output 250,000 tons, and two in the West, capacity 500,000 tons. Two fertilizer plants in West Pakistan and a heavy engineering complex at Islamabad are also being built.

Notable advances have been made in the last two years in the paper and jute industries. In 1947 Pakistan was entirely dependent on imports of paper but in 1970 the country was self-sufficient. The number of jute looms had increased by 15% (to 23,000) in 1970.

The greatest success of the third five-year plan (July 1965–June 1970) has been the tremendous increase in food production. Production of rice, the leading food grain, reached 14m tons in 1969–70 and some of the crop is being exported. Wheat is even more important in narrowing the food gap; the 1969 record crop of 7.3m tons is encouraging. In the fourth five-year plan much emphasis will be placed on replanting and fertilizer subsidy schemes, pest controls and longer tenure of land to encourage new planting.

Many people in East Pakistan demand autonomy and the central government will need to give priority to development spending in East Pakistan if demands for autonomy are not to become more frequent.

Trade with the U.K., 1969: exports to, £40m; imports from, £46m. Trade with the U.S.A., 1969: exports to, $121.9m; imports from,$130m. (See *Hurricanes*.)

PANAMA

39,890 sq.m. Pop. 1.40m. In order to reduce the economy's dependence on bananas large areas of cotton and oranges are being planted in the rich agricultural area of Chiriqui. Fishing is now more important, with shrimps producing 11m dollars in 1969. Panama is offering various industrial incentives and, in the Free Zone in July 1970, 190 companies representing

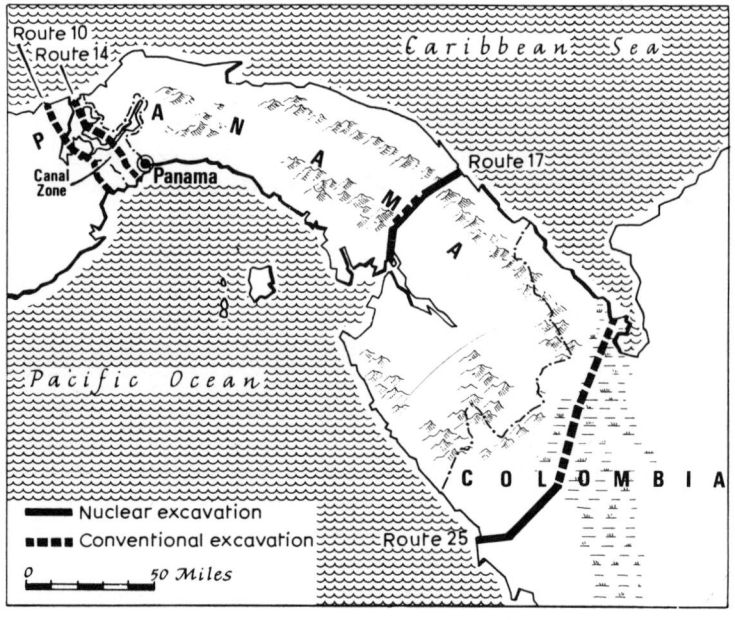

Proposed routes for nuclear canals in Panama

Papua and New Guinea

560 firms from all over the world were operating. The Panama Canal brought in 130m dollars in 1969 (120m in 1967).

Trade with the U.K., 1969: exports to, £6m; imports from, £2.5m. Trade with with U.S.A., 1969: exports to, $33m; imports from, $44m.

PAPUA AND NEW GUINEA

93,000 sq.m. Pop. 2.2m. Despite immense problems, the country is steadily developing into a nation that should eventually become economically self-sufficient and politically self-determined.

The territory consists of the eastern half of the island of New Guinea and of some 600 other islands, extending over an area of more than 180,000 sq.m. Physical communication is hampered by the rugged terrain, jungles and swamps and by its monsoon climate. As a result, population density is low, with the 2m people living in small, widely scattered communities. Coastal settlements rely heavily on shipping services, while the other main form of transport is by air.

Despite these difficulties, a significant rate of economic growth has been achieved in recent years, chiefly through extensive Australian aid. A major achievement has been the expansion of agricultural production, and, to maintain this momentum, new crops, such as tea and palm oil have been introduced. Subsistence farming is gradually giving way to the production of cash crops, chiefly copra, cocoa and coffee. Under a five-year plan the output of most agricultural and forest products is rising considerably. Coffee is, however, an exception because of current world marketing problems.

Although the territory will remain dependent on agriculture, industrial growth, together with the development of mineral deposits, especially copper, is gradually broadening the base of the economy. There are tax incentives to attract new firms including a five-year tax holiday for pioneer industries. A Development Bank provides finance to both small and large-scale businesses. In addition to the processing of primary products, secondary and service industries catering for the growing domestic market include the manufacture of cigarettes, wire products, building materials, furniture, boats and the assembly of electrical appliances.

The World Bank has provided a substantial loan towards a four-year programme to extend and improve telecommunications, and a comprehensive transport survey is also being undertaken.

PARAGUAY

157,000 sq.m. Pop. 2.4m. The decline in demand in recent years for many of Paraguay's principal exports — beef, timber, cotton, coffee, sugar — has had serious repercussions on the economy. Substantial funds, mainly from the IDA and the World Bank, have been spent on the meat industry in efforts to establish modern techniques, increase water supplies and reduce disease.

Food packing and processing, textiles and chemicals are the main industries and a 6m-dollar cement plant was opened in June 1969. In December 1969 the first stage of a 25m-dollar HEP scheme on Acaray River was opened, saving 3m dollars a year on fuel imports. The timber trade, which is virtually completely dependent on the Argentine market, is improving. In an effort to boost this source of foreign exchange, the export of logs is gradually being reduced in favour of concentration on the more lucrative processing of lumber. The tourist industry is beginning to make a valuable contribution to foreign exchange earnings; there were 100,000 visitors in 1969 (41,460 in 1967 and 10,750 in 1960).

Paraguay's main markets are Argentina (25% of total exports), the U.S.A. and the U.K. Its principal suppliers are Argentina, the U.S.A. and Western Germany.

Trade with the U.K., 1969: exports to, £2.1m; imports from, £2.5m (nearly all in machinery and whisky). Trade with the U.S.A., 1969: exports to, $96m; imports from, $111.2m.

PEARLING

Significant changes in pearling have occurred in Australian waters. Before the slump in the mid-1950s Australia accounted for about 85% of world pearl shell supplies. Pearl shell prices have fluctuated wildly and stocks have built up, compelling pearlers to limit their takes severely. The introduction of pearl culture in 1957 arrested the decline in pearling because effort was increasingly diverted from the fishing of mother-of-pearl to gathering live shells for culture farms. The live shell tonnage rose from 5 tons in 1956 to 368 tons in 1966.

The first pearl culture farm was started in 1956 at Brecknock Harbour, about 250 miles north of the old pearling capital, Broome. There are now 18 culture farms, including two in Papua; all but three are operated jointly by Australian and Japanese companies. The Australians establish the farms and supply the live pearl oysters, while the Japanese do the technical operations, cultivate the shell and market the pearls. The industry stretches from Exmouth Gulf to Papua and employs 1,000 people. Only about 30% of the live shells produce a pearl but the pearls grown in Australian waters reach maturity in two years, half the time taken in Japanese farms.

The Western Australian cultured pearls are of exceptional size and beauty and some fetch $A 2,000. In 1969 the value of cultured pearl production was about 4m dollars, with Japan taking 90% of the output. Japan itself produces about 50 tons annually compared with Australia's one ton.

PERU

514,059 sq.m. Pop. 13.3m. The nation's geography revolves around its mining, where foreign investment is strongest. In this industry, too, the problems of achieving a balance between nationalism and foreign participation in the Peru economy is most noticeable. The government is now controlling the marketing of exports of copper and copper ore and the refining of copper within the country. New deposits are being developed at Carro Verde and Quellaveco. Petroleum-based industries have increasing scope with new refineries in eastern and southern Peru.

An important measure is the Agrarian Reform Law to divide very large private holdings, abolish very small farms and form new farming co-operatives.

Peru plans to halt imports of meat and milk by 1979, when home production should be adequate. Cattle have been imported from Colombia to build up the home herds. In 1970 Peru was still the world's largest fishing nation, the catch amounting to 11m tons (10.5m, 1969). Better catches have partly relieved the world shortage of fishmeal; Peru supplies about half the world supply. Rubber manufacture started in 1970 and the sugar industry is rapidly developing, largely with British help.

Trade with the U.K., 1969: exports to, £13.9m; imports from, £11.8m. Trade with the U.S.A., 1969: exports to $328m; imports from, $399m.

PHILIPPINES

114,834 sq.m. (7,107 islands). Pop. 37m. A massive survey of the Philippines' transport system is under way, sponsored by the U.N. Development Programme and the World Bank. Co-ordinated, efficient communications are seen as the basis of the Philippines' development.

Despite some uncertainty and instability in politics, funds

flow into the country. The U.S.A. is a constant source of finance for development projects. Mineral development has been attracting an increasing amount of attention. In 1968 copper became the fourth largest export (after copra, sugar and timber). Valuable deposits of nickel were found in 1969 and surveys during 1968—70 show that the volcanic subsoil is even richer than believed in iron ore, zinc, lead, chrome, gold and silver.

Despite the increase in population less food is being imported following the success of the "miracle" strain of rice, which in 1967 made it possible for the Philippines to meet their own needs and to export rice.

Japanese commercial links with the Philippines have been growing despite opposition by nationalistic groups. British trade is increasing, particularly in the supply of whole factories. For instance, in 1969 a Scottish firm contracted to supply a sugar factory worth £8m.

Trade with the U.K., 1969: exports to, £5m; imports from, £24m. Trade with the U.S.A., 1969: exports to, $435m; imports from, $432.

POLAND

121,000 sq.m. Pop. 32.9m. The change from central planning has been slower in Poland than in many of the Eastern countries and delegation of responsibility has run into considerable difficulty. There is still widespread distrust of new methods and, in contrast with Hungary, no improvement in living standards has accompanied their introduction. Many Poles need two jobs to maintain a reasonable living standard. Production costs remain high because of delays in automation and technology. Poland is still officially convinced that all planning must be within the framework of a comprehensive programme for East Europe as a whole.

Industrial production for 1970 was expected to increase by 7% (the planned figure for 1969 was 8.2%). Chemicals, oil refining, plastics, pharmaceuticals, sulphuric acid and dyes are the chief industries being developed.

Ambitious trade targets have been set for the 1971—75 plan — up to 50% in some areas. Transactions with COMECON countries now account for two-thirds of total trade but there are signs that relations with the West are increasing in importance. In particular, Poland has agreements with France and Italy which provide a part-barter arrangement. For instance, Poland will exchange Silesian copper for French electrical equipment. Poland is also seeking much greater access to the West German market.

The U.K. has been Poland's most important trading partner in the West but Anglo-Polish trade is not expanding as fast as total growth. Ninety per cent of British imports from Poland in 1970 consisted of food and raw materials. Poland wishes to sell more industrial goods.

Trade with the U.K., 1969: exports to, £57m; imports from, £55.1m. Trade with the U.S.A., 1969: exports to,$110m; imports from, $90m.

POPULATION

The Population Commission of the United Nations forecasts a greater proportionate increase in world population during the 1970s than ever before despite growing use of birth control methods. It reports that world urban population will reach 1,780m by 1980 (990m in 1960). Total population will rise from about 3,632m in 1970 to 4,475m in 1980.

Most of this increase, as in the past decade, will take place in the less developed parts of the world, which have annual birth rates of 2.4% and 2.5% against rates of 1.1% and 1.2% in some Western countries, e.g. France. By 1980 there will be 3,247m people in developing regions and 1,280m in advanced nations.

The Commission anticipates that by 1980 New York, Tokio, Shanghai and Mexico City will all have populations of

Portugal

12.5m. Estimates for the 1970s show slight increases in population growths in Africa, the Americas, Oceania and Russia. However, on the whole, the Commission says, "... the general momentum of population growth is not calculated to undergo much substantial change." (See *New Geography 1966–67 and 1968–69*. See also *Ecology, Education* and *Labour*.)

PORTUGAL

34,500 sq.m. Pop. 9.5m. Portugal is short of skilled labour and industrial enterprises are seriously hampered. The shortage is particularly acute in the supply of young male workers of whom about 15,000 are on active service in the overseas provinces (Angola, Mozambique), while the threat of imminent call-up combined with the attraction of higher wages abroad has induced many others to leave the country.

Certainly, some industries have prospered — engineering, wood pulp and chemicals — but the textile and fishing industries are declining. An alteration in the habits of the sardines has meant that they are no longer found along Portugal's coast but further south in the Atlantic. The Portuguese fleet is ill-equipped for such long trips as the vessels have no on-board refrigeration and the industry can no longer compete with its Spanish and Moroccan rivals. Exports of sardines fell by 45% in 1969.

Tourism is prosperous, with 2.75m visitors in 1969; the number of Americans increased by 31%.

Agriculture - employing a third of the population and producing a sixth of the GNP– is inefficient, and in 1969–70 the wheat, fruit, rye, grape and olive harvests all fell. It is interesting that Portugal is encouraging immigrant farmers from the U.K. and elsewhere, both to boost production and provide "model farms", whose methods can be emulated by the local farmers.

A steady transformation of the Portuguese economy

has occurred in recent years. It is notable that the population engaged in agriculture is turning progressively towards other sectors of the economy: in 1959, the percentage of the economically active population in agricultural employment was 41.5%, but the figure fell to 37.3% in 1963, 32.2% in 1967 and 30% in 1969. The rural exodus is not solely a consequence of a transfer from one sector of economic activity to another. There has also been a strong tide of emigration. The official statistics show that the number of emigrants has grown from 33,458 in 1959 to 39,519 in 1963 and 80,452 for 1969. The natural increase in the Portuguese population was 100,301 in 1969.

This structural transformation of the Portuguese economy, which is changing it from an essentially agricultural economy to one that is agricultural but with a secondary industrial activity, has not been subject to systematic long-term planning. Industries such as food, textiles and clothing, machinery and apparatus industries have attracted foreign investors. They can profit in Portugal from relatively low wage costs and the existence of a disciplined labour force which can adapt easily to a rapid training — all of which puts them in a situation in which productivity can compete with that of the more developed industrialized countries. It is for this reason that, even though there is an increasing industrialization in Portugal, it is not the type of industrialization which has enabled other nations to raise themselves to higher levels of economic development.

Trade with the U.K., 1969: exports to, £75.9m; imports from, £76.1m. West Germany is the U.K's most important rival. Trade with the U.S.A., 1969: exports to, $206m; imports from, $182m.

Q

QATAR

22,000 sq.m. Pop. 82,000. In the diversification of industry away from complete reliance on oil production one of the largest projects being planned is a petro-chemical plant to produce more than 200 products, mainly plastics. Norwegian management is to run a fertilizer plant which will export to other Middle Eastern and East African markets. The national cement plant has been expanded to produce asbestos sheets and piping.

Trade with the U.K., 1969: exports to, £25m; imports from, £5m. Trade with the U.S.A., 1969: exports to, $75m; imports from, $30m.

R

RESOURCES

American scientists are predicting a technological revolution in geology, oceanography and agriculture with the launching of "earth resources space satellites". Experimental satellites are already in orbit. The earth will come under the constant examination of sensitive electronic eyes recording depths of snow fields, the volumes of rivers, the progress of crops and the movements of fish shoals. The satellites will provide for the first time an accurate global inventory of natural resources to assist in improved crop management and water use. Space satellite sensors will be able to detect differences in soil, identify specific crops, determine damage by crop disease and predict agricultural production. The satellites can also be used for examining earth structures and detecting mineral, oil and gas deposits in remote areas. The information obtained can be applied to help solve problems concerning natural resources. Because of increasing world population and industrial growth such a survey is vital. (See *Maps*.)

RHODESIA

150,333 sq.m. Pop. 4.75m. Late in 1968 the opinion was widespread that Rhodesia was in serious economic trouble, with mounting African unemployment, the tobacco industry collapsing and agriculture hit by the worst drought in 40 years. But in 1969 a high rate of growth was achieved following a very good year for agriculture. The value of exports rose by 20% though this was still below the 1965 level.

With South African co-operation Rhodesia's economic geography is sound enough. South Africa is a staging post for Rhodesia's exports. Rhodesian maize, chrome, asbestos and other minerals are frequently passed off as South African. Trading sanctions imposed by the U.K. have probably harmed British interests more than Rhodesian ones, since Japan and France have filled the gaps.

Rhodesia cannot afford to stand still; the population pressures are too great. Already more than two-thirds of the population is under 21 and each year 50,000 people come onto the labour market. Sanctions have been directly responsible for 12,000 Africans losing their jobs on tobacco farms alone.

ROUTES

THE NORTH-WEST PASSAGE. Considerable interest in the North-west Passage as a viable trade route has risen since the discovery of oil in Alaska's north slope.

The implications are vast. For the oil to reach its major market near the east coast of America it could be shuttled by an 800-mile pipeline to South Alaska (to which some oil companies are committed) where it could be shipped to west coast states and piped across America to the east, or, alternatively, it could be sent by tanker through the Passage direct to the east coast, which would mean economies of up to 60 cents per barrel transported. Against the cost advantages of the direct shipment of oil are the physical problems which such an undertaking would face. Major problems start with loading the tankers with oil. Natural harbour facilities are non-existent and shallow water extends 20 miles offshore.

The effects of using the North-west Passage as a regular trade route would be many and far reaching. Oil is not the only commodity that could be sent by this route; proven mineral deposits in the Arctic could be transported, promoting substantial growth in that desolate region. There would also be a reshuffle of major world shipping lanes. The shipping distance between Britain and Japan would be almost halved by using the Passage, and with consequent reductions in time and costs of transport there could be an extension of shipping trade between the two nations. Indeed, the Canadian government is already studying the potentialities of the Passage and is planning a Northern Water Rights and Pollution Control Act to assert sovereignty over the area and to prevent misuse of the waterway resulting in pollution, which, owing to natural conditions, would be prolonged for decades.

The commercial opening of the Passage would require a fleet of 30 250,000-ton ice-breaking tankers, each costing 50m dollars, to be in operation by 1980; this would bring a welcome expansion of the depressed American shipbuilding industry. At present, all ships carrying cargo between American ports must be American-built and American-registered. Consequently, despite lack of experience in building ice-breaking tankers, America's shipyards may well gain substantial orders in the near future. Such developments could also stimulate the introduction of submarine tankers to transport oil, underwater drilling rigs and shipping terminals.

Man's ingenuity, coupled with modern techniques, may well be in the process of revolutionizing world shipping as with the opening of the Suez Canal a century ago.

FREIGHT WITHOUT FRONTIERS. A freight train which commenced operations in April 1970 crosses the frontiers of three countries without the usual formalities. Running from Paris to Rotterdam via Brussels and Antwerp, the train cuts 2½ hours from the journey by eliminating the frontier stops. France, Belgium and the Netherlands are operating the train as an experiment, it being the aim of European railways to run many international freight trains without frontier stops. (See *Tunnels*.)

RUMANIA

91,600 sq.m. Pop. 19.1m. Rumania is maintaining a delicate balance between loyalty to COMECON and its own economic and political independence. It constantly asserts national sovereignty but is vulnerable to pressure from the Soviet Union, which is still the largest supplier of raw materials and manufactured goods. Emphasis is very much on industry, particularly electronic equipment, machine tools and chemicals.

Agriculture, employing half the population and contributing a quarter of national income, is relatively neglected. Foreign exchange earnings from tourism are rising — 1.8m visitors in 1969, 22% from the West. The country expected 2.4m tourists in 1970.

Trade co-operation agreements will become increasingly important during the 1971—75 plan as Rumania steps up production of import substitutes. During 1970 purchases from the U.K. included a copper casting plant, diesel engines, a nuclear decontamination plant, pumps, and a vast sprinkler and irrigation system at Sodova-Corabia in south-west Rumania.

Trade with the U.K., 1969: exports to, £25m; imports from, £29m. Trade with the U.S.A., 1969: exports to, $70m; imports from, $80m.

S

SAUDI ARABIA

927,000 sq.m. Pop. 7.1m. Despite the country's great wealth from oil — it is the largest producer in the Middle East (140m tons in 1969) — increased defence expenditure and financial assistance to other Arab countries are beginning to strain resources and to undermine a high growth rate. The prime objectives of government policy are to reduce the economy's dependence on oil.

An assessment of natural resources is being made. Several major projects are also in progress. They include roads linking Saudi Arabia with Qatar and Jordan, a new airport at Medina, a large-scale irrigation and drainage scheme at Al-Hasa and a great desalination plant at Al-khobar. Copper, phosphates and silver have been located in commercial quantities and with iron ore in large amounts at Wadi Fatima there are plans for an iron and steel plant. Other new industries are fruit and vegetable canning and a caustic soda factory.

A complete water survey of the country is in hand — at a cost of 100m riyals. This is necessary since only 1% of the land is under cultivation but agriculture employs half the population and accounts for 15% of the GNP. Preliminary results indicate large reserves of water.

During 1969–70 the largest increases in imports were from the U.K. and Japan, but the U.S.A. is Saudi Arabia's leading supplier.

Trade with the U.K., 1969: exports to, £69m, imports from, £47m. Trade with the U.S.A., 1969: exports to, $210m; imports from, $271m.

SELENOLOGY

A wealth of data has been supplied by the Apollo 11 and 12 missions of 1969. Perhaps the most interesting geography to emerge from Apollo 12's visit (November 19) was that involving the seismograph that was set up and levelled on the moon's surface. In orbit around the moon the astronauts crashed the lunar module into the moon. The earthquake waves from the impact were transmitted back to earth via the seisometer. Instead of lasting minutes the waves took longer than half an hour to die out. The moon seemed to reverberate like a large ball. Evidently, the structure of the lunar-rock is not like that of the earth. Taken at face value, a study of the geological samples supports the view that the moon and earth were formed as separate planets. It is also clear that a process of denudation is operating on the moon.

SHIPBUILDING

TWO SHIPS FROM ONE. A leading Japanese shipbuilder has succeeded in making two ships out of one by cutting a large ship in half horizontally. The upper and lower halves are being rebuilt into two separate ocean oil-drilling rigs. This unique ship operation was performed by Mitsubishi Heavy Industries Ltd. at Yokosuka on Tokio Bay.

The order for the work was placed by the Western Offshore Drilling and Exploration Co. of America. Eventually the oil rigs will be used for probing oil supplies off the coast of Borneo. The original ship was the 24,500-ton *Cruz Del Sur,* an 18-year-old whaling factory ship owned by the Southern Cross Co. the parent company of Western Offshore.

It took only hours to perform the most difficult and arduous part of the job in a water-filled wet dock. The big ship, stabilized with props on both sides, was cut above the waterline and 40 supporting pillars were inserted between the cut edges so that a new bottom could be quickly attached to the upper section. During this initial operation, work began on reshaping and refurnishing the upper deck structures to provide a helicopter landing pad and oil drilling equipment. The dock was then drained and the "two-storied" ship was lowered to the bottom of the dock. Holes were then drilled in the bottom of the lower section. The dock was refilled with water and the top half was floated clear.

The upper section, now displacing 13,000 tons, will be similarly converted. Although the total cost is the same as for building two new rigs, the job will be completed in about six months and each rig will last for 20 years. (A similar operation was carried out in Germany in 1969, but the lower half of the vessel was scrapped.)

LARGEST TANKER. In 1966 tankers of 200,000 tons were considered the ultimate. In June 1970 Globtik Tankers of the U.K. ordered a 477,000-ton tanker worth £17.4m from the Japanese yard of Ishikawajima-Harima. It should be completed by February 1973. The tanker will be time-chartered by the Tokio Tanker Company and carry crude oil from the Arabian Gulf to Japan. The giant tanker will have a service speed of 15 knots and a draft of 91 feet, which may be a problem in some oil terminals. Lloyd's Register of Shipping marine engineers with the Ministry of Technology and other agencies have carried out feasibility tests for a 1m-ton tanker; they have stated that such a tanker could be built and operated.

The oil companies want bigger tankers because huge capacity makes it economical for their ships to bypass the blocked Suez Canal. The transport costs are about 40 cents a barrel in a 200,000-tonner compared with 52 cents in a 70,000-tonner. Each big ship can save a company about 1m dollars a year in transport costs. However, it seems that only the Japanese are making money from building the great tankers. British, Swedish, and West German builders have suffered losses. The Japanese have computer-controlled cutting torches, self-propelled welders and devices that can flip over 80-ton sub-assemblies to make welding easier.

Shipbuilding

SHIPPING TRENDS. At the end of 1969 Japan claimed to be second to Liberia among the world's shipping nations, displacing the U.K. Japan's fleet grew by 4.4m tons during 1968—69 to reach about 24m tons by mid—1969. Britain's fleet showed an increase of 1.9m tons in the same period. The Japanese aim for a 40m-ton fleet by 1975.

Much canned fruit is being container-shipped from Australia to Europe. A nine-ship fleet provides a weekly sailing in each direction. The chief fruits are apples, pears and grapes.

Mini-container ships are being built in the Netherlands, West Germany and Norway. Up to 300 ft. long and weighing between 10,000 and 15,000 tons, these ships are designed to handle roll-on, roll-off cargo. They will be used in island trade, as in the South-west Pacific, and will feed goods to the main ports.

BRITISH SHIPPING. United Kingdom shipowners are consolidating their grip on world sea routes with record orders for new tonnage of every description. In the six months to April 30, 1970, 3,400m deadweight were ordered bringing the total on order to 16,300m, worth an estimated £9000m. It represents 15% of the world total of 108,500,000 tons.

Nearly one-third of the 3.5m tons of container ships on order will operate under the British flag. Of the world total of 33m tons bulk carriers and OBO (oil/bulk/ore) ships, 5.7m tons — about 17% — are for the United Kingdom owners. They will also own 9m tons — more than 14% — of the 63m tons of tankers on order. British owners have sufficient new ships on order to more than double their existing bulk carrier fleet, which is at present over 5m tons. It represents twice the world average.

In the tanker field United Kingdom owners are active and their replacement programme is higher than the world average. The total order book in July 1970 was half the existing fleet — one fifth higher than the world average — and this is a continuing pattern.

New Geography 1970-71

SIERRA LEONE

27,925 sq.m. Pop. 2.51m. Diamonds now account for more than half Sierra Leone's exports but iron ore and rutile are increasing in importance. Coffee and cocoa are the most successful crops but palm kernels are bringing in good revenue — £3.5m in 1969 compared with £1.1m in 1968. In February 1969 Sierra Leone exported its first consignment of flour — 60,000 bags to Gambia. An important pilot project is rice-growing on Turners Peninsula, Southern Province.

Now that the tsetse fly has been eradicated cattle ranching is expected to flourish. The first cattle co-operative ranch was established in 1969 at Talia in the Kenema district.

The government is trying to stop the drift to the towns by spending money on agricultural improvements and on improved social services. The country's road network is being increased and improved following a decision to close all railways. An oil refinery came on stream early in 1969, a fishing industry is being established and the Japanese are building a textile mill. Paints, plastics, footwear, cement and clothing are all made now.

Trade with the U.K., 1969: exports to, £30.1m; imports from, £12m. Trade with the U.S.A., 1969: exports to, $70m; imports from, $71m.

SINGAPORE

224 sq.m. Pop. 2.15m. Rapid expansion is making Singapore one of the most prosperous Eastern countries. During the 1960s the GNP rose by 250%. With the feeling of greater security resulting from a defence force of growing strength, the government has adopted a policy of prosperity through growth. Investment is being encouraged by considerable tax concessions to foreign firms.

Expansion on such a scale makes land scarce for development. The industrial complex at Jurong is too small and the government is now reclaiming 8,000 acres of marshland to provide space for about 200 factories and to allow the expansion of shipbuilding and repair yards. Much of the pressure to obtain industrial space has come from oil companies; more than 30 are engaged in intensive search. The island already has four refineries.

The Singapore Economic Development Board is working hard to attract new enterprises and in August 1970 was negotiating with 20 companies in the U.K. alone. In 1970 Lever Brothers opened a £320,000 factory. An important development is the emergence of Singapore as the Far East's only Euro-dollar trading centre. This further step towards becoming the financial centre of South-east Asia will attract funds.

The development of container port facilities will help the smooth flow of trade in and out of Singapore. Two free trade zones are being developed, one in the port and the other in the Jurong industrial estate.

Singapore's principal trading partners are Malaysia, the U.S.A., Japan and Communist China. A decline in trade with the U.K. has always been assumed to accompany the withdrawal of British troops. However, Singapore's imports from the U.K. rose by 25% in 1969 and exports by 19%.

Trade with the U.K., 1969: exports to, £31m; imports from, £50m. Trade with the U.S.A., 1969: exports to, $207.5m; imports from, $185m.

SOMALIA

288,000 sq.m. Pop. 3m. Despite efforts to settle more people in agriculture 75% of Somalia's population is still nomadic and stock-raising remains the principal form of livelihood. However, a major project is the development of 250,000 hectares in the Juba Valley. The acreage under sugar around the Shebeli River trebled between 1966 and 1970. Climatic conditions have been found to be ideal for grapefruit, which is to supply the EEC market when North African and Israeli fruit is not available.

In 1970, 30,000 cattle were exported to Kenya's canning factories but a new canning factory began operations at Kismayu in January 1970, and in 1971 will process 60,000 cattle.

Somalia has a coastline of 1,125 miles but only three ports; that at Mogadishu is being greatly developed to obviate the necessity of transferring goods to open-sea lighters. Also, the Soviet Union has built a new port at Berbera and the U.S.A. has given 6m dollars for improvements to Kismayu.

In mid-1970 Somalia became an associated member of the EEC; its principal trading partners were, in any case, Italy and the other Common Market countries. Trade with Japan is bound to increase now that there is a direct shipping service. The country has considerable mineral resources including bauxite, uranium and iron ore, and U.S., German and Italian companies are prospecting. For the moment the principal exports are livestock and bananas but fish, hides and skins and frankincense and myrrh contribute to earnings.

Trade with the U.K., 1969: exports to, £105,000; imports from, £1m. Trade with the U.S.A., exports to, $1m; imports from, $700,000.

SOUTH AFRICA

471,445 sq.m. Pop. 19.9m (Europeans 3.7m). South Africa has had two years of unprecedented expansion, with the steel industry outstanding. The chemical industry, oil refining and mining have also grown. The search for oil — to make the country self-sufficient in the event of economic sanctions — has been intensive. In February 1970 the government announced a strike in eastern Cape Province.

Gold production in 1969 reached a record figure of 31.3m oz (31.2m oz, 1968). Platinum is also a prosperous mining industry. Much of the gold is sold to the IMF.

South Korea

South Africa's distribution of trade is interesting. Exports to Europe showed the largest increase in 1969 — rising by R63m to R862.3m. Exports to Africa and America showed small increases but exports to Asia fell by R44.8m. Imports showed increases from all areas except Africa with Europe and Asia having the largest increases — £115.6m and R80.4m respectively. The U.K. is South Africa's biggest buyer and supplier.

Trade with the U.K., 1969: exports to, £302.3m; imports from, £290.9m. Trade with the U.S.A., 1969: exports to, $400m; imports from, $455m.

SOUTH KOREA

37,436 sq.m. Pop. 30.3m. Despite inflation, South Korea is a prosperous country with industrial growth providing the main impetus. Important projects among heavy industries include an iron and steel mill at Pohang, a petro-chemical complex at Ulsan — the basis for an artificial fibres industry — and an oil refinery at Ulsan. Much of the finance comes from the U.S.A. and Japan but the British stake in South Korea is growing, including major contracts for cotton-spinning machinery, chemicals, plants and oil tankers.

The Korean government says that rural and regional development must now wait until the third plan beginning in 1972. Agricultural production was hampered by serious droughts between 1968–70 and a programme of irrigation and mechanization is intended to increase production and lessen dependence on the weather.

The production of silk increased four-fold between 1968 and 1970 but the most remarkable success story is in the exports of wigs, worth no less than 30.5m dollars in 1968 and 35m in 1969. Virtually all wigs go to the U.S.A.

Trade with the U.S.A. and Japan accounted for 65% of Korea's foreign business in 1970 (70% in 1969) but new markets are vigorously sought. Spain, Argentina, Algeria,

New Geography 1970-71

Tunisia and Malagasy became trading partners in 1970. New export products for that year include binoculars, filters, plastics, tape recorders and electric speakers. Shirts with the label "Made in Japan" are actually made in Korea and sold in Japan. No less than 55 countries buy Korean garments.

Another example of the speed of industrial progress is that of the car industry. In 1962 it did not exist. In 1970 Toyota of Japan, Fiat of Italy and Ford of the U.K. were competing with the local Shinjin Motor. Annual sales in 1971 were projected at 35,000.

Trade with the U.K., 1969: exports to, £2.2m; imports from, £2.4m. Trade with the U.S.A., 1969: exports to, $300m; imports from, $504m.

SPAIN

196,700 sq.m. Pop. 32.6m. During the 1960–70 decade Spanish industrial output rose more than 200%, an indication of the country's changing economic geography. During 1970 attention was mainly given to cement, cellulose pulp, oil refining and iron and steel industries. A sharp increase in shipbuilding orders has created a heavy demand for steel; Spain finished a ship a day between June 1969 and June 1970. Only six deposits of oil or natural gas have been found but the discovery of uranium near Salamanca is of great importance to Spain, already one of the richest uranium-bearing countries.

A notable change has occurred in the pattern of grain crops. Wheat used to be the major crop but barley has become more important. Crops of sugar, potatoes, rice and oranges have increased. The replacement of Spain's 30m orange trees at a rate of 3m a year is under way in an effort to eradicate tristeza, a virus disease which affected enough trees in 1968 for a national disaster to be declared. Agriculture should benefit greatly from various irrigation schemes under construction, particularly that in the Guadiana region and those in south-east Spain.

Spain

The south-west and north will benefit most from efforts to improve the country's livestock, a project which is being financed by a 25m-dollar loan from the World Bank and a 6,000m-peseta credit from France.

Spain's first atomic reactor for electrical power was opened at Zorita de Canes, Guadalajara, in July 1968 but the country has eight other major nuclear works in hand, including one at Santa Marina de Garona, in Burgos, to commence operations in 1971 and another at Vandellos near Tarragona. The others are at Castellon, Almeria, Toledo and Vizcaya (Basque), with one in Galicia and another at Zorita. In the extent of its uranium deposits Spain is second only to France in Europe.

An ambitious project is that of trans-pumping water from the Tagus to the Segura so that water now flowing to the Atlantic will reach Murcia on the Levante coast. The tapping starts at Bolarque artificial lake; water is pumped to La Bujeda Reservoir, flows along the Altomira-Alarcon canal and by a system of canals and tunnels — one of which is 30 km long — it reaches the Fontanar and Talave Reservoirs on tributaries of the Segura. The project covers 270 km., costs 6,500m pesetas and will be complete in 1973.

Spain had no fewer than 20m visitors in 1969 and expected 21m in 1970, though they are spending, on average, less than in previous years. However, tourism remains Spain's greatest foreign exchange earner.

Spain's exports are much more diversified in destination. Trade with Eastern bloc countries, in particular, is increasing rapidly and the only area to which exports have lost ground is Australia and New Zealand. Sales to the Common Market rose by 31% in 1969 and imports by 25%, but the U.S.A. remains the chief trading partner.

Trade with the U.K.: exports to, £99m; imports from, £105m. Trade with the U.S.A., 1969: exports to, $303m; imports from, $536m.

New Geography 1970-71

STEEL

Two new methods have changed the metallurgical industry in the 1960—70 decade — the oxygen injection technique and the continuous casting technique. They have been joined by a new technique which is probably more important — a method of manufacturing steel directly from iron ore without the detour via the blast furnace. The Oberhausen Foundries in West Germany developed the technique and the EEC Steel Community is exploiting it. The importance of the method is that it requires no coke. The ores are converted into metal for steelmaking with the help of natural gas or electricity and nothing else. This means completely new locations for steel works which will not be dependent on coal. Steelworks can now be built near natural gas fields and electric power stations. The importance of the technique can hardly be over-estimated.

SUDAN

1m sq.m (approx.). Pop. 15m. A five-year development plan began in March 1970, with emphasis on agriculture through irrigation. Fourteen pumping stations will be erected on the Nile in Northern Province. The main crops will be wheat and horse beans — which are import substitutes — and sorghum and haricot beans, which will contribute to exports.

Trade with the U.K., 1969: exports to, £2m; imports from, £3.1m. Trade with the U.S.A., 1969: exports to, $5m; imports from, $7.2m.

SWEDEN

173,436 sq.m. Pop. 7.95m. Shipyards and the timber processing industry, as well as the chemical, rubber, plastic

Switzerland

and vehicle industries have all expanded considerably. The trend in Swedish industry is for greater concentration in terms of ownership and the participation of the state is more dominant. For instance, in January 1970 the government bought control of a major pharmaceutical firm and has set up a company to provide equipment for the nuclear power industry. Twelve nuclear power stations are planned by 1980.

An important aspect of government policy is the provision of employment in the rural northern regions, which form the greater part of the country and where mechanization of the timber industries has left large numbers without work. This is in contrast to the urban south where there are too few people for the jobs available. Unemployed northerners are being retrained to work in mines, for instance, or to farm.

Trade with the U.K., 1969: exports to, £330m; imports from, £251m. Trade with the U.S.A., 1969: exports to, $397m; imports from, $441m.

SWITZERLAND

15,950 sq.m. Pop. 6.2m. Unusually for Switzerland, delivery times for Swiss products are lengthening — the result of orders exceeding production and the decline of stocks. Persistent shortage of labour further strains capacity. The bigger industries are merging interests and using more labour-saving techniques.

Compounding the difficulty is the growing public opposition to the volume of foreign labour — 35% of the total in August 1970. It is likely to compel the government to order industrialists further to reduce their quotas of foreign labour.

Exports rose by 14% in 1968 and by 17% in 1969, the largest gains being in chemicals, metal products and machinery. Expansion of the principal markets of Europe and the U.S.A. provides the main impetus. In 1970 Switzerland's manufacturers made 47% of the world production of 150m watches. Switzerland exports 97% of its output.

Switzerland receives an important part of her imports on barges passing up the Rhine to Basle. In 1967 7.5m tons of cargo was imported through the port, compared with 6.9m tons in 1960. However, only 319,000 tons of Swiss exports left Basle by river. While barges remain a relatively inexpensive way of moving products in bulk, such as fuel, metals, cereals, sand, gravel and coal, other faster methods of transport are preferred for sophisticated manufactured products of which Swiss exports mainly consist.

Despite the lack of sea ports Switzerland has a seagoing merchant navy. At the end of January 1970 it numbered 32 ships totalling 303,000 tons deadweight. The ships are employed in world trade rather than EFTA trade.

Despite its small size, Switzerland is falling victim to rural depopulation. Agricultural workers now form only 8% of the total population (20% in 1939). The majority of farms are between 13 and 37 acres; farms of more than 75 acres are rare. It is noticeable that the number of large estates and of small farms is diminishing in favour of medium holdings. Cereal yields are increasing according to plan. The mean yield of winter wheat in 1941—45 was 10 cwt, in 1962 16 cwt and in 1969, 18 cwt. The government is encouraging the growth of wheat, sugar beet and rape.

Trade with the U.K., 1969: exports to, £160m; imports from, £167m. Trade with the U.S.A., 1969: exports to, $441m; imports from, $532m.

T

TEA

Tea-producing countries have been in difficulties because of over-production. Prices at London tea auctions fell by 10% in 1969. In 1970 the producing countries decided on an international attempt to improve prices by reducing supply. Ceylon, for instance, was to restrict the volume of tea exports to 470m lb.

THAILAND

198,247 sq.m. Pop. 34.1m. The American presence has had a great effect on the Thai economy, particularly on manufacturing, services and construction. The building of air bases and roads has helped to open up north-east Thailand. But most industrial development is still concentrated in Bangkok, a major trading centre for South-east Asia, and in neighbouring Thonburi. Two new industrial estates are nearing completion, one in Bangkok and the other in Thonburi.

During 1969–70 Swedish, American, Canadian and Japanese companies, among others, began manufacture of textiles, telephones, steel and paper products. In 1969 no fewer than 2,000 new industrial enterprises were established. The government hopes that local oil - from the Gulf of Thailand and on land near Bangkok and in the north-east — will service the domestic market and Japan.

There was little evidence in 1970 that Thailand's farming is undergoing the "green revolution" of some other Asian countries, though output of rice — Thailand's chief export — was up. Tin, the second largest export, is a prosperous industry because of a world increase in price. Rubber slipped to third place in 1968—69. The most spectacular development has been in kenaf, production of which in 1969 was 400,000 tons — 168% above the 1968 figure, under the stimulus of a near doubling in price.

Thailand's chief trading partners are Japan, the U.S.A., West Germany and the U.K.

Trade with the U.K., 1969: exports to, £6m; imports from, £29m. Trade with the U.S.A., 1969: exports to, $202m; imports from, $331m. (See *Aid*.)

TIDES

In January 1970 oceanographers made the first measurements of tides in the deep oceans surrounding Antarctica. They launched three free-falling deep-sea tide gauges, placed 600 miles apart, at depths of 12,000, 15,000 and 18,000 ft. The gauges remained on the ocean floor for a month after which acoustic signals from their mother ship brought them to the surface. Scientists had believed that because the oceans are "continuous" around Antarctica the tides, unusually large, would significantly stimulate the tides in the Pacific, Indian and Atlantic Oceans. This has been proved true but experiments and calculations are not yet complete.

EARTH TIDES. The land masses of the earth, pushed continuously by the oceans and tugged by the sun and moon rise and fall an average of 12 in. twice a day. This was announced by Columbia University, New York, in February 1970 after lengthy experiments involving sophisticated tidal gravimeters. The sun, 330,000 times more massive than the earth, exercises a tremendous pull on the planet. The moon's mass is only a hundredth that of the earth but its size is made up for by its proximity. Additionally, the scientists found that earth movements are greatly influenced by ocean tides, even far inland. The weight of the oceans appears to be responsible for about 8% of the crust movement. The accuracy of the new measurements raises hopes that new methods of prospecting for oil and predicting earthquakes can be developed.

TIMBER

The need for paper is growing in the world at such pace — the annual increase may now be estimated at 5.5% — that extremely large investments are continuously required to preserve the balance between supply and demand.

By far the largest expansion will take place in North America where the forests of Canada still offer tremendous potential. There is also a rapidly growing supply of pulpwood in the U.S.A. based on the unexpectedly good recovery of once-cutover forests and on improved silviculture. In Europe, Sweden is the only country which has a major reserve of wood for further expansion of its forest industries. These are the countries from which the largest part of the increased need for paper (or pulp) will come during the 1970s. The Soviet Union and Japan are likely to expand their industries more or less parallel with consumption. However, there is always a possibility of export, in particular from the Soviet Union.

Other countries more or less dependent on imports will certainly expand their paper industries as well. In some instances there will be an improved supply of home-grown raw material available, but more often the expansion has to be based on imported pulp or pulpwood. Collecting used paper for reclaiming the fibre will be an additional task.

The world trend, at least in respect of bulk paper grades, seems to be towards large-scale integrated mills which are located close to the source of raw material. In Europe, outside Scandinavia, the main feature of mill development during the next ten years will probably be the modernization and expansion of selected units. Closing down a number of small and obsolete mills might be an unavoidable step in this context. Such an operation was to a great extent carried through in the 1960s in the major exporting countries.

Development of paper consumption in regions
(in million tons per year)

	1950-52	1955-57	1960-62	1967	1975
EFTA countries	4.6	6.4	8.4	10.7	15.8
EEC countries	4.4	7.3	10.8	15.0	24.0
Other countries	1.9	2.5	3.6	5.4	8.8
Europe	10.9	16.2	22.8	31.1	48.6
U.S.S.R.	1.6	2.6	3.5	5.7	11.7
North America	27.3	32.7	37.4	47.9	64.6
Latin America	1.4	2.0	2.6	3.8	7.1
Africa	0.4	0.6	0.8	1.2	2.5
Asia–Pacific (except Japan)	1.5	2.8	5.0	7.6	12.3
Japan	1.1	2.5	5.2	8.8	15.2
World Total:	44.2	59.4	77.3	106.1	162.0

Breakdown by percentage of paper consumption by regions

	1961	1967	1975
Europe	24.8	29.4	30.0
U.S.S.R.	3.6	5.4	7.2
North America	61.6	45.1	39.9
Latin America	3.2	3.6	4.4
Africa	0.9	1.1	1.5
Asia–Pacific (except Japan)	3.4	7.1	7.6
Japan	2.5	8.3	9.4
World Total:	100.0	100.0	100.0

Timber

Some trade flow figures for 1969 (in 1000 metric tons)

Importing Countries	Exporting Countries				
	Finland	Norway	Sweden	U.S.A.	Canada
Pulp for papermaking					
EFTA countries	601	468	1106	168	247
EEC countries	760	228	1414	312	416
Other European countries	137	29	231	21	11
U.S.A.	74	—	125	—	2392
Japan	21	—	3	194	255
Paper and paperboard					
EFTA countries	718	262	712	265	588
EEC countries	909	230	881	337	112
Other European countries	194	34	77	54	30
U.S.A.	289	4	30	—	5898
Japan	—	—	—	22	38

The U.K's timber industry will soon benefit from the investment and long-term planning undertaken half a century ago when the Forestry Commission was established with the responsibility of restoring woodlands depleted during World War 1. The Commission, which accounts for half of the domestic output of softwood and also a small percentage of hardwood, is expecting to double its present output (1.3m tons a year) within ten years and to reach 6.5m tons by the end of the century as its plantations come to maturity.

Even so, the present 10% proportion of the U.K.'s total requirements contributed by domestic producers is not likely to change very much because demand is more than keeping pace. The U.K. is one of the largest importers of timber and timber products, with expenditure in 1970 reaching a record £680m. Moreover, the cost of imports can only continue to grow, particularly in view of the FAO's prediction of a world shortage within 30 years. Even with the considerable extension of acreage planned by 1972 the proportion of forested land in the U.K. — at present about 8% — must always remain very small in comparison with Western Europe (one-third) or North America (two-fifths).

Any possible saving through rationalization is, therefore, of immense value; for example, the experimental introduction of specially designed bulk containers for shipping timber from Canada, together with special landing equipment at ports and standardization of wood sizes, proved during 1969—70 that costs can be reduced by as much as £3 per ton. These arrangements could now be extended to imports of timber from Scandinavia and the Soviet Union. Improved drying processes and the possibility of eliminating sawdust waste (currently estimated at £45m a year) are also beginning to reduce costs, while amalgamations among the small firms constituting the major proportion of the Timber Federation's 830 members are making mechanization, handling and storage possible on a much larger scale.

Prospects for the timber industry are closely linked with the fortunes of the building trade, its largest customer. Even slight setbacks in demand can have a serious impact on importers buying forward on borrowed capital. Stocks which have been built up partly as a hedge against inflation were run down in readiness for the changeover to the metric system which began in 1970, but in the longer term demand is likely to remain high.

TOURISM

The golden age of tourism and business travel has drawn the world's innkeepers into a building boom. Led by aggressive American chains, hotel competition is sharpening rivalry in dozens of countries and the travel boom is transforming entire economies. New construction is aimed not only at American travellers but at Asians and Europeans. Economical jet travel has helped lift the demand for accommodation so rapidly that hoteliers in many countries are swamped with business. The Japanese Expo 70 was so successful and put so much strain on local resources that it contributed to a hotel squeeze in Singapore 3,000 miles away.

The building rush to meet the tourist demand is most apparent in Europe. Five large new hotels opened in London in 1970; Amsterdam increased its hotel capacity 50% during 1968–70. The Soviet Union is building three major hotels for foreign tourists in Moscow, one at Leningrad and another at Sochi, a Black Sea resort. After opening its first European establishment at Leiden, Holland, the American Holiday Inns company is building (1970) 15 more in Belgium, England, Austria, Italy, Germany, Portugal, Greece and Luxembourg. It has plans for another 47 hotels to be completed by 1973. Esso Motor Hotels (see *New Geography 1968–69*) with 41 outlets in Europe in mid-1970 expects to have 71 at the end of 1971.]

Airlines are particularly active hotel builders. Inter-Continental, owned by Pan American Airways, is building in Prague and Bucharest and in June 1970 opened a great hotel in Budapest. Trans-World Airlines has 55 hotels in 33 countries. International Telephone and Telegraph, which owns Sheraton hotels, is building a 1,200-room luxury hotel in Munich and its 1,000-room hotel in Paris will be France's largest. This company is also erecting hotels in Stockholm and Buenos Aires. In mid-1970 Singapore had 25 hotels under way and three were being built in Rio de Janiero.

To meet American competition five European airlines – BOAC, BEA, Lufthansa, Alitalia and Swissair – in cooperation with the banking house of S.G. Warburg and four other European banks – have formed the European Hotel Corporation. This organization is to build tourist hotels in London, Paris, Rome, Frankfurt, Munich and Zurich.

These are only samples of the hotel-building boom which reaches in a less spectacular way into virtually all corners of the world. It further emphasizes that tourism is the most international industry; it also produces more revenue than any other industry in the world.

New Geography 1970-71

TRADE

One of the most interesting aspects of world trade during 1968–71 has been the commercial rivalry of West Germany and Japan. Because of the first postwar "economic miracle" the Germans had a long start in penetrating world markets.

Even in 1968, West Germany's total exports of almost 25 billion dollars were nearly double Japan's exports of not quite 13 billion. Generally, lower-priced Japanese goods have been slicing into the German lead so sharply in so many areas of the world that some Germans are anxious about what they call the "yellow peril" to their foreign sales.

The Japanese gains have been greatest in the U.S.A., the world's richest market. Ten years ago, West Germany shipped 30% of all foreign electrical goods sold in the U.S.A., while Japan shipped very little. Today, the Japanese share has climbed to about half, while the West German share has shrunk to 6% — and even that 6% is being threatened. Japanese firms, having nearly taken over the U.S. market for foreign-made radios, TV sets and tape recorders, are beginning to challenge the traditional German dominance in heavy electrical machinery as well. Volkswagen remains the most popular imported car in the U.S.A. but its sales in 1969 slipped 5% below the 1968 period. One reason was the phenomenal sales gains of 80% for Japanese-made Toyotas and of 52% for Datsuns.

The Japanese challenge has left the Germans far behind in steel production and shipbuilding. Japan's yards now build more than half the world's shipping tonnage, German yards less than 9%. The Japanese say that some of the German orders come from shippers who were turned down by Japanese yards that are booked to capacity for years to come. German exporters are losing their markets in China and the rest of Asia to the Japanese, and are being pushed increasingly hard even in Europe. Export prowess has planted a flourishing Japanese business colony in Germany itself. More than 100 Japanese companies have opened European sales headquarters in Dusseldorf.

The Germans complain, as do many American businessmen, that much of the Japanese competition is unfair. They claim that Japanese manufacturers earn high profits selling in a home market that is virtually closed to foreign competition, then use these profits to subsidize cut-price export sales. The Japanese exporters also receive more government help.

TRINIDAD AND TOBAGO

1,864 and 116 sq.m. respectively. Pop. 1,070m. An ever-increasing number of people are emigrating to the U.S.A., Canada and the U.K. — a situation causing concern. In 1966 emigration was 2,120, in 1968 11,320 and in 1969 more than 15,000. The islands' "Agriculture Year" of 1969, though successful in increasing exports of existing and new crops, does not appear to have checked emigration. The citrus industry is developing more rapidly than most, with 22,000 acres under cultivation. Exports increased from 14,369 lb in 1959 to 70,000 lb in 1969. But copra has declined and the country is now a net importer of copra.

While oil is still the leading industry it is significant that the combined capacity of the two refineries is greater than Trinidad's crude oil production. Therefore, to keep the refineries working economically large quantities of crude oil are imported from Venezuela and the Middle East.

Tourism follows sugar as the third industry but the five trading estates are now the most important part of the country's development. With nearly 150 separate factories they produce no fewer than 200 separate items, ranging from artificial teeth to steel drums.

Trade with the U.K., 1969: exports to, £21m; imports from, £27m. Trade with the U.S.A., 1969: exports to, $79m; imports from, $54m.

TUNISIA

45,000 sq.m. Pop. 4.8m. Progress in agriculture is critical to Tunisian prosperity. The largest part of the economy, agriculture provides work for half the labour force and accounts for a quarter of the GNP. Combining small peasant farms with larger farms has made possible notable progress in diversification of crops, irrigation, mechanization and increased use of fertilizers. In September 1969 the World Food Programme allocated 27m dollars to establish 400 mixed farming co-operatives in central and southern Tunisia. A high-yielding Mexican wheat resulted in self-sufficiency in 1969.

Since 1963 mineral production has risen by more than 50%. Oil, discovered in 1964, was in 1969 the country's second most important export to phosphates. The industrial sector is expanding rapidly. Projects in 1969—70 include the development of an industrial complex in the backward south at Gabes and several factories at Sfax.

Tourism is Tunisia's most successful industry and holds great promise for the future. Since 1968 it has been the largest earner of foreign exchange, bringing in £21m in 1969, when nearly 400,000 people visited the country. Between 1970 and 1974 the government foresees a 20% annual growth in the tourist trade.

In March 1969 Tunisia achieved a "part-association" agreement with the EEC; it is seen in Tunisia as the first step towards full association.

Trade with the U.K., 1969: exports to, £3.8m; imports from, £2.8m. Trade with the U.S.A., 1969: exports to, $19m; imports from, $32m.

TUNNELS

Japanese engineers are working on what is going to become the longest undersea tunnel in the world. Called the Seikan

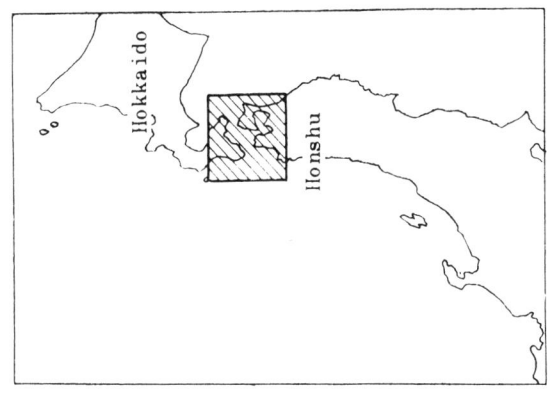

Thoroughfares between Honshu & Hokkaido

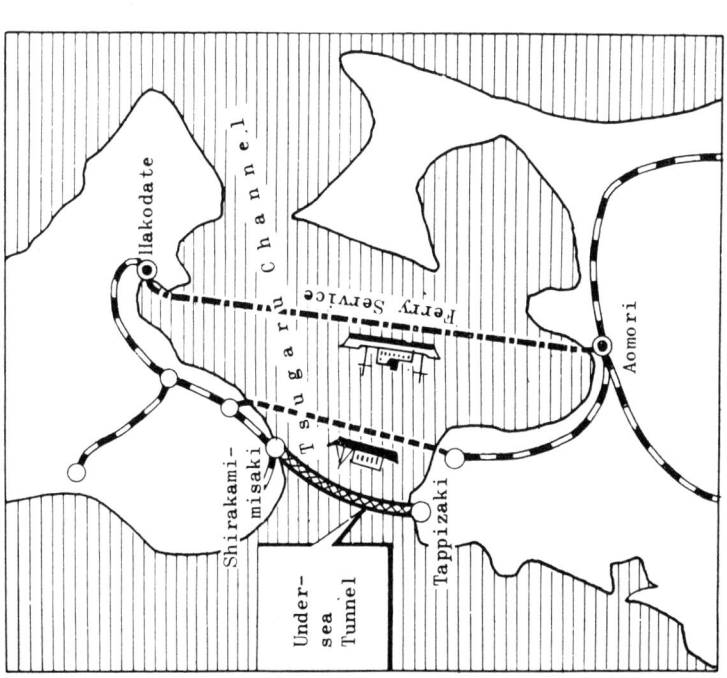

Tunnel, it links Honshu with Hokkaido across the Tsugaru Straits. It will be 22¾ miles — 13¾ of them under the sea. (The longest ocean tunnel in 1970 was the Severn in the U.K., and the longest land tunnel the Simplon, Italy—Switzerland.) The cost will be about £60m and completion is scheduled for 1975. It is for trains only.

Japanese engineers have considerable experience in the problems involved; they have already dug the Kanmon Tunnel from Honshu to Kyushu. The new tunnel will be the final link in Japan's high-speed railway network extending from the southern end of Kyushu to the northern tip of Hokkaido. It is expected to treble freight and passenger traffic.

Japanese tunnels rarely run through uniform hard rock for their entire length. Much of the land consists of strata of hydrogenous and igneous rock in which the dividing line between the two is often softened and weakened by subterranean hot water. In building the Seikan Tunnel engineers have numerous rock faults to negotiate.

TURKEY

294,502 sq.m. Pop. 33.7m. Rapid industrial expansion has caused a shortage of local raw materials and has encouraged a substantial drift from the land but agriculture continues to provide two-thirds of the employment. Rising tobacco stocks and lower foreign exchange earnings (a fall in world prices) underline Turkey's need to diversify agricultural production away from sugar beet and tobacco. Some products — livestock, fodder, fresh fruit and vegetables — are providing the basis for an expanding food processing industry. But because increasing mechanization is causing more unemployment in rural areas there is an even greater need to create new industrial employment opportunities.

The most important public undertaking is a bridge across the Bosphorus, financed by loans from several countries

Turkey

including 8.4m dollars from the U.K. The bridge, linking Asia with Europe, will facilitate trade and tourism. Tourism has a potential which has hardly begun to be exploited. At the moment Turkish travellers abroad are spending more than foreigners in Turkey.

The Keban Dam, harnessing the Euphrates in eastern Turkey, is due on stream in 1971. The dam will provide power for Istanbul and Ankara.

Turkey's major trading partner is West Germany followed by the U.S.A. and the U.K. Trade with the U.K., 1969: exports to, £17m; imports from, £35m. Trade with the U.S.A., 1969: exports to, $91m; imports from, $147m.

U

UGANDA

93,381 sq.m. Pop. 9.6m. The census of 1969 gives accurate regional population figures for the first time: Eastern Region, 2.801m; Buganda, 2.668m; Western Region, 2.416m; Northern Region, 1.640m.

The industrial sector is directing its main efforts towards import substitution, with a plastic pipe factory, an electric light bulb factory, a cement works and a cardboard box factory all newly started. Many others are under construction. Power comes from the Owen Falls HEP scheme.

But agriculture still employs 90% of the total population. While coffee and cotton are the two most important crops tea became number three in 1969, with a record crop of 39m lb. The estimated crop for 1970 was 50m lb. Sugar, tobacco, vegetables, beef ranching, dairy and sheep farming have made good progress.

The economy has been further helped by developments in the mineral industry. Cobalt deposits are being exploited at Kilembe (near the copper mines) and high quality wolfram has been found at Maska.

Tourism is now a significant earner, with 72,500 tourists in 1969 and an estimated 100,000 in 1970.

Trade with the U.K., 1969: exports to, £17.5m; imports from, £10.1m. Trade with the U.S.A., 1969: exports to, $30m; imports from, $20m. Britain is the chief supplier and buyer; the U.S.A. the second largest buyer.

UNITED ARAB REPUBLIC

386,110 sq.m. Pop. 33m. Despite increased exports foreign exchange is scarce and the uncertainty of the political situation will exert a restraining influence on development for some time. The most significant increases are in oil production. In 1970 output was more than 13m tons (9m tons in 1967 when the Sinai fields, producing 70% of the total, were still in Egyptian hands). By 1974 production is expected to be 50m tons, with large surpluses for export: a 200-mile pipeline under construction between the Gulf of Suez and Alexandria will reduce dependence on refineries in the Gulf.

The Aswan Dam project, now completed, has been a focal point of development. As well as harnessing water supplies for irrigation schemes and producing much power for industry the dam is proving a viable commercial venture. Construction costs, remarkably enough, will have been met by the end of 1971. Closely linked to the dam is the iron and steel complex at Helwan (£370m). Fed on abundant supplies of local iron ore, this project is scheduled to employ 20,000 people. Two other steel mills will be in production in 1973. In all 21 new projects were completed in 1969.

The Soviet Union is heavily involved in developing the oil, power, iron, steel and heavy industries. American capital has been channelled mostly into the oil industry and the Japanese are similarly involved. Egypt has barter deals with several countries. Political tensions have, of course, damaged the tourist industry.

Trade with the U.K., 1969: exports to, £12m; imports from, £14m. Trade with the U.S.A., 1969: exports to, $25m; imports from, $60m.

UNITED KINGDOM

93,053 sq.m. Pop. 55.325m. The four most interesting

aspects of new geography for Britain are the changing face of farming, reclamation, water supplies and new towns.*

RECLAMATION. Britain is losing up to 50,000 acres of land a year — equal to the loss of Middlesex once every three years. This land, much of it farmland worth £500 an acre, is swallowed up by "development". Land reclamation from the sea could be the solution and four major schemes are under active consideration. They are for reclamation of a large part of the Wash, much of Morecambe Bay, part of the Solway and much of the estuary of the Cheshire Dee.

The Wash. This scheme would provide Southern England's water requirements, through freshwater lakes, for years to come; 45,000 acres of new farmland; locks for ships to reach King's Lynn, Boston and Wisbech, and a road linking the North with East Anglia.

Morecambe Bay Scheme. This would provide water for Manchester, Liverpool, Preston, the West Riding of Yorkshire and — via the River Wharfe — for Hull and the whole of Humberside; 15,000 acres of new farmland, a 30-sq.m. freshwater lake, and a road across the bay to ease north-south traffic problems.

Solway Scheme. This would provide 16 sq.m. of freshwater lakes supplying water to West Cumberland, including Carlisle and as far east as Tees-side, Newcastle and Sunderland; and thousands of acres of new farm land.

Dee Estuary. This scheme would provide water for Manchester and Liverpool, 26,000 acres of new farmland, and a road carrying traffic across the estuary.

It will be noticed that a major part of all these schemes is water supply, for the thirst for water and the hunger for land are complementary. The need for water storage facilities is urgent.

* It has become clear that users of this biennial analysis would prefer, in the case of the United Kingdom, that major aspects be dealt with in relative detail rather than an attempt made to cover dozens of geographical facets with a few lines given to each.

United Kingdom

WATER SUPPLY. Against a background of diminishing, or at best only constant supplies, demand is rising very steeply. In the South-east, for example, it is expected to double by the end of the century and there are increasingly urgent warnings of shortages in many other parts of the country. At present the provision of water is still the responsibility of a large number of undertakings and has been regarded as an essential social service though an almost entirely local responsibility. Now the essential interdependence of these undertakings is being underlined by the necessity for co-operation in planning.

The United Kingdom is among the select minority of countries where rainfall is sufficient. So far, this country's major problems have been those of storage and distribution, both arising from the wide regional and seasonal variations in rainfall. The average for the United Kindgom as a whole is 36 in. per year but in the South-east and the Midlands, where demand is greatest and is expanding most rapidly, it is only some 20 in. compared with 100 in. in the far more sparsely populated west. Limited storage is, therefore, tolerable only if yearly replenishment is assured, and a succession of dry winters can seriously endanger both underground and surface supplies.

In planning for future U.K. demand, the Water Resources Board envisages that the conservation and distribution arrangements which have been developed over the past hundred years will have to be doubled in the next thirty. River authorities license a total daily abstraction of 23,000m gallons, of which about a fifth is supplied to the public for domestic use and in offices, shops and factories, another fifth is abstracted by industry and, surprisingly, under 1% goes to agriculture. Well over half the total is used as cooling water for power stations and, as with many other industrial cooling processes, most of this is returned to the river.

Since the end of the war, the number of water undertakings has fallen from over 1,000 to some 270. Of this number, about two-thirds are local authorities, the largest being the Metropolitan Water Board which supplies over 360m gallons a day to a population of 6.5m in the London area. The majority of undertakings are still responsible only for their own local supplies (well over a half provide for populations of less than 100,000), though major exceptions are Manchester, Liverpool and Birmingham.

The re-grouping has helped efficient planning, but the size of each authority, although suitable for supplying its own wants, is still not large enough to sustain the necessarily long-term and complicated planning of new supplies. Moreover, responsibility for related problems such as drainage and flooding, the control of effluents and pollution, river navigation, farming, fishing, and recreational rights is divided among a multiplicity of authorities and interests including the Ministries of Agriculture and Housing, river and drainage boards, Public Health Authorities and industrial and agricultural users.

The South-east (defined as the region south and east of a line from the Wash to Lyme Bay) is a "broad deficiency zone". Its population is expected to increase by nearly 50% to 28m by the end of this century and water usage, at another 1,100m gallons a day, will be doubled. The peripheral parts of the region will probably be able to meet this demand from their own reserves but the central area (covered by the Welland, Nene, Great Ouse, and Essex River Authorities and the Thames and Lee Conservancies) will be able to meet only a proportion of its needs by exploration for new reserves, the exploitation of water in the underground strata, desalination and the artificial recharging of underground sources. It has been estimated, for example, that up to 270m gallons a day could safely be drawn from a total of 250 boreholes into the natural pockets of water which exist deep in the chalk and limestone of the Thames Valley. The capital cost would be £8m — but an equivalent supply from surface reservoirs would occupy 30 sq.m. and cost ten times as much.

The alternative to the barrage schemes outlined in the previous section would be at least 30 reservoirs of which a

United Kingdom

third would have to be in the national parks. This would cause controversy. Manchester, for example, ran into massive opposition over its proposals to draw additional water from the Lake District. The new £2.3m upper Teesdale reservoir, designed to meet rising demands in the Tees-side area, was also strongly opposed. In 1970, numerous societies were trying to prevent the construction of a reservoir which would involve flooding part of the Hebden Valley.

The U.K. is at present in the forefront of water research and any cutback in technical research into the treatment of water and in providing for future requirements could prove a dangerously false economy.

NEW TOWNS. While the New Towns Act of 1946 marked a great step forward in the development of urban and regional planning techniques, it also represented the culmination of more than a century's progress towards the creation of good living conditions for the U.K.'s growing urban population in planned communities. Early examples of such new settlements are provided by Bournville (1878) and Port Sunlight (1887), both built for the housing of their workers by wealthy individuals who were appalled by the squalor of the industrial cities.

The principal feature of all the new towns planned and run by development corporations is that they are designed as communities which are balanced in a social sense and self-contained in terms of jobs and facilities. It is this element of independence from existing centres, particularly for employment purposes, that has enabled new towns to be sited as and where required. In every new town the principle of comprehensive planning has been adopted; factories and housing are separately zoned, the latter frequently arranged in a series of "neighbourhoods". Great emphasis is laid on environmental amenities. Many of the earlier new towns were built on relatively sparsely populated sites and have target populations of under 100,000; in a second generation of new towns begun in the 1960s, development in several instances has been centred on towns already established within their

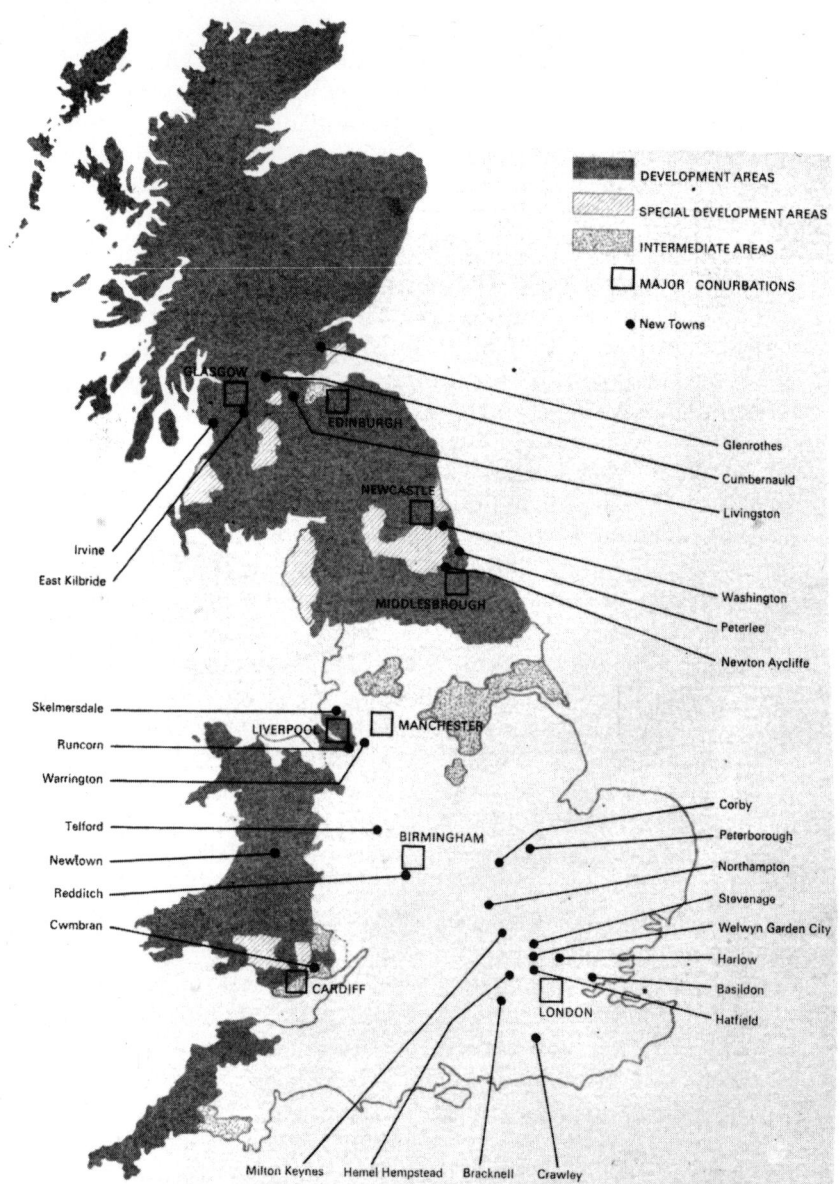

New towns and development areas in the United Kingdom

United Kingdom

regions and projected ultimate populations approach a quarter of a million.

At a time when economic planning was in its infancy and it was thought that the population of the U.K. and, indeed, that of London, would show no significant growth, plans behind the first new towns were concerned with immediate structural problems. Of the new towns established before 1950, only those in the London area represented part of any overall planning strategy — the six built in other parts of the country (Aycliffe, East Kilbride, Peterlee, Glenrothes, Cwmbran and Corby) were intended to correct particular and unrelated sub-regional deficiencies.

Since that time, however, changing economic conditions, both at home and abroad, and a growing awareness of the benefits to be derived from regional planning have contributed to the formulation of a more cohesive strategy. Within this policy directed towards the more equitable dispersal of both population and commercial and industrial activity, the new towns have come to play an increasingly important part. Instead of being regarded merely as population dispersal points, they are now seen as ideal vehicles for the introduction of growth industries to less prosperous areas.

Examination of the reasons behind the designation of the new towns illustrates their position and potential in a regional context. Eleven of the towns are situated in the South-east and are designed to help contain London's growth as an employment centre and solve its housing problem. These include eight of the first new towns (Basildon, Bracknell, Crawley, Harlow, Hatfield, Hemel Hempstead, Stevenage and Welwyn), situated within 20 to 30 miles of central London, and three designated since 1967 (Milton Keynes, Northampton and Peterborough), all of which are larger and at a greater distance from the capital.

Redditch and Telford are being built to fulfil a similar purpose to avoid further congestion in the Birmingham area, while Runcorn, Skelmersdale and Warrington are contributing to the relief of overcrowding in the Merseyside and Manchester conurbations.

Each of the new towns in the North-east (Aycliffe, Peterlee and Washington) was designated to help solve individual sub-regional problems and to contribute to the renewal of an aging infrastructure. All three are now regarded by the region's planning authorities as nuclei of economic growth. Corby was originally developed in order to provide housing for workers in a steel plant but the town, now the second largest in Northamptonshire, is also tending to assume the role of a local growth point.

Wales has two new towns. Cwmbran in the south was among the first to be built, and provides housing for locally employed workers; Newtown, designated in 1967, is intended to assist in halting the depopulation of mid-Wales and to create economic growth in the region. The Scottish new towns (Cumbernauld, East Kilbride, Glenrothes, Irvine and Livingston) have become growth centres within their own areas, bringing new industrial activity to both central Scotland and Fife. Finally, three new towns are being established in Northern Ireland in an attempt to solve the country's two principal problems, excessive concentration in the Belfast area and a high rate of emigration.

Today, therefore, the United Kingdom's 30 new towns, the most extensive development of their type in the world, assume in terms of economic planning an importance far greater than their total population of just over a million would imply. They form valuable weapons within a strategy intent on bringing about a better balance between and within the regions.

In spite of the achievements of the towns, the problem of London has grown worse. As a result of a rapid increase in population within the South-east region, an improvement in transport facilities and, most important of all, a marked reluctance of firms to decentralize office employment from the capital, more people than ever commute to jobs in London. While few of these commuters come from the new towns, it is apparent that, by themselves, the first eight new towns have proved too small and limited a development to make any great impact on the journey-to-work problem, one of the most intransigent currently faced by the planning authorities.

Failure to control the growth of London as an employment centre is one factor lying behind the designation of three much larger new towns at distances of up to 75 miles from the capital. This represents the latest development in the idea of self-contained satellite towns to act as countermagnets to London's influence. This second generation of new towns is conceived within a much larger plan for the dispersal of overspill to many provincial towns throughout the region.

In the North-east mention should be made of Crimlington and Killingworth, though they are not strictly new towns. They are being built by Northumberland County Council to relieve congestion on Tyneside and to stimulate development in south-east Northumberland.

The North-west Planning Region — embracing Lancashire, Cheshire and the High Peak District of Derbyshire — has many deep-seated problems. The oldest and most congested of Britain's industrial areas, it contains nearly 7m people and has a population density of about four times that of Britain as a whole. Employment in the staple industries of coal and textiles is falling and emigration from the region amounts to 10,000 a year. At the same time the Manchester-Liverpool conurbation is grossly overcrowded.

A development of the new town concept may provide an answer to the region's main problems. What is envisaged is a new city in central Lancashire based on Preston, Leyland and Chorley which would ultimately have a population of nearly half a million. If it were to attract population and industry from the conurbations, such a city would make an immediate contribution to the relief of overcrowding and would become a countermagnet to the Manchester-Liverpool axis. At the same time it would constitute a powerful nucleus for the whole of central and north-east Lancashire.

FARMING. Farms are getting larger and farmers fewer, and these changes accentuate existing regional contrasts. Farm

New Geography 1970-71

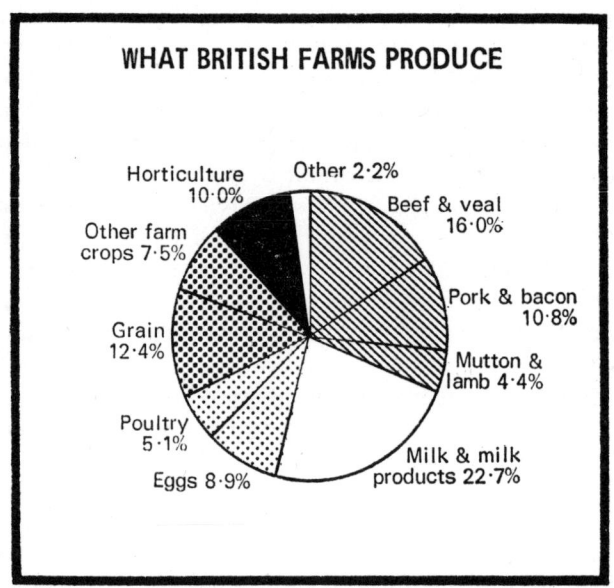

enlargement is marked in eastern areas of arable farming, where farms are already large. In the upland margins farms are small and the range of possible enterprises limited but the government is encouraging amalgamation.

Farmers are able to secure some of the economies of scale by co-operation and the number of business groups has risen sharply in recent years. Much of the rising proportion of produce being processed is also grown on contract, as with peas for quick freezing.

Specialization by farm is accompanied by greater specialization by area. For most of the past hundred years regional trends in crop acreages and livestock numbers have generally followed national patterns, but marked divergences have occurred since the mid-1950s. While the acreage under crops in eastern counties has been rising that in western counties continues to fall. By contrast, dairy cows are increasing in the western lowlands as arable farmers turn to dairy herds and

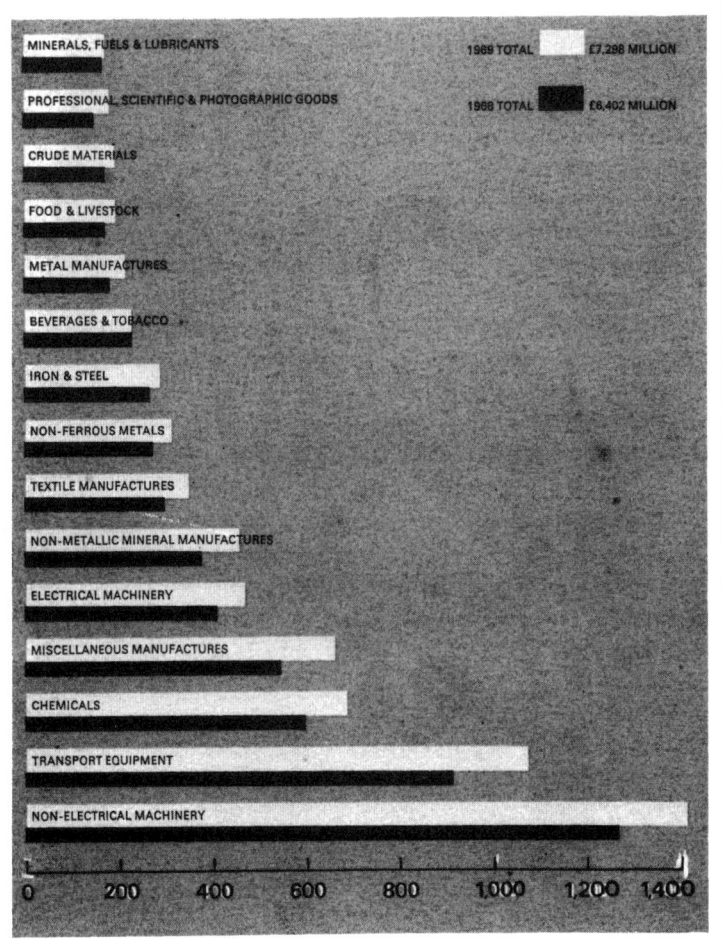

grazing livestock. Similarly, sheep are increasingly localized on the upland margins.

There will probably be 10,000 fewer farms by 1975, and possibly 30,000 or 40,000. Even if the U.K. does not enter the Common Market, the upward trend in the amount of land growing cereals is likely to persist.

The government is also likely to continue to encourage the production of beef, 30% of which is still imported, but rising surpluses of milk will probably lead to a decline in the number of dairy cattle and their further concentration in western lowlands. Numbers of both pigs and broilers will continue to rise. Entry into the Common Market would provide a stronger stimulus to increase output of cereals and beef, but worsen the competitive position of dairy farmers and egg producers; higher cereal prices would encourage the use of grass for livestock production.

Whatever the changes within the farming industry, agriculture's relations with other land uses will also alter. The supply of agricultural land will continue to diminish. In the 1960s, losses for houses, factories and roads averaged 18,000 hectares a year, although this was a quarter less than in the 1930s. More than 4,000 hectares were taken for mineral working, though most will eventually be reclaimed. A further 24,000 hectares of agricultural land were converted into woodland each year, by private landowners and the Forestry Commission.

MINING. At least 30 foreign mining companies — Canadian, American, South African and South American — are actively prospecting in the U.K. and many others are thinking of exploring. The U.K., unlike so many host mining countries, is politically stable and therefore attracts investing companies. Edwin Arnold, in the *Daily Telegraph,* June 29, 1970, noted, "There is a view that the British mining boom is a huge joke and that supporters of the revival are cranks. It is a stupid view." It is indeed. Britain's substantial mineral deposits are virtually untapped. Nobody knew until recently that the massive gabbro rock formation of Aberdeenshire was nickel-bearing. There is probably more tin in Cornwall than has been taken out of it in 3,000 years. Britain also has Europe's largest tungsten supplies at Henerdon in Devon. North Yorkshire has a major world potash field which by the late 1970s will make £35m a year. Consolidated Gold Fields Wheal Jane Tin mine, coming on stream in 1971, will produce 17% of Britain's tin needs by 1974. Arnold considers that given a decade of development Britain could save half her £400m annual bill for copper, lead, zinc and tin. (See *Mining*.)

UNITED SOVIET SOCIALIST REPUBLIC

8.6m sq.m. Pop. 243m. Soviet geography, in the widest sense, is in an interesting stage, made so by the growing complexity of the economy. Agriculture in particular has proved a brake on economic development, although since 1965 annual investment has been maintained at a very much higher level than in previous years and some progress is apparent. Grain harvests, for example, reached a record 170m tons in 1968 and a satisfactory 161m tons in 1969. Fertilization, drainage and irrigation have been widely extended and farm workers' living standards improved. Nevertheless, productivity remains low.

Mechanization is far behind Western standards; costs are high, collective and state farms are generally proving too big to be efficiently administered and there has been an outflow of young and skilled workers. The decline in production last year was largely due to a fall of 25% in the sugar beet crop and of 10% in potatoes. Livestock numbers are declining and the subsequent very serious shortage of meat is having to be met by imports of Australian beef and mutton, Dutch beef, pork, broiler chickens and Canadian grain.

Early in 1969 the Soviet Union announced a new programme to increase the output of mineral fertilizers by an extra 48m tons during the 1970—73 period, with a target of

85m tons in 1972. Supplies of fertilizer have always been inadequate and the emphasis had formerly been placed on the production of a limited variety without regard to different crop and soil conditions.

In mid-1970 further directives were issued. A group of central and republic ministries, as well as the State Bank and the State Planning Commission were told to take the necessary steps to increase the supply of fruit, vegetables and potatoes to the consumer. The Communist Party seems to have set itself the goal of bringing Soviet dietary standards close to those of Western Europe by 1975 — a tall order. The country is running on the spot in many areas of food production, even though the Soviet Union has several times more farm workers in proportion to industrial workers than the U.K. or the U.S.A. The nation is short of food and its foreign exchange earnings are not so lavish that it can make up the gap with massive imports.

There is a notable development in the motor vehicle industry: car output rose by 400% in 1970 and lorries by 150%. The most important plant is the Fiat complex at Togliattigrad; other factories include a new Moscow plant (the Moskvich) at Izhevsk (200,000 cars a year) and extensions to the Zaporozhets factory in the Ukraine.

During the next five years emphasis will be on rapid exploitation of Siberia's vast natural reserves and a growing degree of co-operation with non-Communist traders. Between 1968 and 1970, for instance, the Soviet Union spent 450m dollars on car manufacturing equipment from the West.

The oil fields in Siberia are vital. Total Soviet oil production in 1969 was 328m tons. Over the five years from 1971—75 the target is for 2,700m tons, an ambitious output. Two great power stations are being built at Bratsk and Krasnoyarsk.

Tension with China along the 4,300-mile frontier must continue as China's population expands. The Soviet Union is consolidating its position in its Far-eastern territories by seeking capital from Japan on a long-term credit basis for the exploitation of methane, potassium, phosphates and copper.

United States of America

Another agreement between the two countries is for the sale of £70m of timber to Japan.

Two-thirds of the Soviet Union's trade is with COMECON countries and Cuba. Exchanges with Western countries increased in 1969 to 4,000m dollars compared with 2,500m in 1968. Further expansion is likely to be rapid. In May 1970, France granted 840m dollars in credit to finance the purchase of French capital goods.

The U.K.'s principal exports from the Soviet Union in 1969 included diamonds (£65m), timber (£44m), hides, skins, metal ores, textile fibres, iron and steel. The main British exports were machinery (£46m but £56m in 1968), textile yarns and fibres and chemicals.

Trade with the U.K., 1969: exports to, £197m; imports from, £97m. Trade with the U.S.A. is indirect — that is, routed through other countries and no reliable figures are available.

UNITED STATES OF AMERICA

3,548,974 sq.m. Pop. 203.5m. The attention directed towards the industrial performance of the United States often overshadows the country's importance as a leading agricultural producer. In 1969 farm income rose remarkably to something like 6,600m dollars (4,600m in 1968). Government subsidies approached 4,000m dollars, a growing proportion of which was for buying surplus output. The object of agricultural "support policies" is to try to raise farm incomes without causing massive over-production. The basic principle is land retirement, which is not a new policy but one which is being more intensively applied. The government seeks to buy the cropping rights of farms (the farmer would receive a payment *not* to grow corn, for example) while permitting the acres to be used for other purposes. As a result of this policy, U.S. crop production fell 2% in 1969, to about 4,300m bushels.

Production on a vast scale has made it possible, and indeed essential, for American farmers to develop an exceptionally high degree of efficiency, but it has also meant that they are correspondingly vulnerable to demand both in world commodity markets and at home.

Domination of world trade also carries a heavy responsibility; the United States is one of the largest importers of agricultural commodities and the largest exporter, accounting for around a fifth of the world total. Over two-thirds of the wheat crop is sold abroad (twice the amount exported ten years ago) and nearly a fifth of feed grains. Sales of other commodities including soya beans, dried peas, hides and skins, milled rice, dried milk, tobacco, raisins, fruit and cottonseed range between three-fifths and a fifth of the total output.

Grain production provides a clear illustration of the difficulty of balancing supply and demand. After rapidly declining supplies in the autumn of 1966 had promoted the authorities to encourage the planting of 317m acres in 1967 (an increase of 18m compared with 1966) a record harvest of 1,590m bushels of wheat and 450m bushels of corn was achieved. World production in grain was also at a high level and, with a consequent weakening in the export market, there was for the first time for several years an increase both in feed grain stocks and in the wheat carryover. For 1968, therefore, the acreage of field crops was again reduced to 300m acres but, because of rapidly improving yields, the next harvest was a large one.

In spite of marketing problems, grain production is proving a more attractive proposition than dairying or, in some areas, than livestock farming. As in the U.K., the advantage of this type of enterprise lies in the greater potential for the use of machinery. Soil erosion is coming under control, and crop rotation is considered unnecessary, so that the former pattern of mixed farming, with livestock consuming rotation crops such as hay, is disappearing.

In addition to price supports for all types of grain, there are price supports, acreage allocations and often marketing

United States of America

quotas for most other farm products, although there are no support prices for livestock or for fruit and vegetables.

DAIRYING. Dairying producers have suffered particularly severely from declining demand and depressed prices. The U.S. market for milk has fallen by an annual 25 gallons per head since the war; consumption of "non-fat" products is increasing steadily. Although the number of dairy cows has declined by a third since 1953, output of milk per cow has risen very steeply. The high price of land, particularly near the largest centres of demand, is a heavy burden; few can afford to produce their own feed, and costs are constantly rising. A survey of 12 north-east states, one of the major milk production regions, concludes that half of the present dairy farmers will be out of business before 1975 and that the number of cows will fall by nearly a fifth.

The most hopeful future is for those farmers who are operating with maximum mechanical efficiency, either on family holdings of up to 150 cows (such as those in the north-east states) or on enormous units of up to 3,000 cows — many of which are established along the southern Pacific coast. Here, there is likely to be an even greater emphasis on shift working, on round-the-clock milking, on elaborate indexing and record systems and on specialization so that a milker responsible for perhaps 120—200 cows will have no part in the management, feeding or veterinary care of the herd.

BEEF PRODUCTION. There has been some improvement in conditions for livestock producers; rising cattle numbers have been matched by a faster expansion in demand and even a small rise in meat prices. Nevertheless beef prices are lower than they were 15 to 20 years ago.

INDUSTRY. It is said that the car industry is a barometer for American industry as a whole. Car sales in 1969 reached 9.6m, only slightly less than the record 1968 figure. Imported cars accounted for a larger share of the market — 11.5% — but face increasing competition from American "compact" cars. In 1970 there was a cutback in production

New Geography 1970-71

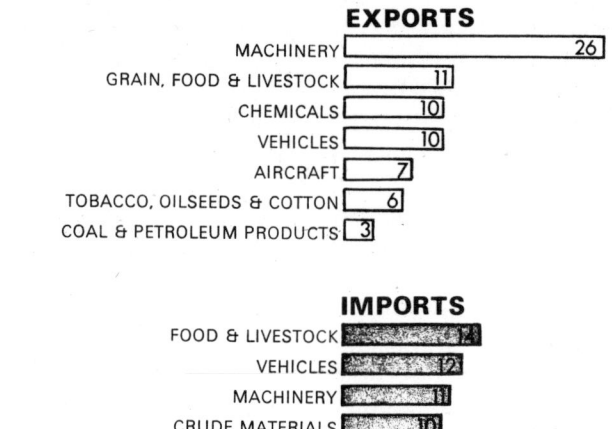

Main U.S. Exports & Imports
AS A PERCENTAGE OF TOTAL

EXPORTS
- MACHINERY 26
- GRAIN, FOOD & LIVESTOCK 11
- CHEMICALS 10
- VEHICLES 10
- AIRCRAFT 7
- TOBACCO, OILSEEDS & COTTON 6
- COAL & PETROLEUM PRODUCTS 3

IMPORTS
- FOOD & LIVESTOCK 13
- VEHICLES 12
- MACHINERY 11
- CRUDE MATERIALS 10
- PETROLEUM & PETROLEUM PRODUCTS 7
- IRON & STEEL 6
- NON-FERROUS METALS 6

thus affecting iron and steel. The car industry accounts for 20% of steel output and 60% of the rubber consumption. Nevertheless, the 1969 steel production reached 141m tons, partly because of voluntary cutbacks by Japan and European countries in their steel exports to the U.S.A.

The U.S.A. has become increasingly alarmed by the shrinkage of its trade surplus from 7 billion dollars in 1964 to less than 1 billion in 1969. Barriers have been put up against products as diverse as Mexican tomatoes and Japanese steel. The Japanese used to buy more from America than they sold but in 1968 a swing occurred, with a 1.1 billion dollar trade deficit for the U.S.A. Textiles have been prominent among imports and some Americans fear that before the end of 1971 the jobs of 600,000 American textile workers will disappear, including many in southern towns.

Uruguay

CALIFORNIA. (Pop. 20m.) California's output of goods and services rose to 100,000m dollars in 1969, more than a tenth of the national total. Manufacturing in California is tremendously wide, with many industries associated with the aerospace industry, which itself employs 600,000 people.

As the nation's leading agricultural state California has also achieved great progress, with cash receipts of 4,400m dollars. Farming is even more mechanized, since labour is very expensive. It is interesting to note that in this leading farming state more than 7m people work outside agriculture.

Because the Californian market is so rich the British Board of Trade and the National Export Council launched in 1969 a five-year trade drive — Target California. The plan is to increase the 1969 trade of 150m dollars to 300m.

One of the most interesting of U.S. geographical projects is the world's largest atom-powered waterworks. On an artificial island a mile off the Californian coast the plant will be able to supply 2m people with electricity by 1972 and 750,000 with desalinated drinking water, 200m litres daily and, eventually, 600m litres.

Trade with the U.K., 1969: exports to, £1,100m; imports from, £860m. (See *Alaska, Fishing, Ecology, Cities, Trade.*)

URUGUAY

72,180 sq.m. Pop. 3.1m. Uruguay is largely dependent on foreign investment for its development, particularly in improving ports and transport, the basis of all other development in this country. The IADB has granted a 20-year loan of 15m dollars for road improvements and the British Petroleum Company 7m dollars for better dock facilities. A group of Swiss banks has lent 30m dollars for tourist industry development.

Agriculture and pastoralism have shown a little improvement, particularly in citrus, rice and dairy farming. Brazil is now buying Uruguay's dairy products, but the country has a great trade deficit with its LAFTA partners. However, trade with West Germany and Italy has been improving while Soviet exports to Uruguay have increased following the signing of a 20m-dollar trade credit in 1969.

New industries being encouraged are forestry, fishing and mining of semi-precious stones. These may help to make good the losses in the wool trade. The international price of wool, which makes up 30% of Uruguay's exports, has been depressed by competition with synthetics to about a third below its usual level. Cost problems also bedevil the meat industry, which has to compete with low-cost producers in Brazil, with the result that large numbers of cattle and sheep are smuggled to Brazil annually, an estimated loss of 16m dollars. Wheat, sugar beet, potatoes, oats and sunflowers have all declined and in 1970 there were large surpluses of wine and butter.

Trade with the U.K., 1969: exports to, £13m; imports from, £5m, mainly iron, steel and machinery. Trade with the U.S.A., 1969: exports to, $55m; imports from, $74m.

VENEZUELA

352,051 sq.m. Pop. 9.9m. A serious effort is being made to broaden trading connections, notably with Eastern Europe and Latin America, under the five-year plan for 1970–74. While the country depends heavily on exports of oil the output of iron ore, in contrast to that of oil, rose rapidly during 1969–70.

The oil situation is disturbing. In 1969 petroleum and its by-products constituted 90% of the nation's exports, a third of the sales being to the U.S.A. But the Venezuelan share of the American market is declining, as it is elsewhere under competition from the Libyan, Algerian and Nigerian fields.

More encouragingly, Venezuela is increasing its steel capacity. Even in 1970 the country imported half its steel requirements, the steel sometimes being made from Venezuelan exported ore. A Venezuelan steel industry could become the mainstay of the Guyana region. Several major schemes are under construction, including an underground railway system for Caracas, a steel rolling mill, a petrochemical complex at El Tablazo and a dam and power project at Santo Domingo.

Much unemployment stems from a movement of population to the towns. For example, the population of Caracas is estimated to be growing at 9% a year against 3.6% for the whole country. Venezuela is rapidly becoming an urban society. Agrarian reform programmes only add to the difficulties as farms become less labour intensive.

Trade with the U.K., 1969: exports to, £65m; imports from, £33m. Trade with the U.S.A., 1969: exports to, $961m; imports from, $666m.

New Geography 1970-71

VIETNAM (North)

63,000 sq.m. Pop. 20m (U.S. Intelligence estimate). It is known that the South Vietnamese economy would collapse in weeks if U.S. support were withdrawn. Less widely recognized is the fact that without vast aid from the Soviet Union, China and other Communist countries North Vietnam would hardly be able to support its own people, much less prosecute a war.

North Vietnam has encountered formidable economic difficulties that are caused only in part by strains imposed by the war. Much of the problem lies in poorly skilled and unmotivated workers. Production goals are so elusive that five-year plans have given way to one-year plans. For example, at the big Hon Gai coalfields in Quang Province production has slipped steadily.

Troubles persist in agriculture, too. More than 70% of the work force is female, a reflection of the losses the country has suffered in nine years of war with the French and another nine fighting for control of South Vietnam. The "miracle rice" strains have failed to take hold in North Vietnam, apparently because workers assigned to collective farms have been unwilling to give the new strains the intensive care they require. To meet the minimum needs of its people the Hanoi government must import 800,000 tons of rice and wheat flour annually.

Since 1965 economic assistance (apart from war aid) from other Communist countries has reached a billion dollars. During 1970 the Soviet Union was supplying 50,000 tons of supplies monthly and Soviet engineers were working on an eightfold expansion of Haiphong port facilities. (This information is from a British Government report, August 1970.)

Vietnam (South)

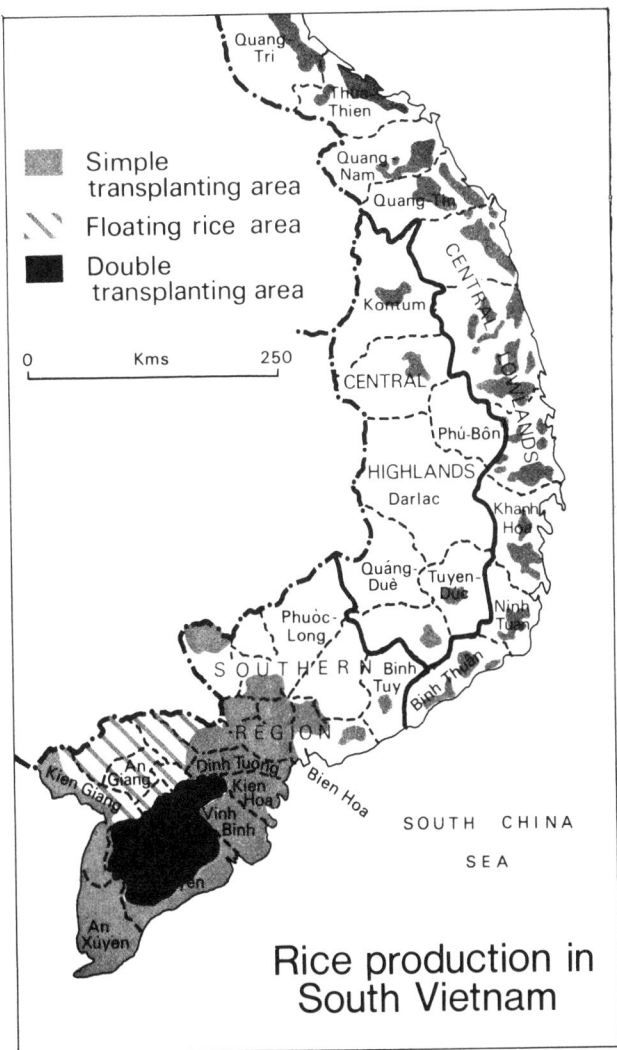

Rice production in South Vietnam

VIETNAM (South)

66,281 sq.m. Pop. 17.8m. The military situation tends to obscure the very important developments in the country's agricultural system. There are great problems, of course. The rice, rubber and sugar cane crops have fallen considerably. However, projects to introduce new, higher-yielding strains are very successful. The potential yield from IR.8 — the remarkable Philippines' strain — can achieve ten metric tons per hectare against the two metric tons harvested in 1967. The growing period is between 20 and 40 days shorter than that of local varieties, allowing two or even three crops in the same field. There is now a National Rice Production Training Centre in Bien Hoa province, which gets much assistance from the American Aid Service — USAID. Officials of USAID say that South Vietnam might again be self-sufficient in rice by 1972.

The most important change in the system occurred in June 1969 when the government introduced a scheme to give free land to the peasants who farmed it, taking it away from the big landlords and the Catholic Church. This is the so-called Land-To-The-Tiller Programme. It effects 800,000 farmer tenants farming 13m hectares.

WEST GERMANY

95,744 sq.m. Pop. 60m. The German boom continues with all industries prosperous. The vehicle industry in particular shows steady development but the chemical and textile industries are also expanding. The state of Germany's economic geography is clearly shown by the labour situation. Only about 1% of the working population is unemployed and there are five vacancies for every man out of work. The number of foreign workers has been rising at an annual rate of 40%; the total at the end of June 1970 was 1.8m.

The government is setting up an institution on the lines of the British Monopolies Commission which will give the government a say in proposed mergers. There have been moves in many industries to rationalize their structures; a notable example is the coal industry where mergers should enable it to compete more effectively with natural gas and oil.

The shipbuilding industry has not expanded as much as others, hit as it has been by rapidly rising costs and revaluation. In December 1969 a £44m order was lost to a British shipyard and with 65% of its ship output sold abroad West Germany cannot now compete so readily with other nations.

SAARLAND DECLINE. With coal and steel under pressure the Saar is apparently becoming more of a burden that an asset to Germany. The government is faced with a choice of two expensive methods of curing the Saar's ills. One is to dig a £160m canal from Saarbrucken eastwards to the Rhine at Ludwigshaven, 75 miles away. The alternative is to bring in new industry to provide jobs for the 55,000 workers who will be out of work if the canal is not built.

Already, since 1960, Saarland mineworkers have decreased from 65,000 to 25,000. But it is in iron and steel that Saarland is most threatened. Saar coal alone is not capable of producing the right kind of coke for a modern steelworks. It has to be supplemented by outside supplies. Indeed, coke made in Saarland from imported American coal is much better and cheaper than the local variety. The traditional Lorraine iron ore which once fed the Saar furnaces is no longer adequate. Today it is more economic to bring richer iron ores from Sweden, South America and Africa, despite the distances, than to use French ores only 60 miles away.

Transport is the key to Saarland's economic success. To remain competitive the Saar steel industry, employing 40,000 workers, must be able to bring in high-grade coal and ore cheaply. This is why the canal is important. The bulk of supplies come by rail but by 1972 the special rates now applying will cease, and ore will cost a ruinous £1 per ton more to transport.

Even with the canal Saarland will need new industries. Ford has built a car factory at Saarlouis which will employ 10,000 workers by 1973. The chemical industry is growing. The ultimate solution may have to be a combination of both major remedies, canal (seven years to build) and government-sponsored industries.

RUHR. The Ruhr (4560 sq.km.) is a region of colossal production and population (nearly 6m) but it has evolved a planned programme of conservation to maintain an acceptable environment. It is clearly the workshop of Western Europe but few people realize that no less than 53.6% is still farmland, 15.9% woodland, 2.3% water and 2% open space (such as parks and airfields). Residents of Ruhr cities — there are 12 with a population of more than 100,000 — have more than eight times as much woodland per head as do Londoners. Credit for the environment, which is steadily improving, rests with the Ruhr Planning Authority, the first organization of its kind in the world. Possessing considerable power, the Authority designates green areas and protects them against urban encroachment. The Ruhr's cities are separated from one another by long north-south green fingers which prevent the fusion of conurbations. Planning permission for deep-mine operators is now very strict; they must, for instance, back-stow 50% of their spoil. The rest must be hauled to huge communal tips which are landscaped and tree-planted. Much spoil is being used as hardcore in the Ruhr's vigorous road and motorway programme. Apart from all this the Ruhr is rapidly cutting down areas of pollution. (See *Ecology*.)

Trade with the U.K., 1969: exports to, £466m; imports from, £414m. Trade with the U.S.A., 1969: exports to, $2,750m; imports from, $1,693m.

WHALING

This industry has reached a critical point. In 1952, when the International Whaling Commission was formed, the Antarctic quota was 15,000 to 16,000 blue whales; the 1969—70 quota was down to 2,700. This reflects the disastrous decrease in whale population. In 1969, for the first time in 50 years, Norwegian whalers abandoned the southern seas. They say that probably no more than 1,000 blue whales exist. Species after species has been driven to extinction because the laws of whaling have never been enforced. The worst offenders have been the Japanese and Russians.

WHEAT

Wheat remains the major grain for human consumption and throughout the world production has risen markedly in the past two decades. From the 1950—51 season to the harvests of 1967—68 the harvested area rose by a third, with a production increase of 81%, mainland China excluded.

The contribution from the major suppliers varies seasonally with weather conditions; even in Western Europe where rainfall is adequate and reliable, frost can seriously damage harvests. The advance of farm technology, more highly mechanized farming systems and development of new strains are combining to deal with problems imposed by physical geography.

Rising yields are startling. In Western Europe average yields rose by 55% between 1949—50 and 1968—69, despite little change in acreage. The yield per acre is 13 bushels. In Eastern European countries the increase for the same period was 66%, though here the acreage is greater.

In Western Europe there is now a much greater proportion of spring wheat, particularly in Denmark which, with Holland, West Germany and Sweden, has the highest wheat yields in the world. Elsewhere in North-west Europe this trend has been reversed, with greater emphasis on autumn and summer wheat.

Higher yields per acre are characteristic of European countries; the product per acre is much lower in the Soviet Union, the Americas and Australia. Still, the trend to higher acre-yields continues and is not yet finished. The future holds great potential for those areas yet to increase their use of fertilizer and awaiting irrigation and agricultural development.

A world wheat glut has bedevilled trade since 1968 and resulted in abandonment of the International Grain Agreement. All wheat producing countries have felt the effects of the glut. Canada is a good example. In 1964 wheat exports accounted for 14% of overseas sales; in 1968 the figure was 6% and in 1969, 5%.

WINDWARD ISLANDS

(Grenada, St. Vincent, St. Lucia, Dominica and the Grenadines). 825 sq.m. Pop. 385,000. While production of bananas, nutmeg, mace, copra, citrus, timber and fishing are developing, two traditional industries are failing — cotton and sugar. Sugar is no longer grown in St. Lucia and St. Vincent's Sea Island cotton, reputed to be the best in the world, is weak in production because of price increases. Much of the islands' future rests with tourism, especially in St. Vincent.

WOOL

A new breed of sheep evolved in Tasmania is likely to be widely bred in many parts of the world. Named Cormo, the breed was developed by crossing the best quality Corriedale rams with superfine Merino ewes. The new sheep combines high body weight and fertility with a heavy good quality fleece at present averaging 11.5 lb.

YUGOSLAVIA

98,725 sq.m. Pop. 20.1m. The high rate of unemployment in the country has resulted in many people seeking work in Western Europe. Even the unemployment rate of 8% in 1970 masks the economic gulf between Slovenia and Croatia in the industrially developed north and the retarded southern states, which include Macedonia and Kosovo.

Paradoxically, the rising costs of hiring Yugoslav workers abroad is encouraging some West German and Swedish firms to move into Yugoslavia to make use of the spare industrial capacity and surplus labour. The unemployment has been caused by inflation but industry itself is prosperous. Growth is specially noticeable in the motor industry. Until 1965 the average annual increase in vehicles on the road was 25,000. In 1969 it reached 120,000 — 90,000 of them produced or assembled in Yugoslavia. The pace-setter is the Crvena Zastava (Red Flag) plant at Kragujevac, turning out cars under licence from Fiat. Many European motor companies are trying to strengthen their position in Yugoslavia. The International Finance Corporation has invested 8m dollars in further expansion of the motor industry.

A consortium of British banks is providing £6.4m towards extension of the Skopje steelworks and a U.S. bank is co-operating with the Bank of Yugoslavia in the development of the port of Koper, just south of Trieste, as a gateway for East-West trade. Two major construction projects for which finance is needed are iron works in north-west Bosnia, where rich deposits of ore were recently discovered, and new plants for the production of aluminium. Yugoslavia is now a leading European producer of copper, lead, silver, zinc and bauxite.

Yugoslavia

With HEP stations being built — power output will be increased five-fold by 1975 — there is plenty of future for alumina. Output should be 200,000 tons annually by 1972 compared to 47,000 tons in 1967.

Another important sector is the shipbuilding industry. The shipyards on the Adriatic coast have accounted during the 1960—70 decade for only 2% to 3% of the world's total merchant tonnage, but this still put Yugoslavia, in 1968, in sixth place as an exporter.

There are opportunities for investment in transport, farming and tourism. For example, Yugoslavia is planning to build 100 new hotels before 1972 and hopes to earn from tourism no less than 900m dollars annually by 1975 (300m dollars in 1969). The IBRD has lent 30m dollars for highway construction to attract tourists even further.

The various provinces or republics are being given greater autonomy, thus allowing the more advanced republics to expand their traditional crafts and service industries which are indispensable to the development of the Yugoslav economy. In 1969 Slovenia accounted for a quarter of the country's exports. Plans to extend the network of canals for freight transport and to modernize the railways should do much for the country's immediate future.

Two-thirds of trade is with the West — the major part with the EEC. EEC exports to Yugoslavia (700m dollars annually) are nearly twice as high as Yugoslavia's sales to the Community. However, in March 1970 Yugoslavia won a long-term contract to sell large supplies of meat to the EEC. Sales of wine, maize and textiles seem likely to increase, too.

Trade with the U.K., 1969: exports to, £28m; imports from, £30m. Trade with the U.S.A., 1969: exports to, $95m; imports from, $180m.

Z

ZAMBIA

290,587 sq.m. Pop. 4.075m. Zambia may be truly described as a one-crop economy consisting of copper, which brings continuously high prices. Copper exports account for well over nine-tenths of foreign exchange. From January 1970 the government acquired a 51% share in the two holding companies — Anglo-American and Roan Selection Trust — which control the copper mines. The importance of copper is overwhelming, since it is the main source of paid employment for Africans and Europeans.

Paradoxically, the very success of copper has led to neglect of agriculture which remains the livelihood of the majority of Zambians. In 1969 the tobacco crop was only 11m lb and realized less than in any year since 1962. Cattle slaughterings decreased and the number of tourists fell below 5,000 for the first time; there were 22,167 in 1965. Non-mining industries also fared badly. In March 1970 the government announced that foreign companies will be able to export profits and this should cause more foreign investment.

Much development is projected. Several foreign companies have been granted mineral-prospecting licences. Work on the North Bank power station for the Kariba HEP project spanning the Zambezi River border between Zambia and Rhodesia began in August, 1970. An Italian oil group has started work on a £15m refinery at Ndola, next to the pipeline terminal. When the refinery is producing, in 1972, the pipeline from Dar-es-Salaam will carry crude oil instead of the present refined oil. Work on the 1,000-mile Zambian-Tanzanian rail link which China is building began

Zambia

late in 1970. Other projects include a car assembly plant at Livingstone and a steel rolling mill at Kafue.

Zambia's leading suppliers are the U.K., South Africa (despite Zambian disagreement with South Africa's racial policies), U.S.A., Japan and Rhodesia. Its chief buyers are the U.K., Japan and West Germany.

Trade with the U.K., 1969: exports to, £105.5m; imports from, £35.1m. Trade with the U.S.A., 1969: exports to, $91m; imports from, $80m.

APPENDIX

Table of Par Rates of Exchange for Sterling and Dollars

	£		$		
Australia	£1.00 =	2.15 A dollars	$1.1230	=	1 A dollar
Austria	£1.00 =	62.3 schilling	$0.0390	=	1 schilling
Canada	£1.00 =	2.58 dollars	$0.9324	=	1 dollar
Denmark	£1.00 =	18.00 kroner	$0.1334	=	1 krone
Finland	£1.00 =	10.00 markka	$0.24	=	1 markka
France	£1.00 =	13.3 francs	$0.1812	=	1 franc
Greece	£1.00 =	7.15 drachma	$0.0335	=	1 drachma
India	£1.00 =	18.00 rupees	$0.1335	=	1 rupee
Israel	£1.00 =	8.50 pounds	$0.29	=	1 Israeli pound
Italy	£1.00 =	1513.00 lire	$0.001600	=	1 litre
Japan	£1.00 =	860 yen	$0.002792	=	1 yen
Netherlands	£1.00 =	8.7 guilders	$0.2755	=	1 guilder
New Zealand	£1.00 =	2.14 NZ dollars	$1.1263	=	1 NZ dollar
Norway	£1.00 =	17.1 kroner	$0.1401	=	1 krone
Portugal	£1.00 =	68.6 escudos	$0.0352	=	1 escudo
South Africa	£1.00 =	1.714 rand	$1.4055	=	1 rand
Spain	£1.00 =	167.00 prsetas	$0.0145	=	1 peseta
Sweden	£1.00 =	13.36 kroner	$0.1925	=	1 krone
United Arab Republic	£1.00 =	1.04 pounds	$2.31	=	1 pound
U.S.A.	£1.00 =	2.40 dollars	$ —		—
West Germany	£1.00 =	8.7 Deutsche Marks	$0.2752	=	1 DM

INDEX

Abu Dhabi, 17
Afghanistan, 17, 56
Agriculture, 18-19, 35, 36, 37, 38, 62, 73, 74, 76, 81, 87-90, 91-92, 93, 103, 107, 108, 110, 114, 115, 121, 123, 129, 130, 135, 136, 138, 139, 140, 144, 150, 152, 154, 163, 165, 168, 171, 177, 178, 182, 183, 185, 186, 190, 199, 200, 202, 206, 213, 217, 219, 223, 225, 226, 228, 236
Barley, 186
Cocoa, 55, 103, 154, 155, 165, 182
Coconut, 25, 50
Copra, 165, 169, 199, 233
Coffee, 39, 50, 55, 60, 75, 76, 107, 129, 136, 154, 165, 166, 182, 204
Cotton, 21, 24, 50, 55, 62, 107, 109, 118, 119, 129, 155, 164, 166, 204, 233
Fruit:
   Apples, 136, 181
   Bananas, 24, 50, 60, 73, 107, 114, 118, 164, 184, 233
   Citrus, 60, 61, 90, 107, 108, 114, 118, 119, 152, 164, 183, 186, 199, 223, 233
   Grapes, 61, 114, 171, 220
   Melons, 119
   Pineapples, 24, 108, 136, 155
   Tomatoes, 21, 44, 119, 138, 155, 222
Groundnuts, 119, 140, 155
Honey, 21
Horse Beans, 188
Kenaf, 192
Legumes, 19, 92, 108, 188
Mace, 233
Maize, 18, 19, 88, 108, 119, 175, 220, 235
Millet, 87
Nutmeg, 233
Oats, 224
Olives, 136, 138, 171
Opium, 117
Peas, 214, 220
Pepper, 30
Potatoes, 186, 217, 224
Rape, 190
Rice, 19, 50, 60, 73, 87, 110, 115, 116, 123, 130, 135, 136, 142, 163, 182, 186, 192, 220, 223, 226, 228
Rubber, 50, 81, 138, 140, 155, 168, 192, 228
Sisal, 129
Sorghum, 18, 87, 108, 118, 188
Sugar, 60, 90, 108, 118, 142, 143, 144, 166, 168, 183, 186, 204, 228, 233
Sugar Beet, 21, 118, 119, 152, 190, 202, 217, 224
Sunflower Seeds, 21, 224
Tea, 30, 50, 115, 129, 142,

165, 191, 204
Tobacco, 106, 108, 119, 140, 174, 202, 204, 220, 236
Wheat, 19, 21, 27, 45, 73, 87, 90, 107, 110, 115, 135, 136, 150, 163, 171, 186, 188, 190, 220, 224, 226, 231, 232
Vanilla, 30
Vegetables, 36, 76, 91, 152, 155, 202, 204

Aid, 17, 23-26, 91, 92, 111
Alaska, 19, 20, 22
Albania, 59
Algeria, 20, 21, 23, 147, 152
Antarctic, 42, 43, 192, 231
Antigua, 41
Arctic, 22
Argentina, 22, 23, 90, 197
Ascension Island, 42
Asia, 20
Asian Development Bank, 25, 26
Australia, 27-31, 40, 43, 59, 90, 111, 118, 145, 146, 149, 167, 181, 217, 233
Austria, 31, 197
Aviation, 26, 31-34, 59, 63, 93, 117 (*see* Transport)

Bahamas, 42
Barbados, 41, 80
Beef, 22, 24, 27, 129, 166, 204, 216, 217, 221
Belgium, 35-36, 80, 112, 146, 176, 197
Bermuda, 42
Bolivia, 23, 36, 147
Botswana, 37-38, 41
Brazil, 23, 39, 223, 224
Bridges, 202
British Antarctic Territory, 42
British Colombia, 47, 48
British Commonwealth, 40-43
British Directorate of Overseas Surveys, 142

British Honduras, 42
British Indian Ocean Territory, 42
British Solomon Islands Protectorate, 42
British Virgin Islands, 42
Brunei, 42
Bulgaria, 43, 44

Canada, 40, 45-48, 90, 103, 105, 106, 146, 147, 149, 162, 175, 193, 196, 217, 232
Canals, 187, 229, 235
Canary Islands, 49
Caribbean Free Trade Area, 57
Cattle, 24, 38, 40, 60, 88, 92, 110, 129, 150, 168, 182, 184, 221, 224, 236
Cayman Islands, 42, 49
Cement, 35, 75, 104, 131, 144, 155, 173, 182, 186, 204
Central America, 50
Central American Bank for Economic Integration, 50
Central American Common Market, 57, 58, 107
Ceylon, 24, 40, 50, 191
Chad, 19
Chile, 23, 51
China, 19, 218, 226
Christmas Island, 43
Cities, 52-54, 151
Climate, 54, 71
Coal, 29, 44, 47, 62, 98, 110, 150, 151, 162, 226, 229, 230
Cocos Islands, 43
Colombia, 23, 55
Colombo Plan, 56
Common Markets, 56-59
Congo, 55, 147
Cook Islands, 41, 59
Coral Sea Islands Territory, 31
Costa Rica, 60
Council for Mutual Economic Assistance, 57, 58, 62, 110, 170, 177, 219
Cuba, 60, 219

Index

Currents, 22, 55, 158
Cyprus, 40, 61
Czechoslovakia, 61, 197

Dahomey, 19
Dairying, 35, 63, 88, 90, 106, 118, 151, 154, 168, 204, 214, 220, 221, 223, 224
Dams, 25, 38, 104, 111, 155, 156, 203, 205
Denmark, 63, 112, 232
Diamonds, 103, 119, 150, 182, 219
Disease, 103, 185, 186
Dominica, 41
Drought, 27, 37, 38, 51, 154, 174, 185
Dubai, 64

Earthquakes, 66-69, 123
East African Community, 57
Ecology, 52-53, 54, 69-72, 170, 171, 230
Ecuador, 24, 73
Education, 20, 38, 73, 135
Egypt, 19, 156
Eire, 24, 74, 75
El Salvador, 75
Emigration, 21, 123, 130, 135, 171, 172, 199, 213
Ethiopia, 18, 76, 89, 101, 118
European Economic Community, 56, 57, 63, 77, 78, 90, 98, 129, 152, 184, 187, 188, 194, 200, 216, 235
European Free Trade Association, 57, 63, 78, 79, 114, 190, 194
Exploration, 80, 154

Falkland Islands, 42
Farming, 213
Fertilizers, 18, 37, 75, 118, 144, 163, 173, 217
Fiji, 42
Finland, 52, 81
Fish Farming, 84-86, 92

Fishing, 20, 21, 30, 39, 60, 71, 73, 83-86, 92, 104, 105, 108, 110, 114, 131, 141, 143, 144, 154, 155, 156, 158, 159, 164, 168, 171, 182, 184, 224, 233
Floods, 86, 112, 113, 152, 155
Food, 39, 83-86, 87-90, 91, 92, 104, 115-116, 163, 168
Food and Agriculture Organization, 19, 55, 83, 88, 91, 92, 104, 118, 195
Forestry (*see Timber*)
Fossil Fuels, 96, 98
France, 21, 52, 90, 93, 176, 197, 219

Gambia, 19, 41
Geomorphology, 99-103
Geophysics, 59
Germany (West), 23, 72, 83, 90, 112, 113, 146, 157, 181, 188, 197, 198, 199, 203, 224, 229-231, 232
 (East), 69, 83
Ghana, 18, 24, 40, 103
Gibraltar, 43
Gilbert and Ellice Islands, 42
Glaciers, 104-105
Gravel, 105
Greece, 106, 107, 197
Grenada, 41
Guatemala, 107
Guyana, 41

Honduras, 108
Hong Kong, 42, 109
Horticulture, 35, 44
Hungary, 37, 110, 197
Hurricanes, 110
Hydro-Electric Power, 23, 24, 39, 51, 76, 96, 111, 114, 129, 136, 142, 143, 155, 157, 166, 204, 235, 236
Hydrology, 39, 112, 113

Iceland, 24, 114

Illiteracy, 37
India, 23, 24, 40, 56, 87, 115, 151, 159
Indicative World Plan (for Agriculture), 92
Indonesia, 56, 115
Inter-American Developement Bank, 23, 25, 26, 50, 223
International Labour Organization, 132
International Development Association, 23, 25, 166
International Monetary Fund, 26, 184
Iran, 56, 116, 117
Iraq, 117
Irrigation and Dams, 24, 25, 50, 77, 116, 117, 118, 119, 121, 123, 130, 136, 143, 155, 177, 178, 185, 186, 188, 205, 217
Israel, 119, 120
Italy, 44, 90, 121, 184, 197, 202, 224

Jamaica, 41
Japan, 17, 20, 67, 84, 116, 125, 146, 150, 167, 169, 179, 181, 196, 198, 199, 200, 202, 222, 231
Jute, 115, 138, 163

Kenya, 18, 19, 23, 41, 129, 130, 156
Korea (South), 25, 56, 60, 86, 146, 185
Kuwait, 130, 131

Labour, 44, 62, 74, 91, 109, 121, 122, 132-136, 138, 140, 144, 154, 171, 172, 174, 189, 190, 202, 223, 225, 226, 229, 234
Latin American Free Trade Association, 57, 224
Lebanon, 136
Leeward Islands, 41
Lesotho, 19, 41

Liberia, 19, 136
Libya, 19, 138, 139, 146
Luxembourg, 197

Malawi, 18, 19, 23, 41, 140
Malaysia, 24, 40, 56, 140, 141
Mali, 19
Malta, 41, 141
Maps, 142
Mauritania, 152
Mauritius, 41, 142, 143
Meat, 22, 27, 60, 106, 166, 168, 217, 224, 235, 236
Metals and Minerals *Alumina,*
  Alumina, 29, *235*
  Aluminium, 60, 71, 114, 136, 144, 149, 154, 157, 234
  Asbestos, 28, 129, 173, 175
  Bauxite, 28, 36, 60, 103, 146, 150, 184, 234
  Bromine, 149
  Chromium, 116, 169, 175
  Cobalt, 204
  Copper, 20, 28, 51, 59, 116, 146, 154, 155, 157, 165, 168, 169, 177, 178, 217, 218, 234, 236
  Gold, 20, 103, 146, 150, 151, 155, 169, 184
  Gypsum, 147, 150
  Ilmenite, 28
  Iron Ore, 28, 29, 31, 40, 62, 108, 116, 138, 149, 150, 151, 154, 169, 178, 182, 184, 205, 230, 234

  Lead, 28, 74, 116, 149, 152, 154, 169, 217, 234
  Magnesium, 159
  Manganese, 40
  Methane, 21, 23, 36, 44, 98, 143, 147, 150, 153, 162, 218
  Nickel, 29, 60, 107, 144-146,

Index

149, 169, 217
Phosphates, 147, 152, 178, 200, 218
Phosphorite, 150
Platinum, 149, 184
Potash, 45, 147, 150, 217
Potassium, 218
Rutile, 182
Salt, 149, 151
Silver, 20, 28, 74, 155, 169, 178, 234
Steel, 21, 28, 31, 81, 82, 93, 116, 121, 123, 127, 163, 184, 185, 186, 188, 191, 205, 222, 225, 229, 234, 237
Sulphur, 107, 117, 146
Tin, 20, 28, 140, 149, 150, 155, 192, 217
Tungsten, 217
Uranium, 36, 147, 149, 184, 187
Wolfram, 204
Zinc, 28, 74, 116, 149, 154, 169, 217, 234
Meteorology, 158
Mexico, 24, 87, 144, 222
Milk *(see Dairying)*
Mining, 28, 147-150, 216
 Deep sea mining, 153, 158
Mongolia, 150
Monsoon, 151, 165
Montserrat, 42
Morocco, 152

Nauru, 43
Netherlands, 52, 80, 112, 147, 153, 176, 181, 197, 217, 232
New Hebrides, 42
New Towns, 52, 53, 209-213
New Zealand, 40, 43, 153, 154
Nicaragua, 155
Nigeria, 18, 19, 24, 40, 146, 155
Nile, 156
Norfolk Island, 43
Norway, 98, 156, 157, 181, 231

Nuclear Power, 23, 44, 96, 98, 153, 162, 187, 189

Oceanography, 22, 99-103, 158, 159, 192
Oil, 17, 19, 20, 21, 28, 31, 44, 47, 55, 62, 64, 73, 74, 75, 88, 96, 98, 103, 107, 108, 110, 115, 116, 117, 130, 138, 150, 151, 154, 155, 159-162, 173, 175, 176, 178, 179, 182, 184, 185, 186, 191, 199, 200, 205, 218, 225, 236
Oil Pipelines, 47, 55, 116, 117, 119, 127, 159, 175, 205, 236

Pakistan, 23, 25, 40, 56, 87, 110, 133, 163
Panama, 164
Papua − New Guinea, 25, 30, 43, 165, 167
Paraguay, 166
Pearling, 167
Peru, 25, 68, 168
Petro-Chemicals, 31, 115, 154, 173, 185, 225
Philippines, 56, 87, 168-169
Pigs, 92, 216, 217
Pitcairn, 42
Poland, 84, 86, 169
Pollution, 69-72, 86, 105, 149, 231
Population, 20, 27, 37, 52, 53, 55, 56, 64, 81, 93, 94, 106, 111, 132, 143, 144, 165, 170, 171, 190, 213, 225
Ports, 26, 31, 48, 60, 74, 93, 94, 111, 116, 128, 138, 183, 184, 223, 226, 234
Portugal, 83, 171, 197
Poultry, 27, 60, 92, 118, 135, 216, 217
Poverty, 37
Power *(see HEP, Nuclear, Thermal, Oil, Coal, Fossil fuels)*

243

Prawns, 28

Qatar, 173

Railways *(see Transport)*
Reclamation, 39, 50, 128, 139, 206
Resources Survey, 174
Rhodesia, 42, 174, 175
Roads *(see Transport)*
Routes, 175
Ruhr, 230, 231
Rumania, 86, 111, 177, 197

Saar, 229, 230
Sahara, 102-103
St. Helena, 42
Saudi Arabia, 178
Scientific Committee on Ocean Research of the International Council of Scientific Unions, 102
Selenology, 179
Senegal, 19
Seychelles, 42
Sheep, 110, 154, 204, 216, 217, 224
Shipbuilding, 69, 141, 176, 179, 180, 183, 198, 229, 235
Shipping *(see Transport)*
Sicily, 122, 123
Sierra Leone, 18, 25, 41, 182
Silk, 185
Singapore, 25, 41, 56, 182, 196
Somalia, 25, 183
South Africa, 60, 146, 147, 184
Spain, 83, 186
Steel *(see Metals and Minerals)*
Sudan, 25, 156, 188
Swaziland, 41
Sweden, 52, 188, 189, 193, 197, 232
Switzerland, 189-190, 202

Tanzania, 18, 41, 101, 156
Textiles, 21, 35, 75, 81, 93, 107, 116, 140, 144, 155, 166, 171, 182, 186, 191, 219, 222, 229, 235
Thailand, 26, 56, 87, 191
Thermal Power, 76, 110, 114, 143
Tides, 192
Timber, 20, 30, 35, 47, 81, 103, 107, 108, 121, 127, 136, 138, 142, 144, 154, 155, 156, 166, 188, 193-196, 219, 233
Tonga, 42
Tourism, 17, 20, 31, 49, 51, 61, 62, 73, 110, 119, 121, 130, 136, 141, 143, 152, 154, 166, 171, 177, 187, 196-197, 200, 203, 204, 205, 223, 233, 235, 236
Trade, 20, 22, 30, 47, 50, 61, 63, 69, 77, 78, 79, 80, 81, 103, 104, 109, 110, 114, 117, 153, 154, 170, 185, 186, 190, 198, 199, 203, 237
Transport
  Air, 31-34, 49, 59, 63, 165, 178, 191, 196
  Containers, 64, 181, 183, 196
  Rail, 26, 29, 30, 39, 92, 111, 136, 140, 176, 230, 235, 236
  Roads, 17, 24, 25, 39, 92, 111, 136, 155, 178, 182, 191, 206, 223, 235
  Shipping, 74, 83, 136, 138, 158, 181, 185, 190
Trinidad-Tobago, 41, 199
Tristan da Cunha, 42
Tunisia, 26, 86, 112, 200
Tunnels, 150, 187, 200, 201
Turkey, 26, 69, 116, 202, 203
Turks and Caicos Islands, 42

Uganda, 41, 204
United Arab Republic, 26, 205
United Kingdom, 23, 40, 81, 82, 89, 90, 105, 110, 114, 146, 150, 181, 195, 197, 202,

Index

205-217, 219
United Nations Development Programme, 168
United Nations Educational Scientific and Cultural Organization, 37, 39, 73, 106, 159
United Soviet Socialist Republic, 23, 52, 84, 90, 104, 111, 131, 147, 177, 184, 197, 205, 217-219, 224, 226, 231
United States Aid, 23, 228
United States of America, 52, 60, 66, 80, 84, 88, 89, 90, 106, 111, 114, 116, 146, 158, 161, 162, 176, 184, 193, 198, 219-223
Upper Volta, 19
Uranium, 36, 147, 149, 184, 187
Urban Development, 52, 53, 64, 128, 142, 170, 209-213, 225, 230-231
Uruguay, 223

Vegetable Oils, 24, 55, 73, 76, 90, 91, 104, 107, 108, 136, 141, 165, 182
Venezuela, 26, 146, 162, 199, 225
Vietnam (North), 226
(South), 56, 227

Water, 25, 26, 38, 44, 49, 50, 51, 76, 104, 112, 118, 131, 138, 156, 187, 205, 206, 207-209, 223
Western Samoa, 43
Whaling, 83, 231
Wigs, 185
Windward Islands, 41, 42, 233
Wine, 61, 152, 224, 235
Wool, 28, 224, 233
World Bank, 24, 25, 26, 39, 50, 127, 166, 168, 187
World Food Programme, 104, 200

Yugoslavia, 69, 111, 234, 235

Zambia, 41, 236, 237

245

Printed in Great Britain
by T. & A. Constable Ltd.,
Edinburgh EH7 4NF